D1556690

Marketing for
Leisure and Tourism

Marketing for Leisure and Tourism

Michael Morgan
Bournemouth University

PRENTICE HALL

London   New York   Toronto   Sydney   Tokyo
Singapore   Madrid   Mexico City   Munich

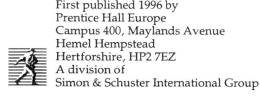

First published 1996 by
Prentice Hall Europe
Campus 400, Maylands Avenue
Hemel Hempstead
Hertforshire, HP2 7EZ
A division of
Simon & Schuster International Group

© Prentice Hall Europe 1996

Typeset in $10\frac{1}{2}$/12pt Palatino
by Mathematical Composition Setters Ltd, Salisbury, UK

Printed and bound in Great Britain
by Redwood Books, Trowbridge, Wiltshire

Library of Congress Cataloging-in-Publication Data

This information is available from the publisher.

British Library Cataloguing in Publication Data

A catalogue record for this book is available from the British Library

ISBN 0-13-150988-8

1 2 3 4 5   00 99 98 97 96

To Bournemouth University for giving me the motive to write this book and allowing me time to do it.

To my colleagues for their help and advice and proof-reading, particularly to Caroline Jackson, Elaine Porter, Chris Dean, Peter Elliott and Norman Freeth.

To my wife, Felicity, and my daughters, Emily and Ros, for putting up with me and my piles of papers while I wrote it.

To everyone I have met in leisure and tourism who has in any way influenced what I have written.

CONTENTS

PREFACE

This book has developed from my experiences as a lecturer in leisure and tourism marketing at Bournemouth University. When in 1987 I changed from being a practitioner to a teacher, I found there were virtually no specialist textbooks on the subject, and I had in effect to invent my own course.

There were plenty of good books on the theory of marketing, but to illustrate how it was applied in practice in leisure and tourism, I had to find my own examples. Fortunately, Sealink had given me experience of running an inclusive tours operation, managing a retail sales office and being part of a product marketing team. The work brought me into daily contact with people from tour operators, travel agents, coach companies, from every level of public sector tourism marketing and, most important of all, with the customers who paid our wages. Added to that was my keen interest and amateur participation in sports and the performing arts. I found that I had plenty of material to bring the subject to life for my students, material I have been adding to ever since.

In 1991 I became leader of a new degree course in Leisure Marketing. This set out to meet the growing need for leisure professionals with marketing skills. This need had always being recognized in tourism and commercial leisure where there was intense competition to find new ways, harnessing new technologies, to give people satisfying leisure experiences. Now pressure was being put on publicly funded arts and recreation to 'identify, anticipate, and satisfy customer needs profitably'. Peter Brown, Business Development Manager of Bournemouth's Littledown Leisure Centre told our students that he had a degree in sports physiology but he spent all his time now doing marketing.

In this course we took a holistic view of the leisure industries. From the customers' viewpoint divisions between leisure and tourism, between public, voluntary and commercial providers, have little relevance. All offer ways of spending spare time and disposable income, and all are therefore in competition with each other. By now there were some interesting books on tourism marketing, and a few on leisure marketing but none that had the breadth of coverage of the industries that our students were looking for. There was therefore no alternative but to write the book myself, and here it is.

The book takes a fairly standard path through the elements of the marketing process, as it is intended to stand on its own as the main marketing text for students doing a marketing unit on a leisure, tourism or similar course at HND or degree level. It should give them a sound introduction to marketing principles and practice, and point them to the key authors for further reading.

The book uses many illustrations and case studies from a wide range of leisure organizations, which should make it a useful source for students studying leisure and tourism at all levels from GNVQ upward. A number of case studies focusing on different aspects of the overseas package holiday market will give the student a good insight into this important sector.

It also highlights areas of importance in leisure marketing which are not given as much attention in other marketing texts, and which should make it of interest to those already familiar with the subject. These include:

1   The key characteristics of leisure activities which are significant to marketing, i.e. the absence of necessity, the pursuit of personal satisfaction, the importance of play, and the social implications (Chapter 1).

2   The way that many leisure organizations exist because of the owner's personal enthusiasm, or belief in the intrinsic value of the subject (artistic, scientific, social or political), rather than a simple profit motive (Chapter 3).

3   The need to examine the external influences on the market (the usual PEST analysis) in terms of the effects they have on the key determinants of leisure demand: time, income and access to facilities. In particular, Chapter 6 draws together statistics which illuminate the crucial relations between age, leisure time, disposable income and leisure expenditure.

4   The fact that the 'product' the customer chooses is often made up of elements supplied by a number of different organizations. Collaborative marketing is therefore a frequent strategy, one that involves a partnership between private and public sectors. Chapter 22 shows how leisure and tourism marketing by a local authority can play a crucial role in the wider economy of the area.

5   The importance of Quality Management as a means of delivering the service that the marketing effort has promised to the customer (Chapter 11).

6   The significant role of promotional literature, PR, direct marketing and sponsorship, particularly for organizations with small budgets.

7   The undervalued area of distribution in leisure marketing. The role of tour operators and travel agents in tourism marketing is examined in depth, of course, but Chapter 13 also looks at distribution channels in professional sport, a highly topical application of distribution theory.

I hope that whether the reader is familiar with marketing or not, he or she will find the book useful and thought-provoking. I also hope they will find it readable. I strongly believe that the ability to communicate is vital in marketing and so have avoided unnecessary jargon, ponderous academic style and the inappropriate use of algebraic equations to describe human behaviour. Marketing is not a mystery to be preserved by a priesthood of academic theorists. I have therefore tried to be both scholarly and accessible.

Mike Morgan

Notes on terms:

To avoid constant repetition the following 'short-hand' terms have been used:

Product refers to anything produced that might satisfy a customer need, both tangible goods and intangible services.

Organization is used to stand for any company, voluntary organization, public sector authority, or other management team responsible for marketing.

Leisure, unless otherwise stated, encompasses tourism, entertainment, recreation, sport, the arts and anything else enjoyed in or out of the home from choice rather than necessity (see Chapter 1 for a discussion of possible definitions).

ACKNOWLEDGEMENTS

Permission is gratefully acknowledged for the use of the following material.

The Sports Council for John Roberts' diagram from *The Commercial Sector in Leisure*, Figure 1.2.

Roger Joiner and the Royal Botanical Gardens, Kew, for Case Study 2.1.

Mintel Market Intelligence for the use of their survey data in Figure 6.2 from 'Leisure Time 2 – Age and Leisure', *Leisure Intelligence*, Vol. 2, 1991.

British Market Research Bureau for the extract from *Target Group Index 1986*, Table 8.2.

Figure 9.1 Every effort has been made to contact the copyright holder of this figure. When the appropriate information has been received we shall be pleased to make the necessary acknowledgement at the first opportunity.

John Weaver and Bournemouth Borough Council for Figures 10.6 and 10.7.

Business Books (Random House UK Ltd) for Figure 15.1, from Simon Broadbent and Brian Jacobs *Spending Advertising Money*.

John Wilmshurst and Butterworth-Heinemann Ltd for Figure 18.1, from *The Fundamentals of Advertising*.

Sunny Crouch for Case Study 22.1.

PART 1

What is Leisure Marketing?

1 Leisure

Definitions and key elements of leisure
Leisure industries
Summary

Definitions and key elements of leisure

This book is for anyone engaged in, studying, or interested in, the marketing of leisure. The first chapter tries to explain what that means and why it differs from the marketing of, say, groceries or electronic components. In simple terms, leisure can include anything on which we spend our spare time and our disposable income. There are many more precise and profound definitions of leisure.[1] For example, George Torkildsen spends much of the first seven chapters of his book *Leisure and Recreation Management* discussing the nature of leisure, recreation, sport and play.[2]

In all the definitions of leisure, certain common elements occur which are significant for the way in which leisure is marketed. These are:

- the absence of necessity,
- the pursuit of personal satisfaction,
- the importance of play, and
- the social dimension of leisure.

The word 'leisure' can be used to refer to leisure time, leisure activities or the state of mind of being at leisure.[3] It is usually the activities (or the equipment needed to take part) that are being marketed, and these will be the main focus of the book. However, as the activity takes place in 'leisure time' and provides the participant with a 'leisure experience', it is important to understand what distinguishes these from other kinds of time and experiences.

The absence of necessity

Leisure, unlike work, allows freedom of choice, freedom to 'do what one wants to do' and to 'do something for its own sake', as Barrett put it.[4] Leisure time occurs, and leisure activities take place, when we are free not only from the necessities of work, but also from the obligations of family and social duties.[5]

Surveys of leisure time, such as those in the UK Central Statistical Office annual report *Social Trends*, divide leisure time from time spent at work or asleep or on 'other essential activities', which are defined as domestic work, and personal care including essential shopping, child care, personal hygiene and personal appearance[6] (see Table 1.1). The problem with this kind of division is that there are different kinds and degrees of necessity. Maw, for example, constructed a time budget model distinguishing between essential, optional and leisure activities according to the degree of commitment involved.[7] To illustrate how arbitrary these distinctions can be, I regularly walk my dog in the woods near Thomas Hardy's birthplace in Dorset. Is this an essential domestic chore, an optional leisure activity or, since I use the time to think about this book, trying out the sentences in my head as I walk, is it part of my working time? Nevertheless, no leisure activity is really essential, and this absence of necessity means that the marketer has to work harder to persuade a customer to choose a particular activity.

The pursuit of personal satisfaction

Some writers distinguish leisure from other activities by the motivation and state of mind with which the activity is undertaken. According to Burton, leisure is 'undertaken freely for purposes of relaxation or entertainment or … personal or social development'.[8] In this respect, practical activities such as cookery, dressmaking, household maintenance, car mechanics, gardening and pet care can be just as much leisure activities as less functional pastimes like bridge, bingo, football or water-colour painting.

Table 1.1   Time use in a typical week: by employment status and sex, 1991–92

	Full-time		Part-time females	Housewives	Retired
	Males	Females			
Weekly hours spent on					
Employment & travel	48.9	43.7	21.1	0.4	0.2
Essential activities	26.8	42.3	57.0	65.5	36.0
Sleep (average 7 h)	49.0	49.0	49.0	49.0	49.0
Free time	46.5	33.0	41.0	53.5	83.0
Free time per weekday	4.8	3.3	4.7	7.0	11.6
Free time per weekend day	11.3	8.3	8.7	9.0	12.6

Source: Henley Centre for Forecasting; *Social Trends* 23 (1993).

All provide competition for activities offered by the commercial 'leisure industry'.

Leisure theorists have proposed various categories of leisure needs, including 'recuperation, entertainment and self-development',[9] 'spiritual renewal'[10] and improved personal relationships.[11] Escapism, escaping the pressures and frustrations of work and social obligations, is obviously a crucial motivation for many leisure activities.[12]

The nature of the personal satisfaction gained from leisure will depend on the individual and the activities. It can be the satisfaction of virtually any but the most basic human needs and desires. The study of consumer motivation and the way choices are made between activities is an important part of leisure marketing, and will be the subject of Chapter 7.

The importance of play

These leisure needs are often satisfied by playing games. In this, we include sports, card and board games, fantasy role-play games, computer games, and drama, particularly improvisation. All of these games have rules which limit the risks to participants, create an even basis for competition, and maintain the suspense of an uncertain outcome. This is often in contrast to the participants' everyday lives.

Within the framework of these rules, players can develop skills, ingenuity and creativity.[13] (In this tension between rules and creativity, games are similar to art and music which also offer the same types of satisfaction.) Because they are outside real life, players can assume roles and status otherwise unavailable to them. They can express themselves spontaneously and exuberantly without embarrassment. They can resolve problems and overcome difficulties (in a crossword puzzle, unlike life, there is always a correct answer!). Games are both escapist and self-developmental. The element of 'playfulness' or becoming absorbed in a game for its own enjoyment, can depend on taking it seriously and giving it one's best effort. Paradoxically, this can lead to the playfulness being lost.[14] How many professional sportsmen would describe their training programmes as leisure?

Leisure marketers need to understand and exploit the appeal of games playing. Leisure activities which allow for the development of skills, the solving of increasingly challenging problems and the expression of creative playfulness are, according to Gratton, likely to remain popular longer than those that are quickly mastered, after which the novelty wears off.[15]

The social dimension of leisure

So far we have defined leisure in terms of personal choice and satisfaction. Most leisure activities, however, are social activities. They are undertaken with other people, often partly for the pleasure of meeting new friends outside the narrow circle of work and family. Marketers need to understand the social as well as the personal influences on the choice of leisure activities.

Leisure also has social implications. Certain activities are encouraged or discouraged because of their social effects. Archery and equestrian sports, for example, were developed as ways of training young men to be warriors. Golf was discouraged because it interfered with archery practice. Even today, providing leisure facilities is seen as part of the solution to such problems as juvenile crime, urban deprivation, and the cost of treating heart and lung diseases on the National Health Service. Physical recreation in particular is recognized to be important to society as well as to the individual, and is promoted by governments using marketing techniques.[16] A recent example of a state's concern for promoting health through leisure activities is the UK Government's report *The Health of the Nation*. The appreciation of art and the preservation of the nation's cultural heritage is also considered to bring social and economic benefits.

For these reasons, facilities for leisure and recreation are often provided by the state, locally or nationally. Swimming baths, playing fields and more recently sports or 'leisure centres' have been funded out of taxpayers' money, as have libraries, museums and art galleries. This has created a marketing environment in which people expect to enjoy these facilities at low cost or none, and so under-value them.

Recently, in the UK and elsewhere, this approach has been challenged by cost-conscious governments. The Thatcher government of the 1980s ruled that local authorities should put out the management of their leisure facilities to competitive tender and where possible run them as commercial enterprises.[17]

The decision to subsidize or not to subsidize an activity implies a value judgement on its social value. Nash's grading (Figure 1.1) creates a scale of value with creative participation at the top and crime and delinquency at the bottom. While this is unexceptionable, his classification appears to label popular entertainment as merely an antidote to boredom, which could be seen as elitist. Leisure marketers cannot afford to dismiss so lightly activities that satisfy real needs and produce a significant share of leisure spending.

On the other hand, to allow leisure provision to be determined solely on commercial grounds, by what people are prepared to pay the full cost for, ignores the fact that neither sport nor the arts have ever existed without some kind of financial backing, whether from the medieval church, the renaissance nobility, the nineteenth-century nation-state or from the philanthropy of wealthy businessmen. Today, leisure marketers have to communicate the benefits of their products not only to the end-users, the public, but to clients such as sponsors, politicians and central or local government funding bodies.

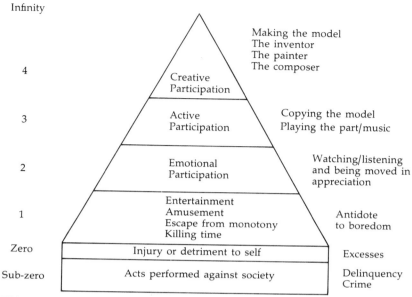

Infinity

4   Creative
         Participation   Making the model
                                The inventor
                                The painter
                                The composer

3   Active
         Participation   Copying the model
                                Playing the part/music

2   Emotional
         Participation   Watching/listening
                                and being moved in
                                appreciation

1   Entertainment
         Amusement
         Escape from monotony   Antidote
         Killing time   to boredom

Zero   Injury or detriment to self   Excesses

Sub-zero   Acts performed against society   Delinquency
                                              Crime

FIGURE 1.1   Nash's conceptualization of the use of leisure time.
Source: Nash (1960) *The Philosophy of Recreation and Leisure.*

Leisure – the significance for marketing

In our brief review of the key elements of leisure, we have seen that a leisure activity is something the individual chooses to do for his or her own satisfaction. It is an opportunity to do something different from the rest of everyday life, to develop new skills, to express another side of the personality, and to meet different people. It is relatively uninfluenced by work, family background or social grouping. The choice is almost endless, and the individual is under no innate compulsion to do anything.

The task of persuading an individual to choose a particular leisure activity is therefore a challenging one and requires a high level of marketing skills.

The leisure industries

The scope of this book

This book aims to help those engaged in marketing for leisure and tourism to develop the skills and knowledge needed to meet the challenge. Before beginning to discuss what marketing is, we will first outline what is meant by the leisure and tourism industries.

The public sector

In Britain, the term leisure management has tended to be used for the management of leisure facilities provided by the public sector. Torkildsen's standard work, *Leisure and Recreation Management*, deals with the public, commercial and voluntary sectors, but his emphasis is on the management of leisure opportunities as 'a tangible means of improving the lot of individuals in society'.[18]

To give an example of the scope of public sector leisure interests, Bournemouth Borough Council's Leisure and Tourism Directorate has as its Mission Statement:

> To provide Bournemouth with the best possible leisure, cultural and tourism services, generating economic, environmental and social benefits for residents, visitors and local businesses.[19]

Under the directorate's three divisions of Arts and Museums, Tourism Services and Leisure Services come responsibilities for art galleries and museums, arts development, sports and recreational facilities, parks and play areas, beaches and countryside conservation, street entertainment, beach huts, tourism promotion and information. The council also own three major conference and entertainments venues and a leisure centre, which are managed as self-contained businesses. The full range of local authority leisure services is shown in Table 1.2.

Table 1.2   Percentage of local authority leisure service departments with responsibility for various amenities (from a survey of 373 local authorities conducted by Loughborough University Business School)

	% of authorities
Swimming pools	90
Leisure centres	83
Sports halls	82
Arts entertainments	71
Tourism	58
Community centres	54
Allotments	52
Theatres and arts centres	50
Museums and galleries	49
Country parks	45
Golf courses	38
Parks and open spaces	37
Playgrounds	17
Nature reserves/zoos	17

Source: Saker and Smith (1993) 'Selling leisure', *Leisure Opportunities* **115**.

Under the terms of the Local Government Act 1988, the management of sports and leisure facilities must be offered to competitive tendering. Whether they are managed by local authority staff as a direct service organization or by private contractors, the council still control the specifications under which they operate and must balance the potential revenue for the council with the leisure needs of the whole community. Both the centre management and the council policymakers need to base their decisions on marketing principles, that is, on a clear understanding of the needs of the communities and customers they serve.

The private sector

The word 'leisure' often appears in the titles of companies in the commercial sector. First Leisure, based in Blackpool, says in their annual report that they are 'committed to bringing quality and innovation to the mass market leisure business'. In their case, this means ten-pin bowling, discotheques and leisure park developments, arcades, piers, marinas, hotels, theatres, snooker, fitness centres and cafe bars. Most are 'low ticket, high-volume markets' offering high turnover, high margins and high profits.[20]

Figure 1.2 shows John Roberts' classification of the extent of activities provided for by the private sector.[21] Some of these, such as transport, accommodation, catering and retailing, are professional and academic specialisms on their own, but they are part of leisure in two ways. First, as travelling, eating out and shopping form part of the overall leisure experience of a day visit to a theatre, sports event or attraction, they form part of the product to be marketed. Second, leisure customers form an important segment of the business of hotels, restaurants or airlines. For these reasons, examples from these sectors will be included in this book.

Tourism

Tourism is also a professional and academic subject in its own right. Like leisure, it is a term used to describe a wide range of activities. The definition adopted by the Tourism Society is:

> the temporary short term movement of people to destinations outside the places where they live and work, and activities during their stay at these destinations.[22]

The activities referred to in this definition could almost all be classified as leisure activities, the only distinction being that tourism activities are practised away from home. As the definition goes on to include day visits and excursions as tourism, the dividing line between leisure and tourism becomes very difficult to see. As Holloway says, 'Tourism is just one form of recreation, one use of our discretionary time'.[23]

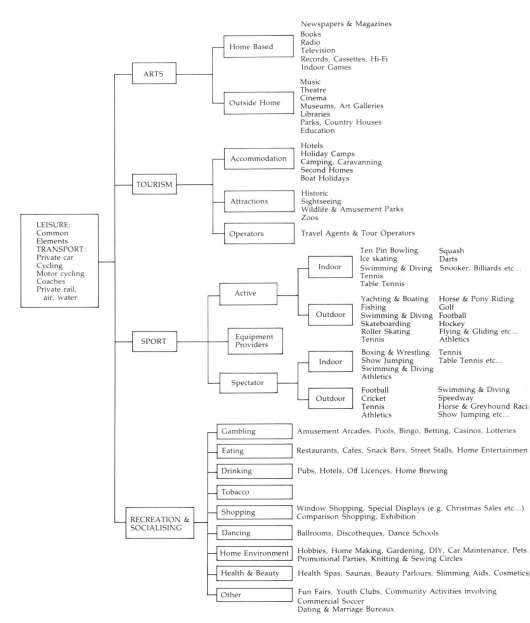

FIGURE 1.2   Roberts' taxonomy of activities undertaken by the commercial sector.
Source: Roberts (TEST).

Tourism admittedly also includes business travel and conferences, which are not leisure activities *per se*. However, business travellers very often take part in leisure activities – shopping, sightseeing and sports, for example – during business trips. Conference venues are often chosen for the leisure facilities available to the delegates. There is also a growing market in incentive tourism which offers leisure trips as rewards for business performance.

Tourism deserves special attention as the biggest single item of leisure expenditure in most people's budgets, and as a major source of jobs and income for local economies. Nevertheless, it shares many of the characteristics of leisure. Tourism is a discretionary activity undertaken for personal reasons, including relaxation, escapism and personal development. It has social and economic implications, both for the originating and destination areas, and so is managed and marketed by the public as well as the private sector. This book will therefore treat tourism as a leisure activity, and tourists as part of the leisure market.

Home-based leisure

A growing amount of our leisure time, activities and spending take place in our own homes. Electronic media bring music, drama and films to our living rooms; video and compact discs mean we can enjoy them when we want them. Computers provide the excitement, escapism and challenge of games-playing without leaving the armchair. Take-away meals and drinks are available to complete the experience. Impending developments in two-way links via telephone lines or fibre-optic cables will greatly increase the choice available and our control over what we take, and when.

The marketing of home-based leisure and the competition it provides for out-of-home leisure activities will therefore also come under the scope of this book.

The voluntary sector

There are thousands of voluntary organizations involved in leisure, ranging from local sports and social clubs to national organizations like the National Trust or the Royal Society for the Protection of Birds. These organizations usually have other than purely profit-making objectives, but nevertheless need to make money to continue in existence and to achieve their other goals. This money may come partly in grants from the public sector or from business sponsorship, but the main reason for their existence, if not always their largest source of income, is their membership. To attract and retain members the voluntary organizations need to identify and satisfy their members' needs. In other words, they need to market themselves as effectively as any commercial organization.

This book will be useful to anyone involved in marketing for a voluntary organization, whether in a paid or an honorary position.

Summary

A large number of organizations are competing for our leisure time and disposable income. They start with different objectives – social, political, charitable or simply commercial – and the range of activities and facilities they offer is immense. What they all have in common is that they need our custom more than we need them. We are free to choose whatever will offer us the most personal satisfaction. Each organization must try to convince us that what they have to offer is the best use of our time and money. The means by which they do this is marketing.

Notes

1. For a comprehensive discussion of definitions of leisure see Bernard, M. (1983) 'Leisure defined: A review of the literature', *Leisure, Recreation and Tourism Abstracts*, **8**(1).
2. Torkildsen, G. (1983) *Leisure and Recreation Management*.
3. *Ibid*, pp. 26–31.
4. Barrett, C. and Winnifrith, T. (1989) *The Philosophy of Leisure*.
5. Dumazedier, J. (1960) 'Current problems in the sociology of leisure', *International Social Science Journal* **12**, 522–31.
6. Henley Centre for Forecasting data, in Central Statistical Office (1993) *Social Trends 23*, p. 140. See also Gratton, C. and Taylor, P. (1987) *Leisure in Britain*, ch. 2, for a discussion of what constitutes leisure time.
7. Quoted in Congreave, I. and Jackson, R. (1972) *The Geography of Recreation and Leisure*, p. 14.
8. Burton, T.L. (1971) *Experiments in Recreation Research*, p. 20.
9. Dumazedier, J. (1967) *Towards a Sociology of Leisure*.
10. Meyersohn, R. (1972) 'Leisure', in Campbell, A. and Converse, P.E. (Eds) (1972) *The Meaning of Social Change*.
11. Russell, B. (1960) *In Praise of Idleness, and Other Essays*, p. 20.
12. Prochnik, W.O. (1975) 'Urban planning for leisure', *Ekistics*, **40**(236): 60–62.
13. For a discussion of play, in particular the theories of Huizinga and Callois, see Torkildsen (1983), *op. cit.*, pp. 50–60.
14. *Ibid*, p. 57.
15. Gratton, C. (1993) *Transnational Corporations in the Leisure Industries*.
16. Recreation is used almost but not quite synonymously with leisure. It is generally used for activities with positive 're-creative' effects on the mind, body or spirit, and therefore with a positive influence on society. See Torkildsen (1983), *op. cit.*
17. *Local Government Act 1988* (Competition in Sport and Leisure Facilities Order, 1989).
18. Torkildsen (1983), *op. cit.* p. 450.
19. Bournemouth Borough Council Leisure and Tourism Directorate (1993) *Business Plan 1993*.
20. First Leisure plc (1990) *Annual Report 1990*.
21. Roberts, J. (1979) *The Commercial Sector in Leisure*.
22. Tourism Society (1976), quoted in Holloway, J. C. (1990) *The Business of Tourism*, p. 9.
23. *Ibid*, p. 9.

2 What is marketing?

Definitions of marketing

Marketing is about *customers*. It is about how to find them, how to satisfy them, and how to keep them. Without customers, there will be no money to pay staff, creditors and shareholders. Without customers, there can be no reason for the organization to exist.

Even the most heavily subsidized public or voluntary organization needs customers. If the organization is not fulfilling a need, if no one comes to its performances or uses its facilities, then how can it justify spending the money given to it by taxpayers or sponsors or as charitable donations?

The British Chartered Institute of Marketing (CIM) defines marketing as:

> The Management Process responsible for identifying, anticipating and satisfying customers' needs profitably.

The word 'profitably' is important. It would be easy to satisfy customers' leisure needs with an unlimited budget. The skill comes in identifying and anticipating what they are likely to spend their hard-earned money on, i.e. what *value* they put on the opportunity to satisfy a need in a particular way.

Philip Kotler, the famous American marketing writer, emphasizes this in his definition of marketing:

> Marketing is a process by which individuals and groups obtain what they need and want through creating, offering and exchanging products and value with each other.[1]

The concept of an *exchange* means that both sides must obtain what they need and want. If you visit your local leisure centre for a swim, you get the enjoyment of healthy exercise in a safe environment. The centre gets your entrance money. If it is a publicly owned centre, the local council also hopes to get the benefits of a contented, fit and healthy population, and a reduction in the number of young people aimlessly hanging around the town centre. The elected councillors also hope to get your vote in exchange for providing good leisure facilities for you.

None of this will happen unless the centre has created good value for you. If the facilities are not what you want, or if the price is too high, you will stay away. The centre will then lose money, and it will not achieve any of the social or political objectives either. Even if the facilities are good and the price is reasonable, however, no one will come unless they are told about it. The process of creating value includes advertising and promotion, making the centre sound an exciting place to visit.

As Kotler's definition shows, marketing can be used in a wider *societal* context to achieve political and social as well as profit objectives.[2] A local authority may set its leisure centre management the objective of achieving the use of the centre by a representative cross-section of the population, including the unemployed, the disabled and ethnic minorities. To achieve such objectives requires as much or more skill in marketing as is needed to meet a purely financial target.

What marketing is not

Advertising on its own cannot succeed unless the product provides good value. You may visit a leisure centre once after seeing an advertisement, but if it does not live up your expectations, you will not go back again.

Marketing is about 'selling products that don't come back to customers who do'.[3] It is not just advertising, publicity or selling. It is the complete process of 'converting consumer spending power into effective demand for a specific product'.[4] Selling is only a late stage in this process.

To discover why this is so, the reader is invited to try selling an item of out-of-date fashion wear to their contemporaries. Flared trousers, platform soles and kipper ties were good examples at the time of writing; no amount of price discounting or lurid advertising claims will now persuade your friends to buy them. This is because you are selling the wrong product to the wrong people, probably at the wrong price and in the wrong place as well.

The marketing process, by starting with the needs and wants of the customer, aims to avoid putting sales people in this embarrassing position.

Marketing as a process

The process of marketing, then, starts by identifying the needs of the customer. As different customers will have different wants, effective marketing often requires a focusing or targeting of particular types of customers or segments of the total market. The organization has to decide what its objectives are, and who are its best target customers. This requires research and planning.

The organization must decide what to offer those customers. This offer involves four key elements, described by McCarthy as the '4 Ps' of the marketing mix:[5]

> *Product*: what to offer.
>
> *Price*: how much to charge for it.
>
> *Promotion*: how to tell people about it.
>
> *Place*: how or where people can buy it.[6]

All of these need to be decided upon with the customer's needs and values in mind.

Marketing can therefore be seen as a series of jobs, a process carried out by various members of the marketing department.

Marketing as a philosophy

To carry out its work effectively, however, the marketing department needs the support of the whole organization. The customers will come with expectations created by marketing. If the other departments such as operations, finance, or personnel allow their own priorities to divert them, then the organization as a whole may not be able to fulfil the promise.

As Peter Drucker said, marketing is too important to be left to the marketing department. It is a philosophy, an approach to business that puts the customer first. 'It is the whole business seen from the viewpoint of the end-user, the customer.'[7] This approach requires commitment from the senior management of the organization and from the front-line staff who actually meet the customers. To achieve this, *internal marketing* is needed, i.e. selling the benefits of the company's policy to those who have to implement it.

Marketing as relationship management

Critics of the standard definitions of marketing by Anglo-American writers accuse them of failing to practise what they preach. The aim is to focus on the customer, but by describing marketing as a process, they start from the firm and not from the market.[8] The concept of the marketing mix can lead to an image of the marketer as a kind of mad scientist brewing up a potent combination of the 4 Ps which will enable him to have his way with the hapless customer. In fact, the customer is an active, and unpredictable, participant in the process.

It is important to remember that the marketing process does not end with the exchange, with the first purchase or visit. The customer must be made to want to come back for more. She must be reassured that she has made a good decision; she must be welcomed and looked after and encouraged to return. It is much easier to keep existing customers than to find others to replace them.

The Swedish writer, Christian Grönroos, proposed a Nordic definition of marketing:

> Marketing is to establish, develop and commercialize long-term customer relationships so that the objectives of the parties are met. This is done by a mutual exchange and keeping of promises.[9]

These long-term relationships are formed between the customer and all the people in the firm with whom she has contact. These are unlikely to be the marketing specialists, but those who answer the telephone, staff reception desks, bars or cafes, or act as ushers, instructors, lifeguards, security or cleaning staff.

Marketing and competitive advantage

If customers are the basis of any marketing strategy, another 'C' must also be considered: competition. As we saw in Chapter 1, there is an almost unlimited number of ways in which people can choose to spend their leisure time. Even when a particular activity is chosen, there is very rarely only one organization offering it.

To succeed in the face of all the competition, the marketer must offer something distinctive. According to Michael Porter, there are basically three basic ways of gaining a competitive advantage:

- lower pricing,
- differentiation, offering a better product than your rivals,
- focus, serving particular groups or segments of the customers better than your competitors.[10]

To this list can be added the concept of the brand image. Promotional techniques can be used to create a 'unique blend of appeals to the reason, emotions and senses'[11] that can make your customers think of your product as distinctive even though there may be few real differences from those of your rivals. To deliver this promise, the whole company, management and staff must work together to meet a common objective.

Leisure marketing – why is it different?

The marketing approach, then, is to see the business from the customer's viewpoint and to get the whole organization working together to develop relationships with the customer based on trust. This is even more critical in leisure services, where there is nothing *tangible* for the customer to examine beforehand or to take away afterwards. The service is *inseparable* from the moment of consumption. The customer pays her money on the promise of receiving an experience. Whether that promise is kept can depend on her interaction with the staff she meets. A friendly welcome or rude indifference can colour her perception of everything that happens while she is in contact with the organization. The quality of the product is therefore *variable* and is not entirely under the control of the marketer. An outdoor event, for example, is very vulnerable to the weather. So too are the sales of ice-cream and T-shirts. The difference is that services are even more *perishable*; the tickets for today's event cannot be stored in a refrigerator until the weather improves or demand increases.

These characteristics – intangibility, inseparability, variability and perishability – are common to most services.[12] In leisure and tourism what is even more significant is that the services are competing for the customer's spare time and disposable income. There is, as we said in Chapter 1, nothing essential about a holiday, a day out or a visit to a leisure centre.

The skill in leisure marketing lies in creating value, in packaging and promoting the experience so that the customer feels she must buy it, and buy it from you rather than your competitors.

CASE STUDY 2.1 *Kew Gardens*

The Royal Botanical Gardens at Kew hold the largest and most diverse collection of plants and preserved plant material in the world. As its publicity leaflet says: 'Kew's purpose is to increase mankind's understanding of the plant kingdom'.

First and foremost, Kew is a research establishment, studying the basic properties of plants and use of plant material for agricultural, industrial and medicinal purposes. Kew scientists' work is contributing to knowledge which may help to develop drugs for the treatment of HIV, Alzheimer's disease and other major illnesses. It is also an educational institution with 75 students.

Almost incidentally to these purposes, the creation of its huge collection of living plants has produced a large and beautiful park with unusual plants and trees and its famous glasshouses (see the accompanying extract from the Friends of Kew publicity leaflet). Because of this, Kew is one of London's most visited attractions (Table 2.1).

Table 2.1 Number of visitors to top UK tourist attractions charging admission (in millions)

	1986	1990
Madame Tussauds	2.4	2.5
Tower of London	2.0	2.3
Alton Towers theme park	2.2	2.1
Natural History Museum	2.7	1.5[a]
Chessington World of Adventure	0.8	1.5
Blackpool Tower	1.4	1.4
Royal Academy	0.6	1.3
Science Museum	3.0	1.3[b]
London Zoo	1.2	1.3
Kew Gardens	1.1	1.2

[a] Admission charge introduced in 1989.
[b] Admission charge introduced in 1987.
Source: British Tourist Authority (1991).

The Royal Botanical Gardens, Kew

- manages gardens of more than 300 acres at Kew, Surrey, and 500 acres at Wakehurst Place, Sussex;

- maintains 39 listed buildings and structures including four of the world's greatest glasshouses;

- grows one in eight of all flowering species;

- holds and researches on over six million preserved plants;

- safeguards more than 80,000 plant products used by mankind;

- has a library of more than 750,000 books, journals and original illustrations;

- employs a dedicated staff of almost 500 who carry out a wide range of activities from research to the maintenance of the estate.

As 80% of its income came from government research grants, Kew traditionally paid little attention to its visitors. From 1916 to the 1970s admission was by a penny coin in a turnstile, and people treated Kew as an extension of Richmond's other parks and riverside walks. From 1980 to 1990, the price had risen to £1, but visitor numbers remained around 1.2 million. Visitors were left to wander around reading the Latin names of the plants from metal plaques. At the weekends when most visitors came, the management and research staff were not there, so any contact was with a small number of staff in ticket offices, constables or the few weekend duty gardeners.

In the early 1990s, with the UK in recession and the Conservative government determined to control the economy by containing public expenditure, Kew, like every other recipient of state aid, needed to look for ways to reduce its dependence on grants. The visitors now were identified as an asset that had not been fully exploited.

With this in mind, in 1990 the admission charge was increased to £3 and in early 1992 a new visitor centre was opened at Kew's Victoria Gate entrance nearest to the Underground station. (Kew is a short journey from Central London by tube train. It is near the junction of several main road routes into London but car parking space is insufficient for weekend peaks.) However, there was still little structured focus for the operation of the Gardens as a visitor attraction.

In 1992, Roger Joiner was appointed as Kew's first marketing manager, and was given the task of developing Kew as a visitor attraction. He was given his objectives to develop and sustain revenue growth in the long term, to demonstrate to the government that Kew was taking steps to help its own financial viability, and to increase public awareness of and support for Kew's underlying mission.

A national survey showed that Kew was already well known: almost 90% of those questioned had heard of Kew, 12% had visited in the last five years, and 13% said they would like to visit it. These results were higher than those for most other national tourist attractions.

Joiner saw potential in the growing public interest in conservation and the environment, which was evident in the growth of support for charities like the National Trust, Greenpeace and the World Wide Fund for Nature. However, a detailed study of published surveys showed that the majority of people are not active conservationists and that concern for environmental issues had begun to fall since its peak in 1989, being replaced by more immediate concerns such as unemployment and recession. Of some 80 million visits to major attractions, only 7 million were to gardens, and these commanded lower entry fees than theme parks or 'experience' attractions.

Joiner's own surveys showed that visitors to Kew understood the purpose of the gardens: 39% said it was research, 33% conservation, 21% the plant collections and 11% enjoyment. But when asked why they were visiting, they gave reasons such as 'for a day out' (21%), 'to show it to friends and family' (20%), 'for a walk' (16%), and 'to look at the plants' (14%). He concluded that it was not a conservation or technical message that they were seeking.

Since 1990 admission charges had been increased steeply, which had the effect of reducing visitor numbers (see Table 2.2). Further analysis

Table 2.2   Admission charges at Kew Gardens, 1990–93.

	1990	1991	1992	1993
Admission	£1.00	£3.00	£3.30	£3.50
No. of visitors	1,200,000	990,000	950,000	940,000
% change on previous year		–17%	–4%	–1%

revealed that overseas visitors remained unchanged, but UK visitors particularly from the local area were deterred by the price increase. The recession and the weather may have been contributory factors, since there is a direct correlation between hours of sunshine and the number of visitors. As overseas visitors made up only 33% of the total, with local residents 38% and other UK visitors 29%, there was some cause for concern.

In order to increase the income from visitors, the new Visitor Centre included a gift shop. Catering facilities – restaurant, cafeteria, bakery and kiosks – are operated by Ring and Brymer, under a contract that provides Kew with further income. Visitor surveys show a high level of satisfaction with these facilities.

QUESTIONS FOR DISCUSSION

1   What are the main objectives of the Royal Botanical Gardens?

2   What part do visitors play in achieving these objectives?

3   What leisure needs or satisfactions could be met by a visit to Kew Gardens?

4   In what other ways could the same needs be met, other than by visiting Kew?

5   Is a visit to Kew good value for money? How do visitors judge this? (Consider overseas and local visitors separately.)

6   What could Roger Joiner do to market Kew more effectively? What decisions does he need to consider for product, price, promotion and place?

Acknowledgement

The author would like to thank the Royal Botanical Gardens, Kew, for permission to publish this case study, and in particular Roger Joiner for providing information and suggesting improvements to the text.

Summary

The aim of marketing is to succeed in business by satisfying your customers more effectively than your competitors do. On one level marketing is a management process that involves researching customer needs and making decisions about the marketing mix – product, price, place, promotion – accordingly.

It is also a philosophy of business, ensuring that the entire organization is run with the customer in mind.

The goal of marketing is to create an exchange in which both parties, the organization and the customer, are satisfied. Advertising and sales techniques may persuade people to buy a poor or inappropriate product once, but they will not return. The real aim is to develop long-term customer relationships.

Leisure services present a special marketing challenge. They are intangible, variable and perishable, and depend on factors that are not directly under the manager's control. They are wholly optional purchases, and compete with a huge range of possible uses of the customer's spare time and disposable income.

Leisure marketing is the art of making these inessential products and services become an indispensable part of the customer's lifestyle.

Notes

1. Kotler, P. (1994) *Marketing Management*, p. 6.
2. *Ibid*, pp. 28, 31.
3. Baker, M. (1985) *Marketing: An Introductory Text*, p. 4. This is one of some 15 definitions of marketing listed by Baker.
4. Rodger, L.W. (1971) *Marketing in a Competitive Economy*.
5. McCarthy, E.J. (1981) *Basic Marketing: A Managerial Approach*.
6. The last of McCarthy's 4 Ps is the one that most often confuses students. 'Place' means the place where people can buy the product. It refers to the set of decisions involving the distribution of the product to the customer through wholesalers and retail shops. In leisure, to add to the confusion, the customers often come to the product, and 'Place' will include decisions about access, parking, and what theatres call 'front-of-house' facilities.
7. Drucker, P. (1954) *The Practice of Management*.
8. Grönroos, C (1989) 'Defining marketing: A market-orientated approach', *European Journal of Marketing*, 23(1): 52–59.
9. *Ibid*, p. 57.
10. Porter, M. (1980) *Competitive strategy*, p. 35.
11. King, S. (1973) *Developing New Brands*, p. 25.
12. Kotler (1994) *op. cit.*, pp. 466–8.

3 Marketing orientation

The philosophy of marketing as outlined in Chapter 2 may seem to be common sense. Of course businesses depend on customers. Of course the customer should be the focus of the whole organization. In practice, however, other preoccupations often conflict with or distort the organization's concentration on satisfying its customers.

The rise of marketing

Marketing writers sometimes present the rise of the marketing approach to business as an inevitable process of economic history.[1] To summarize rather simply what they say, in the past skilled craftsmen produced fine products for the small elite with disposable income to spend. It was the quality of the *product* that mattered. Then, in the nineteenth century, the new technologies of the Industrial Revolution enabled goods to be made and distributed in large quantities at lower cost for the growing urban population. *Mass production* was the key to success – goods which were available for the first time at affordable prices found ready markets at home and overseas.

However, as competition from other producers and other nations developed, the markets eventually became saturated. With a surplus of supply over demand, goods now needed aggressive *selling* to succeed. The early part of this century saw the rise of the sales representative and the development of the advertising industry. Using selling techniques to shift surpluses that had already been created was only a short-term solution. Gradually, industries learned to adapt their output to meet the changing needs of the *consumers* rather than to assume they knew what they wanted. This, as we have seen, is the basis of the marketing approach.

In an influential article in 1960, Theodore Levitt[2] defined the difference between the selling and marketing approaches as:

> Selling focuses on the needs of the seller; marketing on the needs of the buyer.

The crucial difference is that focusing on the needs of the buyer means taking a much broader view of the nature of the business. One of Levitt's examples of what he called 'marketing myopia' was a leisure one:

> Hollywood barely escaped being totally ravished by television. As with the railroads, Hollywood defined its business incorrectly. 'Movies' implied a specific limited product. This produced a fatuous contentment which from the beginning led producers to see TV as a threat. Hollywood scorned and rejected TV when it should have welcomed it as an opportunity to expand the entertainment business.
> Today TV is a bigger business than the old narrowly defined movie business ever was. Had Hollywood been customer-oriented [providing entertainment] rather than product-oriented [making movies], would it have gone through the fiscal purgatory that it did? I doubt it.[3]

It would be wrong, however, to believe that this conversion to a true marketing orientation was something that happened once and for all in the 1950s. As the example of Kew Gardens (Case Study 2.1) shows, it is a process that organizations still go through today.

Defining objectives

All organizations need to carry out regular reviews of their objectives by asking simple but fundamental questions such as those of Peter Drucker:[4]

- What is our business and what should it be?
- Who are our customers?
- What is value to them?

The answers to such questions will help to diagnose whether the organization really is consumer-oriented, or whether it is showing symptoms of other types of orientation. Product, production and sales orientations are not phenomena from the historical past. They can still be found in leisure organizations today.

Product orientation

A product-oriented organization believes that what it offers is of such quality and appeal that, to use the popular phrase, it will sell itself. Managers therefore concentrate on maintaining and improving the technical quality of the product. This is what Hollywood did in the 1950s, producing spectacular wide-screen epics while ignoring the potential of television.

The differences between the product- and the marketing-oriented approaches are shown in Figure 3.1. Product orientation is common in small and specialist leisure organizations, particularly those originating from the founder's personal enthusiasm (see Case Study 3.2, the Weymouth Diving Museum, at the end of this chapter). Enthusiasm and commitment are vital to the success of a new business. The danger is that those involved fall in love with their own product. Love, as we are told, is blind, or at least myopic, and fails to see the product through the eyes of the customer. There is often a disparity between what the organization sets out to provide and what the customer really wants (as illustrated by the Kew Gardens research in Case Study 2.1).

Museums and other leisure attractions with educational objectives have had to learn that just because the expert curators are interested in a topic or exhibit, it does not necessarily follow that it will interest the casual visitor looking for something to do on a wet Saturday afternoon. The exhibit needs to be interpreted and displayed in a way that will be relevant and understandable to the visitors. To quote a government report:

> Traditionally, museums are run by curators. Though highly motivated ... some have had little interest in presenting the results of their work to the public. Marketing and display skills have not always been valued and the presentational skills of organizations like Madame Tussauds or Walt Disney are sometimes viewed with suspicion.[5]

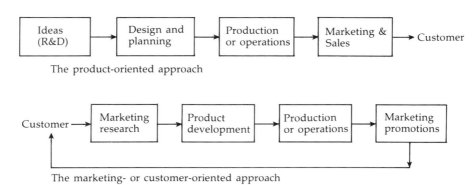

The product-oriented approach

The marketing- or customer-oriented approach

FIGURE 3.1   The product- and marketing-oriented approaches.

A consumer-oriented approach would recognize that the presentational methods used to present the past at Madame Tussauds or on television have helped to shape the expectations visitors now bring to museums and other attractions.

Even an attraction which could be seen as the ultimate in quality and popular appeal, the Crown Jewels of England in the Tower of London, now uses modern interpretative methods to increase visitors' understanding and enjoyment of the exhibits. Videos show the jewels in use at the last coronation, the queue moves through a mock-Gothic area depicting the 40 English monarchs since William the Conqueror, so that the visitors sense something of the significance of the jewels before they reach them. A travelator moves them slowly past the central exhibits so that each person gets a chance of a good view. In the past, visitors found the jewels disappointing after a long queue and few ever returned for a second visit. The new methods aim to increase visitor satisfaction, encourage return visits and enable higher prices to be set. Customer surveys will monitor the success of the improvements.[6]

Production or operations orientation

The production-oriented organization assumes that there is a high level of demand for the product and therefore concentrates on satisfying that demand efficiently and cost-effectively. The emphasis is on maximizing the output while holding down staff and other costs.

In leisure, this would perhaps be better described as *operations orientation*. Organizations running large stadiums for sports or entertainment events necessarily have to be concerned with operations in order to get tens of thousands of people in and out of the venue quickly and safely, to maximize their opportunity to buy food, drinks and programmes, and to avoid illegal entry. Since such events are totally perishable products, filling the place to capacity and minimizing costs are essential to profitability.

In the longer term, however, organizations that concentrate on operations while neglecting the quality of the consumer experience may find their audiences declining. Attendances at professional Football League matches in England and Wales declined from 28.7 million in 1971/72 to 19.5 million in 1990/91.[7] Rather than be crammed into wooden stands and open terraces with poor facilities for eating, drinking or going to the toilet, and with a worsening reputation for hooliganism and other dangers, former supporters have chosen to watch football matches on TV, or to find alternative leisure activities. Only recently have clubs begun to create all-seater stadiums, to provide special areas for families, children and business entertaining, or to provide pre-match entertainment.[8] New sports like ice hockey are creating new family audiences by focusing on the all-round customer experience they offer.

Another symptom of operations orientation is the proliferation of notices announcing procedures and regulations which, though designed with good intentions, have the effect of making it more difficult for customers to get what they came for. This tendency in leisure centres was parodied in the recent BBC comedy series *The Brittas Empire*, but can be found in many real life situations as well. According to the chief executive of Historic Royal Palaces,

> At Hampton Court visitors were walking through rooms they didn't understand, but staff were not supposed to talk to them in case an accomplice was stealing something.[9]

Sales orientation

The sales-oriented organization considers that consumers will not choose to buy the product unless they are persuaded to do so by the active use of sales techniques. These techniques include attention-getting gimmicks, personal sales calls by representatives and sales promotional incentives designed to persuade the consumer to buy now in order to obtain a bargain. All of these have a role in marketing but in a sales-oriented organization they tend to be used as a substitute for marketing to create a demand where none existed.

This approach is illustrated by the excesses of an element of the timeshare industry. Because the concept is unfamiliar, the organizations feel they have to lure people into sales presentations by promises of expensive prizes and then subject them to psychological pressure in order to persuade them to sign contracts immediately. As a result, the whole concept is viewed with suspicion by much of the public.

In ideal circumstances, careful marketing would avoid the creation of surpluses that need to be sold off by incentives and sales promotions. However, the demand for leisure is subject to fluctuations caused by the weather, the economy, changes in fashion or outside events, which make short-term sales incentives almost inevitable.

Tour operators, for example, negotiate with hoteliers and airlines two years in advance in order to bring out brochures 10–12 months before the holiday dates. It is very difficult to forecast the demand accurately and a downturn in the economy or a terrorist incident in a destination can leave the operator with unsold seats. In this situation there is little choice but to offer discounts and other incentives for last-minute bookings. The long-term effect, however, could be to encourage customers in subsequent years to defer booking in the hope of more late bargains.

The sales-oriented approach may also be motivated by a desire to gain market share over competitors or to force weak rivals into liquidation or merger. A strong company may forgo short-term profits to gain a long-term competitive advantage, aiming to increase prices and profits again when it has eliminated its competitors. In 1988, Charles Newbold of Thomson Holidays declared:[10]

> We can live a hundred years without profits if we have to. Like it or not, the industry just has to come to terms with the fact that Thomson Holidays are the market leaders. Nothing will change the situation, we won't let it. In the end our competitors will have to stop selling holidays at prices which do not make money.

This approach can lead to price wars, a decline in product quality as costs are held down, and public perceptions of the product as 'cheap and nasty'. This is the situation in which the tour operating sector in the UK found itself at the end of the 1980s.[11]

However, to maintain market leadership, Thomson did not rely on sales incentives and discounting alone. Price was only part of their marketing mix. They introduced new improved products such as the Sun Hotels scheme, an investment in selected hotels to improve food, accommodation, decor, and entertainment to specifications based on their customer research. They spent more than any of their competitors on advertising to promote their brand image as a quality operator, and they strengthened their distribution network by expanding their Lunn Poly chain of travel agents. This shows how short-term sales incentives and long-term marketing planning can complement rather than contradict each other.

Non-commercial orientation

The orientations described above are common in most industries. In leisure, there is often also an apparent conflict between the marketing approach and the social, political or artistic objectives of the organization.

As discussed in Chapter 1, the social dimension of leisure has led to the view that the provision of leisure cannot be left to the commercial and voluntary sectors. The state needs to be involved in controlling anti-social activities such as gambling drinking or watching violent or pornographic material. It has also taken a leading role in encouraging positive activities such as sport, outdoor recreation and the arts, either by subsidy or by the provision and management of facilities. For example, the 1975 White Paper *Sport and Recreation* stated that the provision of recreational facilities was 'part of the general fabric of social services'.[12]

In marketing terms, the task of identifying, anticipating and satisfying the needs of the public has been taken over by local and central governments who interpret those needs according to their particular social and political values and priorities. They then specify the services required from their leisure and recreation managers and staff. Figure 3.2 shows the contrast in processes between the consumer-oriented commercial organization shown in Figure 3.1 and a public sector organization.

There are many valid reasons for the state to set non-commercial objectives for leisure management. These can be summarized as:

- to support activities that would be commercially non-viable, but have cultural, environmental, social or economic benefits to the community, and
- to provide access to leisure for disadvantaged people who would otherwise be unable to participate.

The public sector can take a wider and longer-term view of the need, for example, to encourage the creative arts, to preserve the architectural and natural heritage, and to provide healthy and non-destructive outlets for the physical energy of the young. However, as Henry and Spink point out, the problem with such objectives is that they can lead to a conflict of priorities and make planning more difficult:

> If one accepts profit maximization as the primary aim of a commercial organization, a coherent and unified hierarchy of objectives can be operationally defined and monitored. The situation is somewhat different for the public sector organization where goals are expressed in qualitative terms, where they incorporate potentially conflicting goals from which it is difficult to establish clear measures of performance.[13]

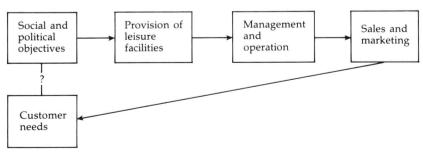

FIGURE 3.2   The traditional public sector approach.

This conflict is illustrated in Case Study 3.1.

CASE STUDY 3.1 *Local authorities, entertainment and the arts*

The Audit Commission for Local Authorities in England & Wales reports that local authorities in Britain spend £45 million a year on grants to arts organizations and £95 million to subsidize over 400 theatres, concert halls and arts centres which they provide and run. It is not only high culture that is supported. Subsidies also go to popular entertainment such as children's shows, pop concerts, variety shows, wrestling and snooker.

Although they do not always say so explicitly, local authorities support entertainment and the arts for five main reasons:

- to promote artistic excellence and provide opportunities for innovation;
- to enhance the quality of life both by promoting a wider range of events than the commercial market would offer and by helping lower income groups by reduced admission prices;
- to provide a focal point for the community – a theatre or arts centre can bring people together and help promote social cohesion;
- to support the local economy by helping to attract tourists and to stimulate investment, as companies seek locations which provide a congenial environment for their staff; and
- to conserve the national heritage – many older theatres, in particular, occupy prominent town centre sites and are architecturally important.

These different objectives are of course hard to disentangle, and it is often difficult to monitor them to assess whether they are being achieved. But the Commission considers authorities could do more to ensure that the money is spent effectively.

Although subsidies are normally granted in order to reduce prices, few authorities identify explicitly the people they wish to help. High-income households are more likely to visit the theatre than low-income ones.

Venues are generally receiving houses – i.e. they are visited by touring companies and shows produced by someone else, but they rarely set up events from scratch. Negotiations and financial arrangements with performers who also appear in commercial theatre and other media are complex, making it difficult to set clear financial objectives. The nature of the building may determine the types of events which can be brought to the area.

The Audit Commission nevertheless recommend that local authorities 'develop more targeted programmes of arts support which *respond to the identified needs of the area*'.

Source: The Audit Commission for Local Authorities in England and Wales (1991) *Review: Local Authorities, Entertainment and the Arts*.

Perhaps because of these conflicting objectives, marketing does not play as prominent a role in public sector organizations. Saker and Smith (1993) found that only 48% of local authority leisure departments employed a person specifically responsible for marketing, and only 14% had a written statement of marketing strategy.[14] Earlier research by Cowell suggests that until recently there was no more emphasis on marketing at the leisure centres managed by the authorities either.[15]

Without a marketing orientation, non-commercial organizations can easily become inward-looking, concerned with operations and technical problems, rather than with their customers or users. If this happens they may find it difficult to justify their funding in times of restraints on public spending. They may also develop

- complacency, leading to inefficient use of resources,
- over-dependence on subsidies, leaving them vulnerable if they are withdrawn, or
- remoteness from the public, leading to charges of elitism.

The absence of the profit motive does not mean that the organization does not need to define its objectives, identify its markets, and communicate its messages clearly. These messages should be targeted both at the users, the customers, and at the politicians (and electorate) who provide the funding. All of this requires marketing skills.

In an attempt to clarify the objectives and increase the efficiency of local government activities, the 1988 Local Government Act requires the authorities to put many of these activities, including the management of leisure centres but not as yet arts venues, to competitive tender. As Figure 3.3 shows, the leisure centre management now have two commercial relationships:

- with the *client*, the authority who specifies the services to be offered; and
- with the *customer*, the user of those services, normally the public.

In both relationships there is an exchange of services provided in return for payment. Both, therefore, require marketing.

Unfortunately, the process of compulsory competitive tendering (CCT) can itself become another preoccupation that distracts the

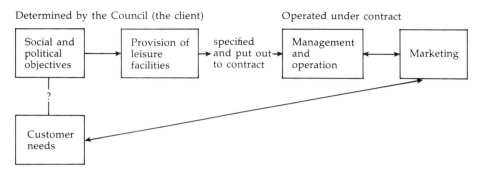

FIGURE 3.3   The approach required under compulsory competitive tendering.

organization from concentrating on satisfying the needs of its customers. If the customer, the final consumer, has not been adequately involved in the contract process, the specification will still result in product- or operations-oriented organizations with all the faults described earlier.[16]

Defining the mission

The overall aim of the organization is often termed its mission or its vision. It is the current business fashion for organizations to prepare mission statements setting out the overall aim so that all who work for the company know and understand it. In practice, such statements can be so broad and bland as to be meaningless. Nevertheless, the exercise of agreeing the statement can be a useful first step in the planning of a strategy.

A marketing-led, consumer-oriented organization will define its mission in terms of its customers and the benefits it offers them. A much-quoted example is Charles Revlon's 'In the factory we make cosmetics; in the shops we sell hope'. Sony's Akio Morita's aim was to give everyone access to 'portable personal sound' when he developed the Sony Walkman.[17]

In the same way, visitors to a leisure centre are buying hope, health, and the other benefits of leisure discussed in Chapter 1. By funding leisure facilities, the state is indeed buying 'the health of the nation'. With the possible exceptions of train spotters and 'booze cruisers', travellers are buying destinations not journeys. Defining the business in this way will avoid marketing myopia. It will remind management of the wide range of ways in which people can obtain the same benefits, and of the large number of organizations competing to offer them.

To survive in their market, the organization must have a strategy which is based on its understanding of those two Cs, its customers and its competitors. It must answer the question 'Who are our customers?' in ways which identify those groups within the larger market whose needs it can satisfy better than its competitors. It must identify and present its strengths (expertise, reputation, facilities, products) which give it an advantage over its competitors in the eyes of those customers. This is the process that will be examined in the following chapters.

Abell recommended doing this by defining a business in terms of three dimensions: customer needs, customer groups, and technologies (i.e. ways of satisfying those needs).[18] The product- or operations-oriented organization concentrates on the technology, which can become obsolete. A marketing-oriented organization concentrates first on the customer's needs, which will always exist.

CASE STUDY 3.2   *The Weymouth Diving Museum*

The Weymouth Diving Museum, which opened in 1988, was the brainchild of Brian Cooper, an experienced professional diver. He tells of a moment standing on a North Sea oil rig with the waves crashing over him when he thought, 'There must be a better way of earning a living'.

He chose Weymouth for the location of the museum initially because it is an area popular with amateur divers who come to dive around the numerous wrecks off Portland Bill. It is also a popular family holiday resort with a large sandy beach sheltered from the prevailing winds. There were already a number of successful tourist attractions, mostly at the Lodmoor Country Park on reclaimed marshland at the eastern end of the town (see Figure 3.4), including a Sea Life Centre, featuring displays of live fish swimming in large tanks which simulate their natural habitats. Particularly popular are the flat fish which come to the surface to look at the visitors. Established in 1984, it attracts 200,000 visitors a year. Other attractions included a butterfly farm (live butterflies in a tropical jungle), a shire horse centre, a model village, and a miniature railway.

Rather than face the cost of purpose-built premises, the Diving Museum was sited in a disused fish warehouse on Customs House Quay in the historic centre of the town. The listed building was renovated and converted by Weymouth and Portland Borough Council and leased to Mr Cooper.

Customs House Quay runs along what used to be the commercial harbour. Berths that used to handle ferries, cargo vessels, and tomato ships from Guernsey were now mainly used for yachts, fishing and pleasure craft, and the occasional tall ship sail-training vessel. With this change of use, the buildings along the quay were being converted to restaurants, cafes and specialist yachting shops.

Car parking near the Museum, and in the centre of Weymouth generally, is limited and expensive. Council policy is to encourage visitors to

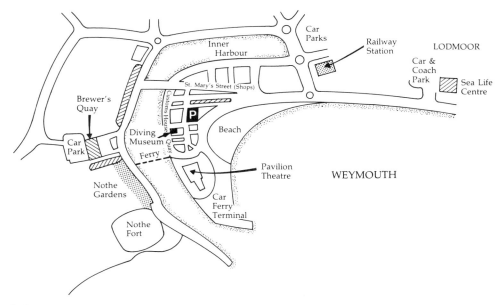

FIGURE 3.4   Map of Weymouth.

park further out at long-stay car parks at Lodmoor or across the harbour. Nevertheless, most tourists spend some time strolling down the quay looking at the boats. Brian Cooper decided that the central location and the picturesque setting outweighed the parking problems.

The building is tall, dark and narrow, but the design of the museum used this to best advantage. The ground floor was occupied by the museum cafe and shop which were open to all, to entice people into the building. Having paid to enter the museum itself, they were taken by lift to the top floor of the building where they could view a scale representation of the wreck of the *Titanic* using the whole height of the building to indicate the depth of the Atlantic. They then moved down through three floors of exhibits telling the history of diving and the story of local shipwrecks. The ground floor contained a miniature submarine and a reconstruction of a diver's decompression chamber.

Several exhibits featured animated figures with recorded voices. A computer game of an air–sea rescue and the opportunity to be photographed 'in' an old-fashioned diving suit were provided to interest children, who also enjoyed scrambling over the submarine. A large tank was used for diving displays at peak times during the summer. The overall effect came somewhere between a traditional museum and the kind of high-tech visitor experience offered at the Jorvik Centre in York, or at Beaulieu.

It cost £300,000 to set up the museum, mostly from bank loans, as Mr Cooper was unsuccessful in obtaining a Tourist Board grant. To recoup this money, he budgeted for 100,000 visitors at a price of £1.80 for adults (compared with the £2.10 charged by the Sea Life Centre). There were reduced rates for children, students, senior citizens and parties. Three main markets were targeted:

1   The special interest group of divers who were visiting the area. The museum would offer them genuine exhibits and insights into the history of diving and of local wrecks.

2   School parties looking for illustrations of science topics or local history. Such visits need to be relevant to the National Curriculum.

3   Holidaymakers looking for an hour or two of interest and entertainment.

The publicity budget was set at £15,000. An A4, three-fold leaflet was produced and distributed to tourist information centres, hotels, cafes, pubs and other attractions. Regular advertisements were placed in the local press. The museum's publicity was also featured on Weymouth Council's stand at exhibitions around the country aimed at coach operators, group organizers or the general public. It was also hoped to attract passers-by along the quay to visit on impulse.

The opening was a publicity dream. HRH Princess Anne was in Portland in her capacity as Commander-in-Chief of a Royal Marines unit, and through a contact of Mr Cooper's was persuaded to perform the opening ceremony of the museum the same day, resulting in regional press and TV coverage.

By the end of the first summer, however, it was clear that things were not going to plan, and that the visitor numbers would not exceed 30,000 for the year. Brian Cooper identified the following reasons:

1   Despite a busy summer for the resort, the museum was not attracting impulse visits. The fine weather, and the free entertainment arranged by the Council – the bicentenary of the visit of King George III, an international firework festival, and the tall ships race – had kept people out of doors.

2   Surveys showed that the museum was being visited by BC1 social grades – the educated middle classes. The C2D working class families who were the majority of Weymouth's holidaymakers were not attracted.

3   Visitor reaction was positive, comparing the museum favourably to others in the area. However, the interactive displays were too few to cope with the large numbers of children.

4   The shop had been reasonably successful, but the cafe had not proved popular and had had staffing problems.

There was also a new competitor being developed across the harbour where an old brewery was due to open as Brewer's Quay shopping village, including the TimeWalk, an historical attraction using animated figures similar in style to the Jorvik Centre in York.

To satisfy his bankers, the museum needed to attract 70,000 visitors a year. Reluctantly, Brian Cooper decided to close between Christmas and Easter and completely review his marketing mix.

QUESTIONS

1   Define the objectives of the Diving Museum using Drucker's three basic questions.

2   To what extent is it fair to accuse Brian Cooper of a product orientation in his ideas for the museum?

3   What are the main strengths and weaknesses of the museum?

4   What changes should Mr Cooper make to his marketing mix?

Summary

Putting the customer at the centre of the organization's activities may seem common sense, but in practice other concerns can distract managers and prevent them from implementing the marketing approach. Product, Production/Operations, and Sales Orientations are not just historical stages in the development of business thinking but can still be found in the leisure industries today. There is also an apparent tension between the marketing emphasis on the paying customer and the social or artistic objectives of non-commercial leisure organizations.

However, organizations that fail to base their business strategy on a real understanding of their customers may find it difficult to survive in a changing environment. For this reason, organizations should regularly review their mission by asking fundamental questions such as 'What is our business? Who are our customers? What are they really buying and why do they buy from us?' The process of using the answers as the basis of the marketing plan is dealt with in the next chapter.

Notes

1. See, for example, Baker, M. (1985) *Marketing: An Introductory Text.*
2. Levitt, T. (1960) 'Marketing myopia', *Harvard Business Review,* reprinted in Cox, B. and Ennis, K. (Eds) (1988) *Marketing Classics,* p. 10.
3. *Ibid,* p. 3.

4. Drucker, P. (1973) *Management: Tasks, Responsibilities and Practices*, ch. 7.
5. Audit Commission (1991) *The Road to Wigan Pier: Managing Local Authority Museums and Art Galleries.*
6. Hewison, R. (1994) 'Sceptered aisles', *The Sunday Times*, 13 March.
7. Advertising Association, *Lifestyle Pocket Book 1992*, p. 86.
8. Inglis, S. (1994) 'A whole new ball game', *Leisure Management*, July.
9. David Beeton, chief executive of Historic Royal Palaces quoted in 'Polishing the Crown jewels', *The Independent on Sunday*, 20 March 1994.
10. Newbold, C., interviewed in *Travel News*, 11 March 1988, p. 7.
11. Astles, R. (1989) 'Overseas package holidays: Where next?', *Leisure Intelligence*, 2: 4.3.
12. Coalter, F., (1990) 'The mixed economy in Leisure', in Henry, I. (Ed.) *Management and Planning in the Leisure Industries*, p. 29.
13. Henry, I. and Spink, J., (1990) 'Planning for leisure', in Henry, I. (Ed.) *Management and Planning in the Leisure Industries*, p. 35.
14. Saker, J. and Smith, G., (1993) 'Selling Leisure', *Leisure Opportunities*, Nos. 115 and 118.
15. Cowell, D. (1978) 'Marketing's application to public authority sport, recreation, and leisure centres', in Torkildsen (1993) *Leisure and Recreation Management.*
16. Audit Commission (1993) *Realizing the Benefits of Competition.*
17. Quoted in Kotler (1993) *Marketing Management*, pp. 68–69.
18. Abell, D. (1980) *Defining the Business*, ch. 3.

4 The marketing planning process

Mission
Analysis
Planning
Implementation
Control
Summary

In Chapter 3 we saw that marketing is based on a customer-oriented vision of the aims and objectives of the organization. This chapter outlines the process by which these aims are achieved. In doing so, it outlines the content of the next chapters of the book.

Perhaps because marketing planning is so important, every marketing writer seems to use a slightly different model of the structure of the marketing plan. All of these models, however, can be seen to have the basic elements of *analysis, planning, implementation* and *control* (as used in the title of Kotler's book). Colloquially, these elements might be expressed as

- where are we now?
- where should we be?
- how do we get there?
- how do we measure success?

Market research is not included as a specific stage in the planning process, but should be used as the basis of the decisions made at every stage. Chapter 5 examines the methods and sources of leisure marketing research.

Mission

As discussed in Chapter 3, the organization should first agree its overall aims or *mission*. This mission will reflect the commercial and non-commercial aims of the organization, and will be expressed in terms of benefits offered to customers. The marketing plan should be designed to fulfil this mission. (The word 'vision' appears to be replacing 'mission', particularly in the strategy documents of public sector organizations such as the English Tourist Board.)

In a large organization, the corporate objectives and strategy will set the direction for the marketing planning process for each business unit, product or profit centre.

Analysis

The first stage in any planning process is to understand the current situation: 'where we are now'. To do this requires an analysis of the organization, its markets – the *company, customers* and *competitors* – and the external forces that influence them. This is sometimes described as a marketing audit; the analogy being with an accountancy audit, since in both cases the processes and outcomes of the organization's activities are critically examined and inconsistencies are highlighted.[1]

The external influences can be summarized under the headings of *political, economic, social* and *technological* (PEST). Chapter 6 examines the current trends in the leisure market and the options they offer leisure marketers.

The analysis can be done in two parts: the general trends or 'macro-environment', and the particular developments affecting the company, its customers and competitors, the 'micro-environment'. The purpose of the analysis is to identify the external *opportunities* and *threats* facing the organization.

The organization should then be assessed in terms of how it is seen by its customers, how it compares with its competitors, and what resources and capabilities it has to deal with the changing market . This is usually summarized under the headings of company *strengths* and company *weaknesses*. This analysis of strengths, weaknesses, opportunities and threats (SWOT) is probably the most frequently quoted tool of business planning. In using it, two major errors must be avoided.

The first is to make it a purely descriptive exercise rather than an analysis. Listing every factor you can think of may be a useful way to begin, but the finished analysis must identify how these factors will affect the business and which are the most significant.

The second is to do the SWOT analysis, fall back exhausted and admire it. The SWOT is not an end in itself, but a means of deciding priorities for action. It should be followed by recommendations on how to exploit the strengths, seize the opportunities, remedy the weaknesses and avoid the threats.

Planning

The SWOT analysis then forms the basis for planning decisions, which need to be made at two levels: strategic and tactical. Strategy is long-term, tactics short-term. Strategy determines the direction that is to be followed; tactics deal with the immediate obstacles in the way. The two should of course be linked. The strategy should be able to be translated into detailed day-to-day tactics. Tactics should not achieve short-term success at the expense of abandoning the long-term strategic objectives.

Marketing strategy answers the question, 'where should we be?'. It says what the organization should be doing to achieve its overall aims given the situation identified in the analysis. The core of any marketing strategy will be the decisions as to which customers to target, and how to make the organization's products more attractive to them than those offered by competitors. As Kotler says:

> the heart of modern marketing is segmenting, targeting and positioning.[2]

These concepts will be dealt with in detail in subsequent chapters. First, an understanding is needed of *consumer behaviour* – the psychological, social and economic influences on how and what people choose. This is the subject of Chapter 7. Chapter 8 shows how this understanding is used in *segmentation*, the process of identifying groups of customers within the total market who share needs and behaviour that can be effectively targeted by marketing activities. *Positioning* the organization and its services so that these customers perceive them to be different from and more attractive than those of your competitors is dealt with in Chapter 9.

Positioning decisions are the core of the organization's *competitive strategy* and will therefore depend on the nature of your competition. Ways of understanding, and dealing with, competition are also dealt with in Chapter 9.

The strategy needs to be expressed not only in general statements about the target markets and positioning, but also in terms of specific marketing objectives: sales targets, market share targets and profit targets.

Implementation

The next question is 'how do we get there?'. To implement the strategy, detailed action plans must be agreed. These plans should include actions for each element of the *marketing* mix – Product, Price, Place (distribution) and Promotion – all of which need to be designed to appeal to your target market and gain a competitive advantage. These '4 Ps' will be examined in detail in Chapters 10–13.

Some writers include an extra P in the marketing mix – People.[3] Certainly in marketing leisure experiences, the interaction between staff and customers is crucial, and internal marketing, informing, training and motivating staff should be part of the implementation plan. This is examined in Chapter 11.

Another extra P is Process. Effective action plans must specify not only what needs to be done but also:

- who is to do it?   Responsibilities
- when must it be completed by?   Timescales
- how much will it cost?   Budgets
- what is the expected result?   Outcomes

The marketing plan will therefore need to be agreed with those in the organization responsible for allocating financial, human and physical resources. The operational implementation is discussed in Chapter 22.

Control

In return for the resources allocated, the organization will expect the marketing activities to produce the promised results. Built into the plan therefore will be the means of evaluating it. If the timescale is not met, the budget is exceeded, and the outcome is below expectations, then those responsible are clearly identified! It is in their interests, therefore, that the progress of the plan is frequently monitored so that any problems are identified and remedied before they cause any serious consequences.

Any attempt to forecast the future is unreliable, and external factors may invalidate the assumptions on which the plan was based. All plans should therefore include the flexibility to modify the plan to meet changing circumstances. Key performance indicators therefore need to be agreed and monitored regularly. A mechanism needs to be in place for reviewing the results and modifying tactics accordingly.

The marketing planning process described here is shown in Figure 4.1.[4] Effective marketing planning depends on the whole organization being involved in the whole process. In many leisure organizations, however, this is not the case. Research by Dibb and Simkin found that most leisure marketing managers they interviewed in a range of UK leisure companies were concerned only with fine tuning the tactics rather than determining the strategy.[5] Because of non-commercial objectives or a set product determined by location, premises or collections, the marketing department 'exists to market/communicate existing policies, services, and products to the organization's various publics'. These policies were determined in theatres and the arts by artistic directors and administrators, in museums and zoos by curators, and in local authorities by bureaucrats. 'The strategic role of

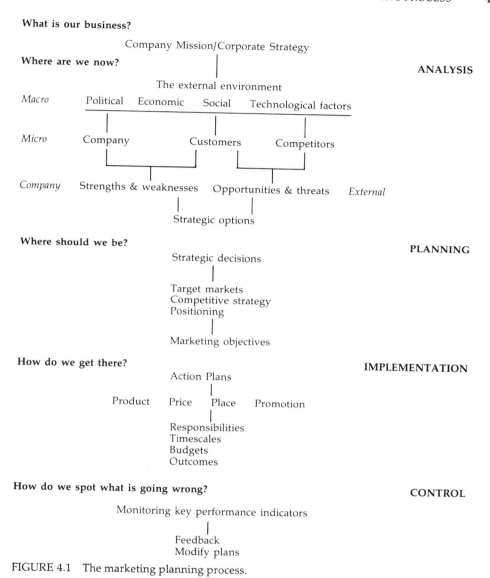

What is our business?

Company Mission/Corporate Strategy

Where are we now?   ANALYSIS

The external environment

Macro   Political   Economic   Social   Technological factors

Micro   Company   Customers   Competitors

Company   Strengths & weaknesses   Opportunities & threats   *External*

Strategic options

Where should we be?   **PLANNING**

Strategic decisions

Target markets
Competitive strategy
Positioning

Marketing objectives

How do we get there?   **IMPLEMENTATION**

Action Plans

Product   Price   Place   Promotion

Responsibilities
Timescales
Budgets
Outcomes

How do we spot what is going wrong?   **CONTROL**

Monitoring key performance indicators

Feedback
Modify plans

FIGURE 4.1   The marketing planning process.

marketing – anticipating and pre-empting the future – is missing, compounded by a narrow definition of competition.'

Such organizations are likely to find themselves struggling to maintain audiences in the face of wider competition from home-based leisure controlled by global multimedia entertainment corporations.

Notes

1. See Kotler, P. (1994) *Marketing Management*, p. 758. To Kotler, a marketing audit is a comprehensive, systematic, independent, and periodic examination.
2. *Ibid*, p. 264.
3. E.g. Moores, B. (1986) *Are They Being Served?*
4. For a guide to the practice as well as a good model of the theory of marketing plans, see Macdonald, M. (1989) *Marketing Plans*, and Davidson, J. (1979) *Offensive Marketing*.
5. Dibb, S. and Simkin, L., (1993) 'Strategy and tactics: Marketing leisure facilities', *Service Industries Journal*, **13**(3), 110–24.

PART 2

Understanding Leisure Markets

5 Research for marketing

Marketing research
The purpose of research
Sources of data
Secondary research
Primary research
Summary

While it is the creative aspects that generally attract people to a career in marketing, success in that career will depend equally on an ability to handle facts and figures. A good marketer can spot an opportunity in a column of figures and understand the implications for the organization of seemingly unrelated facts. Before going into the detail of the decisions involved in the marketing process in subsequent chapters, it is necessary first to understand how to obtain the accurate information on which good decisions depend.

Marketing research

Marketing research is the term used for the whole range of information gathering and analysis undertaken at every stage of the process. Market research, the popularly used term, should strictly apply to research into the market, to which should be added consumer behavioural research, product development research, pre- and post-testing of promotional campaigns, monitoring of the efficiency of the distribution network and evaluation of the overall performance of the marketing plan.[1] The information and methodology needed for each of these will be dealt with in subsequent chapters. This chapter outlines the general principles and practice of marketing research.

The fundamental principle is that research should be a systematic process. It is often compared (for example, by Kotler) with the process of scientific research: defining the problem, observing the facts, forming a hypothesis as to the cause of those facts, predicting the results one would expect if the hypothesis were correct, and testing that prediction. The hypothesis is then confirmed or modified in the light of the results of the test.[2] Marketing research should be equally rigorous, only accepting what can be proved and interpreting the results by comparing them with an expected norm or hypothesis.

The application of the scientific method to the needs of marketing is shown in Figure 5.1. It begins by defining the objectives of the research: what decisions need to be made and what information is needed to make them? This information can be obtained from primary research – first-hand surveys obtaining new data direct from the target market – or secondary research,

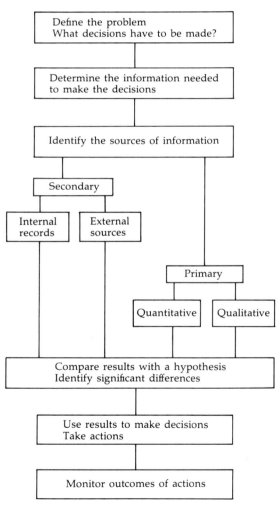

FIGURE 5.1   The marketing research process.

using data already available, for example, within the organization or from government statistics and commercial research publications.

The significance of the data can only be properly understood if it is compared with what is already known about the subject, e.g. to a hypothesis or norm. For example, are the customers drawn from all age groups and social classes in the same proportion as would be found in the population as a whole, or are certain groups significantly over- or under-represented? Do the local results match those from national surveys? Has the composition of the market changed since the last survey?

To judge the significance of the results and to monitor a continually changing market place marketing research should not be limited to occasional surveys in response to particular problems. A marketing information system should be set up to supply managers with the key data they need to run their business on a regular basis so that emerging trends can be quickly identified.

The purpose of research

Research can be used to aid decision making at every stage of the marketing process. In practice, however, many organizations make only limited use of research. In their survey of local authority leisure departments, Saker and Smith found that most research studies were undertaken to determine the use of specific services or general user satisfaction.[3] There was little emphasis on non-users or new service possibilities. They found a lack of a strategic approach to information gathering, raising questions as to the authorities' ability to develop appropriate new services tailored for potential local customers.

In a survey of 76 visitor attractions in southern England, Sheathe found that fewer than half the privately owned attractions did any kind of market research, including desk research, compared with 86% of local authority owned attractions.[4] The research was generally used for decisions about advertising and promotion, although a few organizations also used it for decisions about facilities, pricing, shop products, signposting, staff training and visitor flow management.

While too little information can lead to poor decision making, there is also a danger of gathering too much data without a clear idea of how they will be used. Research is expensive, particularly if outside agencies are employed, and care should be taken in drawing up the research brief. Middleton suggests the client brief should:

- identify the marketing context and perceived problem,
- specify the expected use of the results,
- indicate the timescale for completion, and
- state appropriate budget limits.[5]

The agency then defines the problem in research terms and suggests an appropriate methodology. Equal care is needed if the research is being conducted in-house.

Secondary research

Sources of secondary data

Despite the name, secondary research should always be done first. Primary research is only used to fill in the last gap after the secondary sources have been consulted. Figure 5.2 depicts the research process as the piecing together of a jigsaw picture of the organization's market. The top line of the jigsaw shows some of the internal sources of information: booking details, sales figures, and customer complaints and comments. The organization may also gain market information from its salesforce, by monitoring the response to its publicity and from a variety of informed sources within the industry sector. It may also consult published research by government or commercial agencies. Only when these secondary sources have been consulted should primary research be considered.

Secondary sources

Booking details
Every contact the customer has with the organization creates an opportunity to find out something about him or her. Whether the contact is by phone,

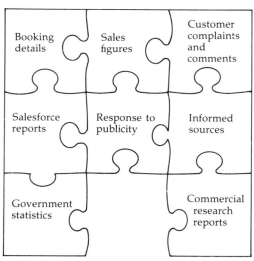

FIGURE 5.2   The marketing research jigsaw.

post or in person, a record can be kept of names, addresses, the source of the enquiry, and the type of transaction. Booking forms can be a particularly rich source of data on customers and their purchasing preferences. The form can be analyzed to provide statistics on:

- Age: especially if there are special rates for children and senior citizens.
- Family or group size.
- Special needs: diets, disabilities, babysitting, business facilities, etc.
- Date of booking: are they booking early or at the last minute?
- Source of booking: via an agency or in direct response to an advertisement or guide.
- Method of payment: cash, cheque or credit card.
- Type and class of product purchased.
- Price they have been prepared to pay.

These data can be used to develop new products and facilities, to plan advertising campaigns and distribution strategies, or to target and customize mailings.

The addresses are very useful not only for mailing publicity to existing customers but also to suggest where other potential customers might be found. A simple analysis can be used to determine the catchment area within which most customers live. Geodemographic systems such as ACORN (see Chapter 8) can be used to analyze mailing lists into postal code districts and to identify the types of housing and neighbourhoods where new customers are most likely to be found.

Sales figures

By monitoring sales figures over time and by type of purchase, an organization such as a leisure centre will know which facilities are increasing or decreasing in popularity, and where there is excess or insufficient capacity at certain times of the day, week or year. They will be able to gauge the effect of promotional campaigns, price changes, programming and other marketing decisions.

Customer complaints and comments

Letters of complaint, or of praise, from customers will give managers detailed insights into how their service is being received. However, these snapshots represent only the extremes of reaction. Most people will go away moderately satisfied or mildly dissatisfied, and will tell their friends rather than write to the company.

Managers should therefore attempt to find out the reactions of a more representative sample of customers by giving them a survey form to complete at the end of their visit. For package tour operators this is comparatively easy to do: questionnaires can be given out and collected back while the customers are 'captive' on the return flight. Thomson claim a 75% response rate for their 'customer satisfaction questionnaires', a detailed four-page document, the results of which are used to decide whether to re-employ a resort representative or even whether to renew a contract with a hotel.[6] Thomson reps wait with trepidation for their monthly 'CSQ ratings'.

It is harder for a visitor attraction or leisure centre to achieve a high response rate. Visitors may not notice the questionnaires in the rack as they leave, or may not bother to return them. Reply-paid cards and offers of prize draws may improve the response. The Big Sheep farm in North Devon, for example, offered a sheepskin as an appropriate prize in their draw.

Sales reports
The sales force are the eyes and ears of the business. In organization to organization selling, for example, a charter airline with a tour operator or a sports goods manufacturer with a retail chain, the sales manager and his client will agree a forecast of demand for the product for the coming year or five years. This then forms part of the airline or manufacturer's business plan and aids them to allocate resources. The reliability of the information is, of course, dependent on the experience and expertise of the parties concerned.

In other situations, the contact may be less formal but the people in personal contact with the customers can still be useful sources of information. The marketing manager should create a working environment in which customer comments are recorded and passed on by the front-line staff.

Response to publicity
Replies to advertisements should be recorded to measure the effectiveness of different media. Coupons in direct response advertisements generally include a code to indicate the publication and the date. Where no coupon is included, different box numbers or named members of staff can be given in each publication. If telephone responses are expected, a dedicated phone number can be used, or an agency can be employed to take the calls and send out further details.

At the Heights of Abraham in Matlock Bath, for example, leaflets carry a 'money-off' coupon which is coded to indicate where the leaflets were displayed. When the coupon is handed in, the clerk types the code into the ticket-issuing computer, revealing for example that source 40 is the Buxton Tourist Information Centre. A more direct approach is for sales and enquiry staff to ask each customer where they heard about the firm or its offer, and to record the answers.

As well as helping to plan future campaigns, information about which newspapers and magazines customers read can be used to create a profile of their interests and lifestyles.

Informed sources
There are many ways in which the leisure professionals can keep up-to-date with trends and developments in their sector. For example, trade journals carry news of competitors' and clients' activities and articles on current market trends and new products. Leisure and tourism journals include *Leisure Management, Leisure Week, Travel Weekly, Travel Trade Gazette, Travel Agency* and *Travel GBI*.

Professional bodies have their own journals and hold meetings, conferences and social events at which members can build contacts, discuss matters of mutual concern, and learn the trade gossip. Relevant bodies include the Institute of Leisure and Amenity Management, the Institute of Sports and Recreation Management, The Chartered Institute of Marketing (Travel Industry Group), the Tourism Society, the Institute of Travel and Tourism, and the Association of British Travel Agents. The Tourism Society, for example, holds a seminar each year at which leading figures in the industry give their views on trends for the coming year.

The growing number of academics specializing in leisure and tourism are likely to develop a wider more objective view of the industry than a busy manager has time to do. Practitioners and academics can forge links through professional bodies, consultancies, student placements or projects, or through academic journals such as *Leisure Studies, Tourism Management*, and a growing number of others.

Government statistics
The UK government carries out surveys which provide useful information on general social and economic trends. The leisure marketer will find the data on population, households, income, expenditure and leisure activities in the annual publication *Social Trends* particularly relevant.

The results of the International Passenger Survey and the British National Travel Survey appear in the British Tourist Authority's *Digest of Tourism Statistics*. Data on British overseas and domestic travel also appear in the Department of Transport's *Transport Statistics in Great Britain*. Worldwide tourism arrivals and departures are monitored by the World Tourism Organization's *Yearbook of Tourism Statistics*.

Commercial research reports
For detailed research into particular markets it is necessary to use commercial reports produced by specialist research companies. Leisure is well served by such organizations as Mintel's *Leisure Intelligence Reports,* and Leisure Consultants' *Leisure Forecasts*. The Economist Intelligence Unit publishes reports on a wide range of business sectors. Particularly relevant are *International Tourism Reports* and *Travel and Tourism Analyst*. Other widely quoted commercial agencies include the Henley Centre for Forecasting and Keynote Publications.

Domestic tourism is covered by the *Insights* reports by the English Tourist Board, though the publications of the Tourist Boards and the Arts and Sports Councils should perhaps be classed as government rather than commercial reports.

Leading tour operators and travel agency chains subscribe to syndicated research into current sales of holiday products carried out by Stats MR.

Leisure and tourism also feature in 'omnibus' surveys of consumer behaviour such as the *National Readership Survey* and other media surveys. The most comprehensive of the omnibus surveys is the British Market Research Bureau's *Target Group Index*. Based on an annual sample of 25,000 people who complete a 90-page questionnaire entitled *What do you buy?*, the *TGI* can give subscribers a detailed profile of the users of a particular brand or product, their age, class, education, region of residence, income plus their reading and viewing habits. As it is based on data from a single source, it can also calculate the favourite beers of those who holiday in Greece, or the savings habits of regular badminton players. It can also provide psychological profiles based on the answers to a large number of attitude questions. Current editions of the *TGI* cost thousands of pounds per volume, and so tend to be bought by large companies and by advertising agencies. Smaller organizations are more likely to rely on their agencies to have access to the data. Nevertheless, use of secondary data can be more cost effective than primary research.

Primary research

Once it has been decided that the information required can only be obtained by primary research, the key elements of the research plan are:

- which target group should be surveyed (referred to as the *population*);
- how many of this population need to be questioned (the *sample size*);
- how the sample is to be selected;
- how to contact the people to be questioned (the *respondents*);
- the type of survey to be used;
- the design of the questionnaire;
- the analysis of the results; and
- the presentation of the findings.

Defining the population

Suppose a leisure centre needs to decide how to improve the utilization of its squash courts. It could survey those who do use them, to find the reasons why they choose the centre and what they see as its strengths and weaknesses. This would be relatively easy to do but would not reveal the reasons why other people do not use the courts.

The problem here is who to ask. A street survey in the town would include many people who are never likely to play squash anywhere. The centre needs to decide how to define the potential market for its squash courts. Is it those who regularly play squash elsewhere? Or anyone who has ever played the game? Or anyone who takes part in any sport or fitness activity? Should it include those who feel that they ought to take more exercise? What age range should be included, and what geographic catchment area?

Secondary data could help to choose the target population. There may be commercial reports giving the profile of a typical squash player. The trade press may have examples of how other centres have expanded their market for the game.

The decision on who to include in the survey would be determined by what use the centre could make of the results. There would be no point in identifying a large potential market among those who have never played squash unless the centre could afford a substantial promotional campaign to make them more aware of the benefits of the game. It might be more realistic to aim at winning existing players from other clubs in the area.

Sample size

Let us suppose the leisure centre manager decided, for example, that the survey should include all adults aged under 45 years who take part in active leisure activities and who live in a 20 mile radius of the centre. There may be 30,000 people aged between 15 and 44 years living in this catchment area. Less than 33% of these are likely to take regular moderate exercise,[7] but this does not mean that the researchers need to survey 10,000 people to produce reliable results.

Opinion pollsters usually survey around 2,000 people to produce a statistically valid sample of the voting intentions of an electorate of over 40 million. Market researchers usually use samples of a few hundred people. The principle behind this practice is that a sample taken from a larger group will tend to have the same characteristics as the larger group.[8]

There is of course the danger that the sample will contain some unrepresentative elements. If the survey only asks ten people how much exercise they take, it could accidentally pick on five fitness fanatics. If, however, it goes on to ask another 50 people, it is likely that the fitness fanatics will be balanced by a number of total 'couch potatoes', and in between the extremes a more representative pattern will begin to form.[9]

Although the accuracy of the results increases with the size of the sample, the increase in accuracy becomes less and less significant as the size increases. Readers are recommended to consult specialist research or statistics text books for the mathematics, but it is possible to calculate the optimum size of sample to give acceptable limits of accuracy, say ±10%, with a high level of confidence, usually 95%.[10] The accuracy will be less reliable when the population is more or less evenly split (e.g. 49% answering 'yes', 51% answering 'no' to a question) than if it shows a large majority in either direction.

Table 5.1 illustrates that with a sample of 30, when the sample shows a 50% result it could represent anything from 69.6% to 30.4% of the population, and for any other result the margin of error is larger than the original statistic. With a sample of 400, we can be 95% confident that the result is accurate within 3–5% either way. By doubling the size of the sample to 800 we reduce the margin of error only by around 1%.

It is also important to remember that the limits of accuracy refer to answers involving the whole sample group. If smaller subgroups within the sample are to be asked specific questions, then each subgroup needs to be of a sufficient size to make the answers statistically reliable. For example, in a sample of 400, if it is found that 20 people, i.e. 5%, play hockey, then it is probably safe to assume that this represents reasonably accurately the proportion of hockey players among local sportsmen (±4%). It is not safe, however, to assume that the replies of these 20 hockey players represent the views of all hockey players in the area on, say, the quality of facilities provided. If the survey wishes to gain reliable information specific to hockey players it needs to increase the sample size, to at least 100 in this subgroup.

Choosing the sample

The statistical theories referred to above only apply to a *random sample*, that is, one that is selected in such a way as to remove any personal influence on

Table 5.1   Confidence intervals and sample size.

	Percentage split found in sample				
	50	40/60	30/70	20/80	10/90
Sample size	Confidence intervals (±%)				
30	19.6	–	–	–	–
50	14.9	14.6	–	–	–
100	10.3	10.1	9.5	8.0	6.0
400	5.0	4.9	4.6	4.0	3.0
800	3.6	3.6	3.3	2.9	2.2
1,000	3.2	3.1	2.9	2.5	1.9
2,000	2.2	2.2	2.0	1.8	1.3
10,000	1.0	1.0	0.9	0.8	0.6

who is interviewed. This assumes that all the names and addresses of the target population are known. The list, known as the sampling frame, could be numbered and the numbers selected using random number tables. Interviewers would then be sent to each address selected.

It can be seen that this could be a time-consuming, expensive and possibly impractical method, and marketers often use other types of sample instead. A *convenience sample* is simply one that is convenient and easy to find. Interviewers could stand outside a rival squash club and interview anyone prepared to talk to them. This would be useful but would not be representative of all sports players in the area.

A more accurate sample could be obtained by selecting people so as to create a cross-section of types (age, sex, income, etc.) similar to that found in the population as a whole. This could be simply a matter of *judgement*, or using secondary research, a *quota sample* could be constructed based on a national survey by Mintel or from the *TGI*, for example, giving the percentage of squash players by age, sex and class. Interviewers would be told to find a certain number of people in each category. The results could if necessary be weighted to make them correspond more accurately to the known characteristics of the population.

Survey methodology

Depending on the required results, surveys may either be qualitative or quantitative.

- The *quantitative approach* seeks to find out the quantity of people in each category who behave in a certain way or hold certain views. It uses a structured questionnaire and calculates the percentages and other statistical measures for each answer. It can produce a factual description of the average customer and measure how many choose particular products or activities.

- The *qualitative approach* is more concerned to understand how and why the customer makes a particular choice. It emphasizes the quality of the insight gained into the mental and emotional processes of the customer. It consists of extended personal interviews or small group discussions led by a skilled interviewer. The interviewer encourages the group to talk freely about their experiences and feelings connected with the product or service.

The drawbacks with this latter type of survey are that the group, however carefully selected, may not be representative, and can be swayed by one forceful individual, or by the desire to tell the interviewer what they think he wants to hear.

Qualitative methods are often used to obtain customer reactions to new product ideas or to advertisements. They can also be used, as Crouch says, early in the research process to generate hypotheses which a subsequent quantitative survey will investigate further.[11]

Observational research is a type of quantitative research which could be used in leisure facilities. Observers armed with clipboards or click-counters record the movements of visitors through the facilities. The results could be used, for example, to redesign the layout and signing in order to reduce queues and congestion, or to increase the numbers visiting the gift shops and refreshment areas.

Contacting the respondents

The quantitative survey can be conducted in a number of ways, by face-to-face interview, by phone, by post or by leaving the questionnaires for the respondents to pick up and fill in. The choice of method should be made with the respondents' viewpoint in mind. They are more likely to cooperate:

- if the purpose of the survey is made clear,
- if they have the time and place to complete the questionnaire at once,
- if there is some incentive for them, and
- if they do not have to make a special effort to return the form.

The face-to-face interview meets these requirements best (the opportunity to talk about oneself to a charming interviewer can be sufficient incentive for many people!). However, it does take more time and is therefore more expensive.

Postal surveys, even with incentives and reply-paid envelopes, have lower response rates; Crouch estimates 50% to be the average.[12] They also carry a risk of bias since only those with strong views will have the motivation to reply.

Telephone surveys are increasingly used, but have their drawbacks. In business surveys, the interviewer may be blocked by a secretary or assistant from talking to the decision maker. Many British people regard being rung at home by commercial companies as an invasion of their privacy and may refuse to cooperate.

Questionnaires may be handed out at entrances or exits, included with other documentation (booking confirmations, delegate packs, etc.) or mailed as part of after-sales service. The problems of getting a representative response to customer satisfaction surveys has already been discussed.

Questionnaire design

According to Crouch, questionnaires have four main purposes:[13]

- *To collect relevant data.* When drafting each question, the researcher and client should always ask, 'What use will the answers be?' This relates back to the definition of the purpose of the research, but also tests whether the question is phrased so as to produce the desired information.

- *To make data comparable.* The wording of the questions and alternative answers should be clear and not capable of more than one interpretation. A pilot survey on a few people is useful for detecting any ambiguities.

- *To minimize bias.* Care should be taken to avoid wording questions that lead the respondents to feel that one answer will be regarded as more acceptable than others.

- *To motivate the respondent.* The respondent must be made to feel that answering the questionnaire will be interesting, useful, and will not take too much time. The purpose of the survey must be explained, and reassurances given that the results will be confidential and that it is not a disguised attempt to sell something. It should begin with interesting questions, not with requests for personal details like 'How much do you earn?', or 'How old are you?'. The length of the questionnaire should be kept to a minimum and the respondent should be thanked at the end.

Some of the more common faults in questionnaire design are illustrated in Figure 5.3.

Analysis of the data

The questionnaire should be designed to make analysis as simple as possible. Closed questions, where the respondent ticks a box to indicate the chosen answer, are easier to complete and to analyze than open questions in which the respondent is asked to make comments or suggestions in his own words. Closed questions can be dichotomous ('yes' or 'no') or multiple choice, giving a list of possible answers. Such lists need careful testing. It is advisable to include 'Other (please specify)' in case an important alternative has been forgotten.

Questions of opinion, attitude or belief usually offer some kind of scale ranging from 'excellent' to 'very poor', 'strongly agree' to 'strongly disagree'. These are often five-point scales allowing an even balance of positive and negative responses and a central point for those with neutral feelings on the subject.

The researcher needs to decide before commencing the survey what links or cross-tabulations are to be made between answers to different questions, e.g. attitudes to exercise analyzed by age, frequency of exercise by occupation, or belief in the importance of exercise compared with actual exercise taken. Only relevant questions should be asked or the questionnaire will become too long. The structure of the questionnaire

QUESTIONNAIRE

This fictional questionnaire illustrates some common faults in questionnaire design. Identify the faults, explain what is wrong and redraft the question.

1 How old are you?
2 What do you think of Bournemouth?
3 What do you like best about Bournemouth?
    Beaches ( )
    Shops   ( )
    Parks   ( )
    Shows   ( )
4 Are you a frequent or occasional visitor?
5 How many holidays have you spent here?
6 What are the principal motivational factors behind your vacation purchase decision?
7 How many advertisements did you see for last summer's International Festival?
8 Do you agree that these events are a waste of money better spent on cleaning the place up?
9 How do you spend your spare time?
    Going to plays and concerts ( )
    Reading   ( )
    Voluntary work   ( )
    Hobbies   ( )
    Watching TV   ( )
    Hanging round the shops   ( )
    Doing absolutely nothing   ( )
Send the completed questionnaire to P.O. Box 149, Grimsby

FIGURE 5.3   Common faults in questionnaire design.

should allow results to be easily input into the computer analysis programme, which needs to be set up to allow for the cross-tabulations. As already mentioned, the number of subgroups to be analyzed will affect the size of the sample needed.

Anyone involved in marketing research, whether as a researcher or client/user, needs to be familiar with the basic principles of statistical analysis, e.g. frequency, average, dispersion, significance and probability. There are many specialist books dealing with these techniques.

Presentation of results

Marketing research reports, like all marketing communications, should be designed with the end user in mind. In this case, the user is likely to be a busy manager. Although he will want to be assured that the research has been systematic and is statistically reliable, and will want to have the detailed analysis included for reference, he will not have time to wade through pages of tables. The report should *begin* with a summary of the significant findings, their implications for the business, and recommend-ations for action.

Summary

Marketing research is the planned, systematic collection and analysis of data designed to help the management of an organization to reach decisions and to monitor the results of those decisions once they have been taken.[14] Research should be undertaken at every stage of the marketing process. Secondary research, using the information available from internal records and published reports, can provide much of the data needed without recourse to expensive primary research. When undertaken, primary research should be carefully planned. It should aim to provide the organization with relevant, comparable, unbiased data that will be of practical use to the business. Those being questioned are more likely to cooperate if they feel that the questionnaire is interesting, important and easy to complete.

Like all aspects of marketing, research should be based on a clear view of the objectives of the organization and of the needs of the users.

Notes

1. Based on Middleton, V. (1988) *Marketing for Travel and Tourism*, p. 109.
2. Kotler, P. (1994) *Marketing Management*, p. 141.
3. Saker, J. and Smith, G. (1993) 'Marketing activity', *Leisure Opportunities*, **116**: 34–35.
4. Sheathe, R. (1991) *What Role Does Market Research Play in the Marketing of Attractions in the Southern Region?* Bournemouth University.
5. Middleton (1988) *op. cit.*, p. 116.
6. *Travel News*, July 1988.
7. In Allied Dunbar's *National Fitness Survey 1993*, it was found that 36% of men and 24% of women took 30 minutes moderate exercise five times a week.
8. This is known as the law of statistical regularity; see Baker (1985) *Marketing*, p. 190.
9. This is known as the law of the inertia of large numbers.
10. For example, Crimp, M. (1981) *The Marketing Research Process*, pp. 56 ff, or Veal, A.J. (1992) *Research Methods for Leisure and Tourism*.
11. Crouch, S. (1986) *Marketing Research for Managers*, p. 76.
12. *Ibid*, p. 103.
13. *Ibid*, p. 145–47.
14. Holloway, J.C. and Plant, R. (1992) *Marketing for Tourism*, p. 30.

6 The external influences

To understand the current situation in which the organization finds itself, it is necessary to identify some of the external factors that affect the behaviour of its customers and competitors. In Chapter 4 it was suggested that these factors could be grouped under the headings of political, economic, social and technological factors (PEST). These should form the basis for an analysis of the opportunities and threats facing the organization, and its strengths and weaknesses in being able to deal with them.

In applying these formulae, however, there is a danger that the result becomes an incoherent list of seemingly unrelated issues. What the analysis should be concentrating on are the effects of these factors on the demand for the organization's services.

The four key variables

From the discussion in Chapter 1, the demand for leisure activities can be said to depend on four key variables:

- spare time available to carry out the activity,
- disposable income to pay for the facilities and equipment,
- access to the facilities, and
- the customer's choice from the alternatives available.

The analysis of the external environment should be an analysis of the factors that affect each of these variables.

The spare time available will depend on *social* factors such as the customer's occupation, age and family status. These will affect not only the time available but the priorities placed on how this time is used.

Disposable income will obviously depend on *economic* factors such as employment, earnings, the cost of living and inflation.

Access to facilities is largely dependent on *technological* factors, i.e. whether the facilities are provided at an affordable price in a convenient location. Changes in technology can make leisure activities accessible to a wider market.

The customer's choice is also affected by *market* factors such as competition and the influence of the media and fashion.

Political and legal factors can affect all of these areas. Economic policies on taxation and interest rates, for example, can affect disposable income. Opportunities for new developments in technology and access can be restrained by planning controls and safety regulations, or encouraged by grants or tax incentives. The competitive market can be directly influenced by subsidies or state ownership of facilities.

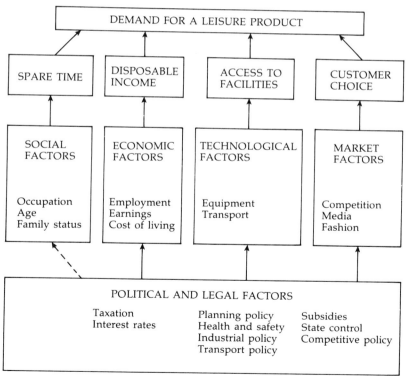

FIGURE 6.1   The influences on leisure demand.

Figure 6.1 shows these relationships diagrammatically. Changes in any of these external factors can affect the demand for a product. This chapter outlines some of the most significant trends in these areas.[1]

Social factors affecting leisure demand

Age

People's choices of leisure activities change as they go through life. Their physical capabilities decline with age; their needs for socializing and personal fulfilment change with their status at work and in their community; the time and money they have to spend on leisure changes with their work and family commitments.

Identifying the ages of potential customers will help the leisure marketer design products and promotions that will appeal to their particular needs, motivations and price sensitivity. In general, the most attractive age segments must be those with a high disposable income matched with a large amount of time available for leisure.

In a Mintel survey of how leisure time varies with age,[2] respondents were asked 'How many hours do you have to do what you like ...'. Figure 6.2 shows the average number of hours per week for each age group. Not surprisingly, the under-20s, many of them students, and retired people aged over 65 have the most free time to 'do what they like', while those aged between 25 and 44 have the least because of family and career commitments. If we superimpose on this graph a line representing income the result would be something like Figure 6.3.[3] At times when our income is at its highest, we have least leisure time. Students living on grants and loans, and retired people living on state pensions may have the time, but not necessarily the money to do what they like.

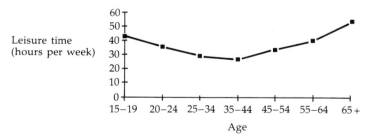

FIGURE 6.2   Average leisure time by age group, June 1990.
Source: BMRB/Mintel (1991).

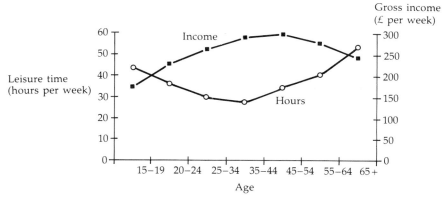

FIGURE 6.3   Leisure time and income by age group.
Source: Department of Employment, *New Earnings Survey 1993.*

If then we show on the graph the expenditure on 'essentials' like food, housing, clothes, transport and children, the result would look something like Figure 6.4.[4] The people with the highest disposable income are likely to be those in their early 20s (pre-family stage) and those aged over 45 (post-family stage). Children are expensive in terms of both time and money. In the late family stage the average figures suggest that many families must rely on a second wage earner to pay for leisure goods and services.

The age groups can be described in various ways. The Henley Centre defines four ages, as shown in Table 6.1.

The Second Age can be divided into various categories:

- young single wage earners, some living with parents, some independent;
- young couples, known as DINKYs (Dual Income, No Kids Yet);
- young families;
- older families.

The Third Age is arguably the most attractive to marketers, particularly couples whose children have left home (who are therefore known as 'empty nesters'). They have paid off most or all of their mortgages, they are still in employment or have retired with a good occupational pension, and have the health and mental alertness, as well as the time and money, to try any leisure activities that appeal to them. They are therefore relatively heavy spenders on leisure services.[5]

Changes in the size of each of these age groups is therefore of vital importance. The changing age pattern of the UK population is

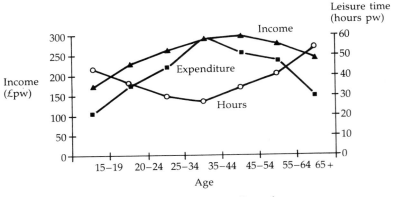

FIGURE 6.4 Leisure time, income and expenditure, by age group.
Source: Family Expenditure Survey 1992.

Table 6.1 The four ages

		Approx. age	Approx. no. in UK (millions)
First Age	Dependence	0–14	25
Second Age	Responsibility	15–49	15
Third Age	Personal fulfilment	50–74	14
Fourth Age	Decrepitude	75	2.6

Source: Henley Centre for Forecasting (1994) *Leisure Futures*, **1**: 7.

shown in Figure 6.5 as a series of tidal waves.[6] Each generation is a peak or trough on this line moving through time, which is continually changing the shape of society in the process. The relative size of each age group affects their overall purchasing power, which determines their importance to marketers and the media, and consequently their influence on fashions.

Take for example the peak in 1947, the post-World War II baby boom. This generation left school in the 1960s at a time of full employment and after the abolition of National Service in Britain. There was an unprecedented number of young people with money to spend on clothes and entertainment which made possible the rise of youth culture and youth markets in the era of the Beatles and Carnaby Street.

The predominant position of the youth market in areas like music, fashion and leisure has continued until now, but it may be coming to an end. The declining birth rate in the 1970s has led to a trough in the number of teenagers in the mid-1990s. Youth unemployment, the reduction in state benefits for young people living away from home, and the gradual

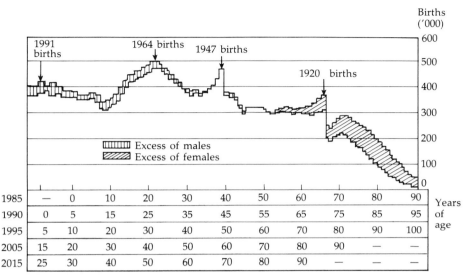

Births
('000)

Age at mid-year extrapolated forward to show the changing age profile

FIGURE 6.5   The demographic tidal wave: UK population by age and sex, 1985. The two lines represent the numbers of males and females born in each year. The scales below show the effect as the generations move through time. The births in 1986–92 have been added to show how the birth rate has levelled off.
Sources: Adapted from Office of Population Census data (*Social Trends 1987* and *Annual Abstracts of Statistics 1993*).

replacement of student grants by loans have all affected the purchasing power of the 16–24 age group.

The most significant age cohorts for leisure marketers at the time of writing would seem to be:

- The 1960s baby-boomers now in their late 20s and therefore in the young family stage. There has already been a modest increase in the birth rate. Their disposable income will be limited by high mortgages and the costs of child rearing, but they represent a growing market for holidays and leisure activities centred on the family.

- The post-World War II baby bulgers now in their mid-40s. They will soon be becoming 'empty nesters' and may use the freedom, time and money to resume the concerns of their youth. This will have a major and unpredictable influence on leisure and fashion.

- The post-World War I baby boomers who reached retirement age in the mid-1980s. The size of this group, coupled with longer life expectancy, has meant there are more people aged over 65 than ever before.[7] Their numbers will not increase significantly in the short term, although there are long-term worries that by 2031 79% of the population will be either dependent children or pensioners.[8] This will have profound effects on the way the economy and society are organized.

In the shorter term it is the changed expectations of retired people rather than their numbers that will affect the demand for leisure services. Today's 65 year olds may have been born in the 1930s and grown up during a war, but they have lived since through an era of increasing prosperity and material comfort. They are more likely than previous generations to own their own home and to have an occupational pension. They may have been used to exerting influence through company structures or trades unions. They are likely to be less frugal and more demanding than traditional images of the old age pensioner suggest (UK readers may recognize elements of TV comedy figures like Victor Meldrew in this!).

This section has been based on a frozen photograph of the position in 1994. While some of it may need revising in the future, the principle remains that marketers need to pay close attention to the movement of the age cohorts and the attitudes and expectations they take with them through the ageing process.

CASE STUDY 6.1   *Club 18–30*

The unique selling point of Club 18–30 was that it offered holidays exclusively for young people. 'Find yourself in the wrong place, with the wrong people – old buffers, young fogeys, a domino convention or two – and your fun factor plummets', warned its brochures. The Club became synonymous with all-night beach parties, pub crawls, drinking games, wet T-shirt contests, sun, sand, sex and sangria. In the 1980s, with the 1964 birth peak generation falling into the 18–30 age bracket, and holiday prices held low by intense competition, the Club prospered, selling around 70,000 holidays a year.

By 1990, however, it found its numbers falling and the average age of its customers rising to around 22 compared with 20 in 1987. The number of teenagers, the Club's future market, had fallen sharply and the existing customers were growing out of the unsophisticated type of holiday it offered.

Club 18–30 therefore decided to modify its image and grow up with its customers. It banned large, single-sex groups and focused on a new repeat business potential – 'the happy pairs who met and fell in love on a Club holiday the previous summer'. Specially chosen Club Couples hotels offered guests a bit more privacy and peace while remaining with like-minded young couples rather than 'old fogeys'.

For its traditional singles customers, mass pub crawls were replaced by visits to medieval banquets or 'Spaghetti Western' film sets. Drinking games were replaced by reps' cabarets and 'other, more wholesome forms of entertainment'.

Press releases for the new products stressed that the Club's image was a distortion, the result of press victimization, when in fact it was other young people who were causing the trouble. Corfu airport officials were quoted as saying that Club 18–30 were the best behaved, best controlled, and best looked after clients they dealt with.

The effects of this repositioning of Club 18–30 were never fully tested as the brand's parent company International Leisure Group went into liquidation in 1991. The new company formed by Club 18–30's management after the crash was called simply 'The Club', with no mention of age at all. This might be thought to reflect the change of image, but was in fact due to legal problems.

Significantly, by 1995 the Club was using the old name again, and exploiting its old reputation in a series of comically explicit advertisements designed by Saatchi and Saatchi. Perhaps the lesson in this is that the effects of demographic change should not be exaggerated. There may be fewer in the age group, but still enough to form a very lucrative market.

Source: 'Changing face of Club 18–30', *Travel News*, 1 March 1990.

Employment

The establishment of the right to holidays with pay, the gradual reduction in the length of the working week, and the increase in holiday entitlements have been crucial ingredients in the development of leisure and tourism. It may be unwise, however, to assume that these trends will necessarily continue at the same rate. Already the increase in overall leisure time is slowing. These improvements in working conditions were negotiated between organized trades unions and employers in conditions of growth and prosperity. In the 1980s the social consensus was challenged by proponents of free-market economics who argued that the improvements in wages and working conditions were making the developed industries of the West uncompetitive against the emerging industrial nations of the Far East.

In Britain, during what have been termed 'the Thatcher years', these views became the accepted thinking of the establishment. Traditional industries and state organizations went through a painful process of change, and the power of the trades unions was effectively broken by legislation and the threat of unemployment. The decade 1980 to 1990 saw only small increases in leisure time, of less than one hour per week, and in the length of the annual holiday, by less than three days. As a Leisure Consultants' report put it:

> some people gained leisure time, often enforced in the form of unemployment or early retirement; but more worked longer hours, as overtime increased and more people, especially women, have taken up part-time work.[9]

People's experience of employment is changing radically as traditional heavy industries move from Europe to the Third World, public utilities are privatized and local and central government services are contracted out. Whereas workers would once have typically belonged to a large organization with the security of its own promotional ladder and company pension scheme, they are now just as likely to work for a small company, or to be self-employed, competing for work as short-term contractors. Government ministers stress the need for a flexible workforce willing to retrain and change jobs several times in a lifetime. This is a new experience, particularly for clerical and managerial workers.

In this competitive environment, whatever the official working week, people are expected to work whatever hours are needed to finish the job. Seabrook points to the way in which the managerial elite, rather than enjoying the privilege of leisure, seems possessed by the need to be seen to be as busy and hardworking as possible.[10]

A wide gap is developing between those in full-time employment and an 'underclass' of unemployed and casual workers, who have plenty of leisure time but not the money to take part in socially acceptable leisure activities. They have been described as 'time-rich but money poor', in contrast with those in work who are the opposite.

While the links between unemployment, poverty and crime are disputed, many commentators, including Leisure Consultants, see this emerging underclass as contributing to 'a deterioration in the urban environment, a rise in public crime and fears for personal safety in public places particularly at night time'.[11] This deters people from taking part in leisure activities out of the home and increases the demand for home security and home-based entertainment.

Family status

The statistics on households and families reinforce what has already been said about the importance of the pre- and post-family stages in the family life cycle. The most common household type in England, Scotland and Wales in the mid-1990s is a married couple without children.[12] The proportion of people living in a traditional family of a married couple and dependent children (average 2.5) fell from 52% in 1961 to 40% in 1992. There has been a big increase in the proportion of people living alone (now 11%) and in single-parent families (10%). The leisure industries should provide for these singles and couples, and avoid stereotypical images of the family in their publicity.

The nature of the family is also changing. Over one-third of all marriages in 1991 were remarriages.[13] Increasing numbers of children have a parent who only sees them at limited times under access agreements after divorce. In these circumstances the parent is very likely to treat them to presents or by taking them on a trip to a leisure activity.

Even within a settled family household, there are indications that people are spending less leisure time sharing the same activities. Only 31% of households have just one TV set, which would force the whole family to watch it together; and 28% have three or more sets, most often located in bedrooms.[14] Ownership of home computers, video players and portable radio/cassette players with headphones is also growing, creating the ability for each member of the household to watch, listen to or play with their own choice of entertainment on their own. What is emerging is a 'cellular family', each member of which needs to be seen as a separate unit for leisure consumption.

The changing role of women

Women have been accounting for an increasing proportion of employees in the UK, to the point at which there are now nearly equal proportions of male and female employees. Three out of four white women of working age are now economically active (compared to much lower proportions of women of Asian origin).[15]

In many areas full-time male employment is being replaced by part-time female employment. For example, the Meadowhall leisure shopping complex near Sheffield has been built on the site of the Hadfield steelworks, which at its height employed 15,000 men. There are now 7,500 people employed at Meadowhall, of whom 80% are women and the majority part-time workers.

The increased economic power of women has combined with the wide acceptance of feminist ideals and the principles of equal opportunities to create a large market of women anxious to express and develop themselves through leisure activities. Nevertheless, women, whether working or not, still have less free time than men because they are still expected to do the bulk of shopping, housekeeping and childcare duties.[16] Because of this they are less likely to take sufficient healthy exercise, and one of the challenges facing leisure managers in the 1990s is to devise forms of activities that are convenient and attractive to busy women.[17] The growth in the popularity of keep-fit and aerobics classes is some indication of the potential demand.

Economic factors affecting leisure demand

Although leisure time has not increased as significantly in recent years as is sometimes supposed, leisure spending certainly has:

> Between 1979 and 1989 consumer spending on leisure in the UK generally grew by 150% in value, by one third in volume (removing the effect of price changes) and 50% in volume if spending on alcohol is removed from the figures.[18]

Leisure spending has consistently grown faster than spending on other categories.[19] Home entertainment, overseas holidays, eating out and participation sports have all benefited. Those in work have seen their real disposable income increase and have spent it on ways of making their limited leisure time as satisfying as possible. This has created opportunities for businesses offering new technologies, new activities, or new styles of presentation which give a sense of excitement, status and value for money.

These changes have taken place mainly in conditions of rapid if inflationary growth in the mid-1980s. The general condition of the national and international economies obviously has a strong effect on the demand for leisure. But just as important as the direct effects of inflation, taxation and unemployment on people's incomes is their psychological reaction to their own economic circumstances and the general feeling about the economy conveyed by the media and by word of mouth.

People's reactions to economic changes are more complex than simple economic models might suggest. While the overall rate of growth in leisure spending decreased in the recession of the late 1980s, leisure spending as a percentage of total consumer spending fell by only 1%.[20] People do not necessarily simply spend less on the same things. They may reduce spending on some items such as short breaks in order to save for special purchases such as a long-haul holiday. Instead of trading down to a cheaper version of the same thing, they may switch categories completely, to something that may be less expensive but still offers quality and status. For example, they may switch from a hotel package in the Mediterranean to a camping holiday in Brittany.[21]

Similarly, as the economy emerges from recession, consumers do not necessarily revert to their old habits. Confidence and a sense of job security may take longer to re-establish. Replenishing savings may seem a higher priority than spending on inessentials. However the economy develops in the future, commentators are convinced that a concern for value for money will remain a priority.

As well as the overall economic state of the nation, leisure marketers need to be aware of a number of changes that may affect particular segments of their markets. For example:

- *Inherited property.* People in middle age now often inherit property from their parents which has increased greatly in value over the years. This can be another boost to their spending power in the 'empty nester' stage. (Not everyone will benefit, however, as the property may instead have to be sold to pay for residential nursing care for the elderly parents.)

- *Negative equity.* Conversely, young couples who bought property at the height of the boom in the mid-1980s now find that it is worth less than the amount it is mortgaged for. This limits both their spending power and their mobility.

The impoverishment of young people as a result of changes in the state benefits and student grant systems has been mentioned above.

The global economy

Most leisure sectors now have to take into account international as well as national economic factors in their planning. Tourism demand, for example, is influenced by the relative strengths of the economies of the originating and destination countries, which affect the exchange rate and the purchasing power of the tourists' money. Like many other industries, sports equipment and electronic entertainment are dominated by multinational companies who analyze and exploit local economic conditions to gain the maximum competitive advantage.[22]

Technological trends in leisure

While the underlying benefits of leisure remain the same, companies are continually developing new improved ways of delivering those benefits. They do this partly to gain a temporary advantage over their competitors, and partly to keep up with their customers' expectations. Every form of leisure entertainment has to compete with the immediacy, special effects and star names offered by television. Technological innovation is one way of doing this.

To speculate on what the next developments in leisure technology will be is to approach the realm of science fiction. One sure prediction is that the pace of change will increase rather than slacken. Hi-tech companies adopt strategies of continuous product development and zero-product-improvement time in order to keep ahead of their rivals.[23] Customers are encouraged to 'upgrade' to the latest model to avoid finding their equipment obsolete. The only limits on the march of innovation are increasing public concern for safety and environmental protection, and the ever-increasing costs which mean that only large organizations are able to finance the research and development.

Apart from television, two of the most significant technological developments of modern times have been the computer and the telephone. Computers have revolutionized the ways in which organizations conduct their business. Travel agents now have access to the reservations systems of airlines, hotels, car hire firms and theatres through one 'gateway', and can book and pay for an entire itinerary while their client waits.

The *multimedia* developments of the next few years will combine the home entertainment of television, the information processing of the computer and the two-way communication of the telephone. The technological innovations that make this possible are CD-ROM, digital transmission and fibre-optic cable. Between them they will increase dramatically the amount of information and entertainment that can be stored and transmitted worldwide via what US Vice-President Al Gore called the 'information superhighway'.

Technically, anyone with a television screen, a personal computer and a modem link to the superhighway will be able to select and interact with data and images for work purposes or for entertainment. Leisure applications could include:

- Interactive video games and filmed entertainment will be available on demand when the customer wants them.
- A massive increase in cable TV channels will be on offer.
- Home shopping: the customer will be able to view the merchandise, or the holiday destination, on screen, place an order by keyboard and input a credit card number to pay for it.
- Interactive news. Instead of reading what the editor chose to include, viewers will be able to select the topics that interest them and read them in as much or as little depth as they wish.

If these applications become commonplace, the effect will be to accelerate already apparent changes in the media industries, such as:

- a much wider choice of home entertainment and information channels will be available;
- a fragmented audience: viewers will be able to select their own special interests, and so will be less accessible to mass advertising, political or public interest messages;
- advertising revenue will be spread more thinly over more outlets.

Each TV station will have less revenue for programming and will have to rely more on subscription income. The demand for programmes will increase but the revenue to pay for locally produced original work will be less. Global companies who own Hollywood studios and their back catalogues of films will be able to sell programmes to a worldwide market at prices well below the cost of local productions. This could lead to an even greater dominance of American material, threatening local cultures and national identities. The cost of the technologies and the need to have a global market to achieve economies of scale will be barriers restricting access to the market and placing control of world media in the hands of a few companies like Rupert Murdoch's News Corporation.

Existing media, such as newspapers and public service broadcasters like the BBC will have to redefine their roles in this new environment. Issues of balanced reporting, freedom of the press, and the independence of national governments will be raised.

One issue that is already causing controversy is the coverage of sport. Satellite TV stations need top sporting events to sell subscriptions to their channels. BSkyB have acquired exclusive live coverage of Premier League football, England cricket tours, major golf tournaments, and English club rugby. The sports governing bodies have accepted that the games will be seen by fewer viewers because BSkyB is paying more than the terrestrial stations (BBC and ITV) offered. It is argued that certain sporting occasions such as the FA Cup Final, Test Cricket and the Grand National should always be shown on public terrestrial TV, but exactly which should be protected in this way is likely to cause continuing debate.

As sport becomes a TV entertainment, the traditional rules, timings of matches, league formats and even the clubs themselves are under pressure to change to suit the TV audience. (At the time of writing, the British Rugby League have agreed to merge several famous clubs and switch to summer evening matches in return for £75 million from BSkyB.)

Other implications of the multimedia revolution include the effect on retailing. Will shopping cease to be a regular chore and become an occasional pleasure, part of a leisure day out?[24]

The range and sophistication of home entertainment will affect out-of-home leisure. Museums, leisure attractions, spectator sports, shopping malls and leisure centres will have to match the style and impact of media entertainment in order to hold their customers' attention. This will increase the market for interactive displays, animatronics (electronically operated animated characters) and virtual reality simulators. Themes from TV and media will be essential marketing tools. The pattern for this has already been set by Disney's theme parks, of course. The cost of these technologies will pose problems for the small privately owned attraction or local museum, which again could lead to a concentration of ownership in the sector.

CASE STUDY 6.2   *Brewer's Quay, Weymouth*

Weymouth Borough Council's Local History Museum used to be typical of local museums. Situated in an old school building a little off the main shopping and tourist areas, it held a fascinating collection of old objects arranged thematically and interpreted by a few captions. When the site was required for a shopping centre, the collection was moved to form the basis of a tourist attraction called the TimeWalk, which is the central feature of a development called Brewer's Quay.

Brewer's Quay was created by Devenish Ltd in their former quayside brewery and contains specialist shops, stalls, cafes and pubs, as well as a brewing museum. The TimeWalk was designed by Heritage Projects, the company that built the Jorvik Centre in York. Visitors are guided through scenes from Weymouth's past by animatronic cats! The collection is now easily appreciated by the casual visitor because of the entertaining way it is presented. In its collaboration between local authority and private industry, and in the style of presentation, the TimeWalk can be seen as a model for the survival of local museums.

The scheme has been criticized because serious researchers, amateur or academic, can no longer study the collection in detail. It is also now experiencing declining visitor numbers since the presentation does not change and therefore does not attract repeat visits from local residents or regular holiday visitors to the resort.

Market factors affecting leisure demand

Fads, fashions and lifestyles

The demand for particular leisure activities can fluctuate wildly. As Gratton points out, the inessential nature of leisure activities and the wide choice available means that demand is more volatile than for other goods and services.[25] He goes on to suggest that leisure operators should spread the risk by offering a portfolio of different leisure products rather than relying too much on one.

A problem facing leisure marketers is to distinguish between changes in demand which are short-lived fads or fashions, and those which reflect more lasting trends of the kind discussed above. Kotler defines a fad as being 'unpredictable, short-lived and without social, economic or political significance'.[26] Recent examples might include frisbees, skateboards and BMX bikes. While the latter two might have started as expressions of youth culture and have survived as speciality sports for a minority, their popularity as mass activities was short-lived, as councils who invested in special facilities for them found out to their cost.

Fashions are rather longer-lasting and, especially in their early stages, express a mood created by the social, economic and political circumstances of the times.[27] They tend to start with influential groups such as the rich, media personalities, or with the young who are freer to experiment, and are then taken up by a wider public.[28] They also reflect the consensus of the leading designers in the particular industry on which styles to produce and promote. Leisure managers will be aware that this process operates among the designers of publicity material and among interior designers. There are often fine lines between being too experimental, too much the same as everyone else, and too old-fashioned.

Fashions in clothes and popular music, for example, used to be more universally adopted than is the case today. The proliferation of commercial radio stations, lifestyle magazines and of independent record labels means that people have more opportunity to choose the type of music to suit their personality, age and the statement of attitudes they wish to project to their peer group. When in the 1960s the record industry was dominated by a few major companies and there was only one radio station dedicated to pop music, choice was limited and superstars were easier to create.

A similar situation is developing in sport. Whereas previously most people had only the opportunity to play and to watch soccer, rugby, cricket, tennis and athletics, schools and the media now offer a wide range of sports and other physical activities. One consequence is that sporting talent is spread more thinly which reduces the chances of Britain producing a world class team in any one sport.

In this environment of consumer choice, certain styles continue to survive or reappear when they fit the mood of the time or the desire for novelty and change. Underlying the fluctuations in fashions, certain long-term trends in people's values, attitudes and lifestyles can be detected. Among the most significant for leisure are:

Individualism
Participation in individual sports and other active recreational activities has grown faster than that of team games.[29] This can be linked to a general movement of attitudes towards individual success and fulfilment and away from concepts of community and society. It is a mood that led to, and was encouraged by, right-wing governments in the UK and the USA in the 1980s. Competition leads to choice, which leads to a fragmentation of markets. The break-up of the family and the increasing mobility of the population – changing jobs, houses and even partners – mean that people are less able to identify with any outside institutions and are forced to rely on their own efforts. Paradoxically, this can lead to a strong urge to find something to identify with, which can be exploited by advertising and by political movements.

Health consciousness
The percentage of smokers in the UK adult male population fell from 52% to 31% between 1972 and 1990. The percentage of women smokers fell from 41% to 29% in the same period.[30] People are generally more concerned with the effects of their lifestyle on their health, even though messages about what to eat and what to avoid are often confusing and contradictory. As

fewer people are working in jobs involving hard physical work, to keep fit they have to take exercise in their leisure time. Swimming, rambling, 'keep fit' classes and jogging are the most popular ways of doing this.[31] Interest in health and fitness is being developed at progressively younger ages with almost 90% of 20–24 year-olds and 80% of teenagers already concerned about their health.[32] There has been a big increase in the number of health and fitness centres in the UK, and also in the demand for leisurewear such as tracksuits, jogging vests and trainers. Cynically, it might be said that it is more important to look active and healthy than to do any serious exercise. The 1992 Allied Dunbar *National Fitness Survey* found that 80% of the sample expressed a strong belief in the value of exercise to health, but only a minority actually engaged regularly in moderate or vigorous physical activity. Tests showed that most people were less fit than they thought they were.[33] Clearly there is still potential to expand this market.

Environmental consciousness
Linked to a concern for personal health, there has been a growing awareness of the problems of pollution and the using up of finite natural resources. Membership of 'green' pressure groups like Friends of the Earth and environmental charities like the Royal Society for the Protection of Birds continues to grow. There is a marketing advantage in advertising the organization and its products as environmentally friendly, but some companies have been criticized for taking a superficial approach, sticking a green label on an existing product rather than seriously reviewing the environmental impact of their activities and modifying them accordingly.[34]

Environmental concerns may take lower priority than employment in times of recession, but concerns for such issues as air quality and asthma, sewage disposal and sea bathing, the ozone layer and skin cancer are unlikely to lessen. The question is whether a concern for single issues will turn into a willingness to change lifestyles and accept higher costs in order to solve environmental problems. At the 1993 Rio Conference governments expressed their commitment to work towards a wide range of improvements in the global environment, but in practice they will only move as fast as their voters and the industrialists are prepared to go.

Tourism encapsulates this dilemma well. Should tourism managers assume that their customers will be willing to pay extra for environment-sensitive developments, and to avoid certain protected coastlines or wilderness areas altogether, or is most people's interest in the environment confined to a desire to find somewhere quiet, 'unspoilt', but affordable for their own holiday?

Consumerism
The principle of consumer rights has been growing since the pioneering work of Ralph Nader in the USA in the 1950s. In the UK the rights of

customers to an agreed standard of service, and to a mechanism by which they can complain and receive compensation, has been enshrined in the John Major government's Citizens' Charters. Consumerism can present an opportunity for a company to gain a competitive advantage by offering more generous guarantees and a higher-quality service than the minimum required by law. Quality management and customer service will be looked at later in Chapter 11.

Competition

This chapter has concentrated on what is sometimes called the *macro-environment* – the broad trends and influences that affect the whole of the leisure market, and indeed the whole of the economy. In addition, some trends and influences are specific to a particular sector of the industry or to a particular locality in which the organization operates. A major factor in this *micro-environment* will be the actions of competitors, and indeed the nature of the competition. Although this will be dealt with in Chapter 9, it should be noted that a review of the external environment would normally include it at this stage.

Political factors affecting leisure demand

Some of the areas in which political decisions influence the demand for leisure are shown in Figure 6.1. Underlying these are two crucial questions of political philosophy: the role of competition and the role of the state. Chapter 3 discussed the current debate on the role of the state and of market forces in the provision of leisure facilities. Clearly, any change in policy will affect the industry and its customers, as has been dramatically illustrated by the experiences of Eastern European countries.

Legislation, at both the national and the European levels, in areas such as consumer and environmental protection, competition and working conditions is likely to become increasingly stringent. Organizations need to anticipate the effects of such legislation on their businesses. They can then make their views and concerns known while the legislation is being drafted, and have contingency plans to adapt if it is passed.

Summary

As this chapter has shown, we live in a world of accelerating change. Any organization that fails to anticipate and adapt to change will fail. Managers, and particularly marketing managers, need to develop a wide awareness of social, economic, technological and political developments that may affect their customers' leisure time, disposable income, and their choice of leisure activities. Reading a serious newspaper regularly is not a leisure activity – it is essential to survival!

Notes

1. For a concise guide to statistical trends in leisure time, participation and expenditure, see Gratton, C. and Taylor, P. (1987) *Leisure in Britain*.
2. Mintel (1991) 'Leisure time 2: Age and leisure', *Leisure Intelligence*, 2: 1. Reproduced with permission from Mintel Ltd.
3. The figures used in the graphs in Figure 6.3 as follows:

Age	Hours[a]	Income[b] (£pw)
15–19	43.2	172
20–24	35.9	227
25–34	29.5	263
35–44	27.1	289
45–54	34.3	297
55–64	40.5	277
65+	53.6	243

[a] Hours are time 'free to do what you like' (BRMB/Mintel, 1991).
[b] Income is average gross weekly earnings (*New Earnings Survey 1993*).

4. The figures for essential expenditure are based on the *Family Expenditure Survey 1992*, p. 54. The total average weekly expenditure per household has been used, excluding leisure goods and services but including alcoholic drink and tobacco. The survey age bands are different from those used in the other sources, so the graph in Figure 6.4 is only an approximation to illustrate the general trend.
5. *Market Report: UK Leisure and Recreation* (1991).
6. Based on a figure in *Social Trends 1987*, p. 30, adapted in Morgan, M. and Vaughan R. (1993) 'Market trends in leisure', *ILAM Guide to Good Practice in Leisure Management*, Release 3, p. 10.1.03 and further adapted here.
7. *Social Trends 1994*, p. 24.
8. Henley Centre for Forecasting (1994) *Leisure Futures*, 1: 16.
9. Martin, W. and Mason, S. (1992) *The Thatcher Years* (Leisure Consultants). In a more recent article, these authors calculate that average leisure hours rose by 3% between 1982 and 1992 compared to 8% in the previous 10 years. See Martin, W. and Mason, S. (1994) 'Current trends in leisure: Taking account of time', *Leisure Studies*, 13: 133–39.
10. Seabrook, J. (1988) *The Leisure Society*, pp. 9–20.
11. Leisure Consultants (1994) *Leisure Forecasts 1994–98*, p. 23.
12. *Social Trends 1994*, p. 35.
13. *Ibid*, p. 37.
14. TGI survey, quoted in the Advertising Association's *The Lifestyle Pocket Book 1992*.
15. *Social Trends 1994*, p. 58.

16. *Ibid*, p. 130.
17. Allied Dunbar (1992) *National Fitness Survey* (Summary) pp. 8–10.
18. Martin and Mason (1992), *op. cit.*, p. 5.
19. *Social Trends 1993*, p. 82.
20. *Leisure Forecasts 1994–98*, *op. cit.*, p. 22.
21. Mitchell, A. (1990) 'Marketing out of the downturn', *Marketing*, 26   April, pp. 25–26.
22. For a discussion of international service marketing see for example Terpstra V. and Sarathy R. (1994) *International Marketing*, ch. 16.
23. Kotler (1994), *op. cit.*, pp. 426–27.
24. The sources of the section on multimedia include the following:

    Buckingham, L., Culf, A. and Goldenberg, S., 'The battle for global vision', *The Guardian*, 23 October 1993.
    Bowen, D. 'Multimedia is the Message', *Independent on Sunday*, 7 November 1993.
    Friedland, J. 'Get set to fast forward to the future', *The Guardian*, 1 January 1994.
    'Survey: Television', *The Economist*, 12 February 1994.
    Keegan, V., 'Fibre firepower', *The Guardian*, 25 February 1994.
    Bowen, D., 'After the media earthquake', *Independent on Sunday*, 6 March 1994.
    Quinton, F., 'A remote way to bring holidays into the home', *Travel Trade Gazette: UK and Ireland*, 13 April 1994.

    Multimedia is a rapidly advancing technological and business development. Readers are therefore recommended to look for articles in the current trade, business and national press to keep up-to-date.

25. Gratton, C. (1993) *Transnational Corporations in the Leisure Industries*.
26. Kotler (1994) *Marketing Management*, p. 152.
27. *Ibid*, p. 358.
28. The adoption of innovations will be considered further in Chapter 7.
29. *General Household Survey 1990*.
30. *Social Trends 1994*, p. 99.
31. *TGI* survey 1990, quoted in P. Smith (Ed.), *Report: UK Leisure and Recreation 1991*, p. 185.
32. Mintel survey, quoted in Hughes, A. (1994) 'Family business', *Leisure Management*, July.
33. Allied Dunbar (1992) *National Fitness Survey*, p. 10.
34. 'Green ploys may lead to backlash', *Marketing*, 14 September 1989.

7   Consumer behaviour

The consumer decision-making process
Extended problem-solving behaviour
Other forms of problem-solving behaviour
Consumer needs
Information processing
Social influences on consumer behaviour
Case Study 7.1: Women, sport and Islam
Case Study 7.2: Consumer behaviour: The package holiday
Summary

Understanding how and why your customers make their choice of leisure services or products is central to effective marketing. The study of consumer behaviour can draw on a wide range of psychological, sociological, and economic research and theories. This chapter will show how these can be of practical use to the marketing manager.

The consumer decision-making process

We shall start by looking at the process by which people reach a decision to buy a particular product. One of the most widely used models of the consumer decision process is that proposed by Engel et al.:[1]

- Problem recognition
- Information search
- Evaluation of alternatives
- Choice of purchase
- Evaluation of post-purchase experience.*

(*I have changed the wording used from the original in order to produce the memorable acronym PIECE.)

   Let us apply this 'PIECE process' to the choice of a holiday. First, the customer must become aware that he needs a holiday. In any year over 40%

of British people do not take any form of holiday away from home.[2] The company must decide whether to concentrate on selling its brands to those who are actively looking for a holiday, or to try to expand the market by persuading some of those 40% that a holiday would be beneficial (or affordable) after all.

Once the customer decides to have a holiday, he will begin to look for information on what is available. He may simply seek the advice of friends. He may go to a travel agent, particularly for an overseas holiday, he may send away for resort guides, or he may look in the holiday classified advertisement section in the weekend papers and book direct with the operator or cottage owner. The company needs to know where customers normally look for information on their type of holiday, and make sure that their brand appears there.

The travel agency will have up to 200 holiday products on sale. The customer is unlikely to look at more than half a dozen. Research has shown that people make their choices from a very limited 'set' of alternatives. Kotler says that there is the *awareness set* – the brands the customer has heard of, which could be only a small percentage of those available. Of these, he will only seriously study a smaller *consideration set* – the brands he has used before, or has heard good reports of, or has been attracted to by advertising or special offers. As he gathers information about these, only a few will exactly meet his requirements and become his *choice set*.[3] The company needs to know where their brand stands in relation to each of these sets. Do they need heavy advertising to improve awareness, and enhance their reputation, or should they concentrate on matching their product more closely to what the customers are looking for?

The customer then evaluates the alternatives and makes a choice. This will involve checking the features of the holiday against a mental list of *attributes*: for example, he may want a quiet location, close to the beach, with baby-listening service and a children's club, in a certain price range. According to Fishbein and others, his choice will depend on the relative value of each attribute to him, and how well he believes the particular brand provides that attribute.[4] The company can carry out research asking potential customers to rank in importance the attributes they expect from a holiday, and to rate different companies according to how well they provide the key attributes. The company then has the choice of changing the attributes of the brand or of trying to change consumer perceptions and attitudes.

Howard suggests that, in addition, the *confidence* the customer has in his beliefs about the company is also important and needs to be measured.[5] The brochure may look wonderful but if he has never heard of the company he may feel safer remaining with a firm he has used before.

Having made his choice, the customer returns to the travel agent to book it. It is by no means certain that he will come out with the holiday he intended to book. He may receive additional advice – the agent may deter him from using a particular company which has caused them difficulties in the past; there may be a more attractive offer available; or the holiday may simply be fully booked. The company needs to know how likely it is that the customer's decision will be influenced at the *point of sale* (in some sectors, 80% of consumer decisions are made at the point of sale; in travel it is unlikely to be as high). The tour company needs to make sure that the agent is equipped and motivated to sell their brand, a subject we shall examine in more detail in Chapter 13.

So the customer pays a deposit in January and the balance in March for a holiday in July. At this stage all he has in exchange is a promise, contained in a brochure. It is very likely therefore that he will experience what is know as *post-purchase dissonance*, an uneasy feeling of doubt about whether he has made the right choice.[6] He will continue to *evaluate* the company right up to the moment he returns home from his holiday. The company must seek to reassure the customer by sending out confirmation letters and tickets promptly. The quality and style of the documentation will also help to establish that he is dealing with a reputable, efficient, and friendly organization. If his dealings with the company do not reassure him, he might at worst cancel his booking. More likely it will make him critical and wary when he takes his holiday. He is more likely to complain, and is less likely to choose that company again or to recommend them to his friends. Since some companies such as Vacances Franco-Britannique claim that 75% of their bookings are repeats or recommendations, a good after-sales service, reducing post-purchase dissonance, can save the company a lot of money on advertising for new business.

Figure 7.1 summarizes the implications for the company's marketing strategy of each stage in the consumer decision-making process and some examples of the decisions to be made after research.

Stage in consumer decision process	Implications for marketing strategies	Decisions
Problem recognition	Targeting of marketing campaign	Existing users? New users?
Information search	Distribution of publicity	Retail channels? Direct response?
Evaluation of alternatives	Product design Promotional message	Change product? Change attitudes?
Choice at point of sale	Marketing to retailers	Ensure availability Incentives to sell
Evaluation of post-purchase experience	After-sales service	Efficient service Quality presentation Friendly relations

FIGURE 7.1   Implications for marketing of the consumer decision process.

Extended problem-solving behaviour

What we have described is termed extended problem-solving behaviour.[7] Obviously it does not apply to all consumer choices. We do not consciously go through all these stages when choosing an ice-cream or a drink. If we did, the queues would be interminable! We only carry out such a thorough search and evaluation when dealing with something new to us or something that is an important purchase, like the annual holiday.

When considering which holiday to book the customer is in a state which Krugman termed *high involvement*.[8] Involvement is defined as the level of importance the consumer attaches to the decision. This depends on the risks involved – not only the financial risk, but also the personal risk of wasting his precious annual leave entitlement on a bad trip, of being criticized by his family or laughed at by his friends.

In high-involvement purchases the customer actively seeks information and weighs up the evidence before deciding. Although this may make him cautious and in need of reassurance, it is a relatively easy task to sell to him. He will come to the shop or read the advertisement with interest and take your arguments seriously.

Other forms of problem-solving behaviour

Someone who is new to an area may go through a form of the problem-solving process to decide which pub, nightclub or sports centre to go to. It may be what Howard called *limited problem solving*, where the search is confined to what is available (what is advertised in the local paper, for example) and evaluation may take place after trying the place once.[9]

Once the initial decision has been made, however, repeat visits become routine. Provided the experience is satisfactory, the *routine problem-solving* decision is a simple process of recognizing the need, 'Let's go out tonight!', remembering the previous experience, and making the decision. She has become what is often called a *brand-loyal customer*. The term may cause managers a false sense of security, since what is called loyalty may be no more than inertia. It is easier to do the same thing again than to go through the uncertainty of making a new decision.

A nightclub, which has regular customers who declare themselves satisfied with the club when surveyed, may nevertheless find itself deserted when a new club opens in town. What has happened is *variety-seeking behaviour*, a change in purchasing habits made simply for the novelty of doing something different. For this reason, a successful organization should never cease to advertise and to improve and refurbish its products and image; otherwise it will leave itself vulnerable to variety-seeking behaviour by its clients.[10]

Routine purchases are usually made in a state of *low involvement*. This is particularly true of regular household purchases like toilet paper. Low-involvement purchases are harder to market. No one is going to seek advice from a chemist on which brand of toilet paper to buy, nor will they nudge their partner in the ribs to pay attention when a toothpaste advertisement comes on television. Advertisers need to attract their attention by entertaining and original commercials (like the Andrex puppy running off with the toilet paper) in the hope that when they next visit the supermarket they will remember the ad and decide to choose the brand for a change.

Consumer needs

These models of consumer problem solving are concerned with understanding *how* the choice is made. It is also necessary to understand *why* it is made, what needs the customer is seeking to satisfy by the choice.

The CIM definition of marketing quoted in Chapter 1 is 'identifying, anticipating and satisfying customer needs'. In practice, customer needs can be identified in a number of ways.

Community needs

Leisure managers can take the approaches classified by Bradshaw in attempting to define what he called the *social needs* of their community.[11]

In planning for the leisure needs of the community a national or local government may use the *normative* method. Experts may advise them that according to research 'people should be moderately or vigorously active at least three times a week in order to reduce their risk of heart disease or stroke'.[12] The government could plan to publicize this advice and provide the facilities for people to take moderate or vigorous exercise. It could decide that this requires a certain area of open space per thousand population or for all urban residents to be within 30 minutes' journey of a leisure centre. Setting standards in this way inevitably involves value judgements and does not address the problem from the individual's viewpoint.

Facilities provided by this approach may not meet the *felt* needs for leisure among the local population. Felt needs are defined by Bradshaw as what a person thinks he or she wants to do.[13] When Tower Park Leisure began to plan a development on a derelict site outside Poole, for example, they first carried out a survey asking local people what leisure facilities they would like to see in the area.[14] The respondents' answers were in part based on their knowledge of leisure facilities that were available elsewhere in the country but not in Poole. They were defining their needs by the *comparative* method, which is also often used by planners and developers.

The test of how well these methods anticipate the needs of the population is of course whether the facilities that are built as a result are actually used. There is often a difference between people's felt needs and their *expressed* needs (expressed in the sense used by Bradshaw means expressed in action not words). The most obvious way of identifying needs is to look at what people are actually doing, to identify which activities are growing, what facilities are being used to capacity and those declining in popularity, and to allocate resources accordingly.

These sociological approaches to leisure needs may help to decide what facilities are needed, or what gaps exist in the market, but they do not help to define individual needs and so are of little use in formulating a promotion strategy to persuade people to use the facilities.

Individual needs

For this, we need to understand their *individual needs*. In psychological terms a need is a deficit, a lack of something, a discrepancy between the actual state and a desired state.[15] Before a person will act to remedy this lack, this discrepancy, he first must recognize the need, and then must feel the lack strongly enough to motivate him to do something about it. Marketing can make him recognize a need and motivate him to act; it can also persuade him to try a new way of satisfying his need; but it cannot create the need. Critics such as Marcuse accuse marketing of encouraging 'false needs' for consumer goods and activities which are not essential and have socially or environmentally damaging consequences.[16] Most writers, however, consider that all purchases and activities are motivated by fundamental human needs, however undesirable particular ways of satisfying them may be.

There have been many different attempts to classify and explain these fundamental needs. The founders of modern psychology, such as Freud and Jung, put great emphasis on the unconscious mind, tracing many adult actions back to experiences of early childhood relationships with parents and siblings or to 'sublimations' of sexual impulses. Freud, for example, said that all travel is the expression of the unconscious desire to escape from a dominating father figure. While this may be true, it is difficult to see how it could be of any practical use to the tourism marketer.

Motivational research in the 1950s attempted to understand consumer behaviour in terms of hidden psychological motives.[17] Baking a cake was said to be an expression of a woman's desire to give birth. This approach is now discredited, although the use of sexual imagery to sell unrelated products has not entirely disappeared. The modern TV audience is now too aware of this type of technique to take 'sexy' adverts seriously, and they can only work when used with subtlety and humour.

Later theories allow for a wider range of human needs. One of the most commonly used in marketing is that of Maslow,[18] who proposed a hierarchy of needs, expressed as a pyramid as in Figure 7.2. At the base of the pyramid are basic physiological needs for food, drink, warmth and rest, which are necessary for survival. These and the next layer of security and safety needs, Maslow argued, must be satisfied before people start to be concerned about social needs or the need for self-esteem and status. Self-developmental needs, the motives for much leisure activity, are at the top of the pyramid, and only come into play after all the other levels have been satisfied.

Though writers on leisure have, as we saw in Chapter 1, proposed various categories of 'leisure needs', it is debatable whether separate categories are meaningful. So-called leisure needs can also be seen as being physiological (relaxation), social (improving personal relationships) or self-developmental using Maslow's hierarchy.

An implication of Maslow's theory would be that a person who is unemployed will be too concerned about the lack of money for basic needs, the absence of security, and the loss of status, to spend his ample leisure time in creative and self-developmental activities. This is not always the case, and illustrates the weakness of Maslow's theory. As Torkildsen points out, needs are not so easily divided and are often overlapping and occur simultaneously.[19] Nevertheless, Maslow provides a useful concise yet comprehensive list of human needs. He also emphasizes that humans are not merely concerned with satisfying basic animal needs but also strive for creative personal achievement and development.

The concept of different types or levels of needs is also found in Herzberg's distinction between *hygiene factors* (or dissatisfiers), which cause

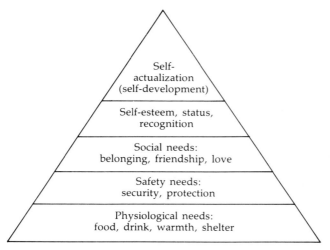

FIGURE 7.2   Maslow's hierarchy of human needs.
Source: Maslow (1954) *Motivation and Personality.*

dissatisfaction if they do not exist but which are taken for granted if they do; and *motivators*, which are actively sought for their intrinsic satisfaction.[20] This can help in understanding the evaluation of alternatives stage of the consumer decision-making process. In choosing a holiday, people will expect to have clean, comfortable premises and an efficient service, and if they do not get these they will complain and go elsewhere next time. However, what will make people choose one destination over another are the opportunities it offers for activities, sightseeing and entertainment.

The same product or activity can satisfy different levels of needs. A car can provide a safe, comfortable and efficient way of getting to work, while at the same time it can convey the owner's status, and give him a sense of achievement from his driving skills. It therefore has *practical* uses but also *symbolic* uses. Lannon and Cooper point out that much of modern advertising works by communicating the symbolic meanings of the product, how it fits the consumer's lifestyle and expresses his identity rather than the practical benefits it offers.[21] Taking physical exercise has practical benefits in improving fitness and preventing heart disease, but people are more likely to be motivated by the effect it has in creating an image of youthfulness and energy, or by fantasies of emulating their sporting heroes.

People's needs from leisure change with age and their stage in the family life cycle. As well as the practical differences in their physical capability, spare time and disposable income we examined in Chapter 6, the symbolic role of leisure activities changes. At different ages, according to Rapaport and Rapaport, people have different preoccupations which manifest themselves in interests which are channelled into various leisure activities:

> Any particular activity – say walking in the park – has different meanings for different kinds of people in relation to the interests they are pursuing. It may be a way of being alone for a young courting couple; a way of exercising a pet for an old lady living alone; a way for a middle-aged man to fend off a coronary to which he is at risk, and so on. Similarly a given preoccupation (for example with a sense of excitement and stimulation) may be expressed differently by different individuals: through sports cars, drugs, sexual adventures or in mountain climbing. Some may experience stimulation by visiting art galleries.[22]

The nature of the preoccupation or need will determine the attributes that are most important to a particular person when choosing a particular activity or product.

Information processing

The product the consumer actually chooses will be the one that he *believes* will best satisfy his needs. This may not be the best quality product or even the most suitable product for him. The decision is not made by a rational comparison of all the facts available. It is the result of a very subjective processing of the information to which the consumer has been exposed.

McGuire developed a five stage information processing model:

- Exposure
- Attention
- Comprehension
- Acceptance
- Retention.[23]

The consumer must be exposed to information, usually through advertising or by seeing the product on display. However, he is likely to be exposed to anything from 500 to 2,000 promotional messages a day, so whether he pays any attention to this particular one will depend on how well it stands out (its saliency) and whether it appears relevant.[24] Even if he pays attention, he may not understand the message in the way the advertiser intended, or he may not accept what it is saying because it conflicts with his previous experience or attitudes. Finally, the message needs to be memorable or it will be forgotten when the consumer comes to make his choice.

The consumer's *perceptions* of the product are selective and subjective because he does not approach the decision with a clear open mind. He brings with him all his previous experience, which he uses to try and make sense of the mass of conflicting stimuli with which advertisers bombard him.[25] Edward de Bono said that the mind is a pattern-making system: it is always trying to make new images and information fit into what it knows already.[26] This concept helps to explain why people are selective in their attention, why advertising meanings can be distorted to fit their preconceptions, and why they remember some messages better than others. Understanding how the mind works can, however, be used by marketers to attract attention and create memorable messages.

Effective advertising often starts with a familiar situation or phrase and changes it slightly. This element of surprise means that it is less likely to be ignored than something either completely unfamiliar or completely predictable. Because the brain has to work out the difference and fit it into its existing patterns, it is also more likely to be retained in the memory than a straightforward statement. This is an example of *cognitive learning*, or learning by elaboration.[27] It works on the same principle as educational methods which make students learn by doing assignments, in contrast with learning by repetition. Repetition is of course a common feature of radio and TV advertising, effective at first but liable to become counterproductive if over-used.

Another advertising approach is to show an unfamiliar product in a situation which evokes a pleasant emotional response. A happy young couple are seen drinking a cola or martini. After several exposures we learn to associate the emotions with the drink. This is learning by *classical conditioning.*[28]

The third form of learning is by experience. In this case, our experience of the product creates a set of positive or negative associations which influence subsequent decisions. This is known as *operant conditioning* or learning by reinforcement. A favourable experience reinforces our behaviour and encourages us to repeat it. The role of advertising in this case is simply to encourage us to try the product.[29] The reinforcement can be intrinsic, from the experience of the product, or extrinsic, by means of some additional reward such as a free gift, coupons or regular user discount.

As a result of our experience and learning, we develop beliefs and *attitudes*. Attitudes are enduring favourable or unfavourable thoughts and feelings towards something. They develop slowly as the result of our own experience and the influence of our peers, society and culture. As such they are difficult to change, particularly in important areas like diet and lifestyle. As with perception, the mind tries to reconcile new information with its existing pattern of attitudes towards the topic. If this is impossible, the individual feels uncomfortable and may refuse to accept the information as correct or ignore it completely. This feeling is known as *cognitive dissonance* and may help to explain why a third of adults continue to smoke cigarettes from packets with health warnings printed on them.[30] Because of this, it is usually easier for a company to fit its product and marketing message to people's existing attitudes than to try and change their attitudes. However, the example of smoking shows that over time attitudes can be changed.

Social influences on consumer behaviour

From what has already been said it is clear that the consumer's decision is not made in isolation. According to Maslow, the need to belong is more powerful than the need for self-esteem or self-fulfilment. It is not surprising therefore that our attitudes to products or activities are influenced by those we live and work with, and by the society and culture in which we live. We shall next look at some ways in which this influence works.

The Rapaports say that individuals' lives develop along three lines – family, work and leisure – which combine to form whole lifestyle patterns.[31] Each line involves relationships with people who influence consumer behaviour.

Family influences

For many important leisure purchases, the family acts as a single decision-making unit. The leisure activities of children and teenagers are approved and funded by their parents. A family holiday has to provide something for every member of the household. In analyzing the ways in which such decisions are made, the roles usually seen in an industrial organization can be distinguished.[32] All members of the family are *users* of the product (unless of course the children are being sent off to a summer camp). The children are *influencers*, in that the parents want to make sure they will be happy and cooperative, but the choice must be *approved* by the parents. The main wage earner, usually the father, will be the *decider*, but it could well be the mother who acts as *buyer*, visiting the travel agent while in town shopping.

Just as in selling to an organization, the marketer needs to understand the dynamics of the decision-making unit in order to sell to the family market. Should the publicity for an activity holiday stress the excitement and adventure elements to the kids, or the educational value and high safety standards to the parents? Philips and Sega both developed CD video game systems. Philips positioned theirs as an educational package for parents to buy for their children, whereas Sega, in a series of outrageous youth-orientated advertisements, appealed to the teenage market direct by positioning their MegaDrive CD alongside rock music and nose-rings as something older people wouldn't understand.[33]

Reference groups

The peer pressure teenagers exert on others in their class or gang to adopt the same tastes in music, fashion and behaviour is an extreme example of the influence of what Hyman termed a *primary reference group*.[34] Other examples are the family, colleagues and neighbours, people with whom we interact regularly. *Secondary* groups with which contact is less frequent but which are still influential include church, trades union and community groups, including leisure organizations such as sports or social clubs. A person may have different roles and status in each group and present a different aspect of his personality. He will want his appearance, his behaviour and possessions to be acceptable and impressive to the others in these groups.

He may also model his behaviour on a group to which he would like to belong, his *aspirational group*. This could be his superiors at work or a higher social set in his neighbourhood. Today it is equally likely to be people he has seen on TV – sports stars, rock musicians, characters in soap operas, etc. Such people are also described as *role models*.

Showing the right role model or reference group using or endorsing a product can help an advertisement to be noticed, accepted and retained in the memory. Conversely, the wrong model or group can put people off buying the product because they do not want to be associated with that type of person.

Opinion formers

Within the group certain people will be opinion leaders who adopt new products or fashion first and influence the others to follow. It would clearly be advantageous to identify these and target them. This is relatively easy if the opinion leaders are media personalities or journalists who can be invited to product launches and opening nights. It may also be possible for organizations to keep a record of people's purchases on a database and identify those who regularly buy new models.

Rogers saw the *adoption* of a new product or idea following a normal distribution curve.[35] In each product area, certain people are innovators, eager to try out new experiences. Early adopters examine the new idea more carefully but still act as opinion leaders for the majority. The late majority are more sceptical about change, while the laggards tend to be tradition-bound and unwilling to discard what has worked for them in the past.[36]

Traditionally, innovations in fashion and leisure have tended to 'trickle down' from the rich, who have the time and money to risk on innovations, to the other classes who copy the behaviour of their aspirational group. More recently, the young have led, with their greater disposable income and their need to experiment and to rebel against current norms. Symbols of rebellion and dissent, like the Afro hairstyle or the baseball cap worn backwards, are borrowed from ethnic minorities by young people (copying their media role models) and then gradually adopted by older adults who want to look young and informal, until the original meaning is lost.

Personality

The speed with which an individual within a group adopts an innovation will depend on their personality. The personality is the expression of enduring inner psychological characteristics[37] which govern how a particular individual responds to their own inner needs and to the influence of others. Personality has been difficult to define in ways that are of use in predicting consumer behaviour, but attempts have been made in terms of self-confidence/insecurity, assertiveness/submissiveness, adventurousness/caution, impulsiveness/self-control, or as extrovert (outgoing, gregarious)/introvert (reflective, shy).

In analyzing the development of tourist resorts, Plog identified the early adopters of a new destination as allocentric, that is outward-directed, interested in encountering people and situations that were very different from themselves.[38] Using a distribution curve similar to that of Rogers, he showed how the allocentrics' example was then followed by less adventurous mid-centrics, and the area began to develop the usual characteristic facilities of a tourist resort. When these were sufficiently established, it attracted psychocentric types who were inward-looking and liked to be in familiar surroundings and company. By this time the resort had lost the characteristics which originally attracted the allocentrics, who therefore moved on in search of somewhere more authentic and unspoilt.

Culture

The sum of the shared attitudes, values and behaviour of the group is known as its culture. Culture is what the group has in common and which divides or distinguishes them from other groups. Historically, each nation developed its own distinctive culture protected from outside influences by geographical, language and religious barriers. Today, on the surface these barriers are being broken down by the ease of travel and communication across frontiers. We all live in what McLuhan called the Global Village, watching the same news and programmes on our televisions. Nevertheless ethnic strife and civil wars currently raging throughout the world should warn us that despite, or even because of, this global culture, the need to identify with one's own small group and to defend its culture against others is still very powerful.

The effects on consumer behaviour of cultural differences between nationalities are a major concern of international marketing. But even within the same country or city, there are significant cultural differences, between ethnic minorities, between social classes, and even between age groups. These are likely to be seen in attitudes to the family, to work, to the role of women and to the way relationships are conducted in business and socially (see Case Study 7.1).

CASE STUDY 7.1   *Women, sport and Islam*

The religion of Islam has about one billion followers throughout the world, who come from diverse local cultures. In the UK there are a million adherents with ethnic roots in the Indian subcontinent, the Arab world or Africa, plus a number of Anglo-Saxon converts.

The popular image of the Muslim woman is of a figure hidden in a enveloping dress or *chador* who plays no role in male society. In fact, according to Shahizah Daiman, a Malaysian Muslim woman lecturer in PE, many beliefs and practices labelled as 'Islamic' owe more to the influence of culture than to the teachings of true Islam. This includes the attitude that women are inferior and subordinate to men: 'It is not Islam that oppresses women but human beings with all their weaknesses who have failed to understand Allah's intentions'.

Most of the rulings of the *Qur'ān* regarding women were set down as restrictions on men with a view to preventing them from transgressing against women, as is their natural disposition and their actual practice in many societies.

Islam does not call for segregation between men and women. Nevertheless, to avoid temptation when assembled together, they should not be crammed together so that their breaths and bodies are very close to each other. The dress should be modest. The prophet directed that except for face and hands, no other part of a woman's body should be exhibited.

Culture and tradition have extended this to complete segregation and isolation of women, which is criticized by some Muslim women as denying them the benefits of the communal life of Muslims.

It is generally agreed that every Muslim man or woman has a responsibility to maintain their well-being, be it physical, mental or spiritual. Recreation and physical activity ought to play a part in this. And women as mothers have the responsibility of educating their families on the importance of fitness and health.

The problem arises when the women themselves do not realize the importance due to lack of awareness. Through generations of cultural tradition that claims to be Islamic, women feel they ought not to be out in public performing physical activities, or taking time off for themselves. In most developing countries women are active in the labour force, and to then take time off from their families seems selfish to traditional husbands or fathers. Competitive sport seems even more unlikely – what with intermingling of the sexes (if the coach, for example, is male), inappropriate dressing, and a feeling that sport has become too commercialized.

Nevertheless, Shahizah Daiman hopes that in following the guidelines for a true Islamic society, strategies could be found for the increased involvement of Muslim women in sport.

Source: *Sport 2*, May/June 1994.

QUESTION

1 What actions would a leisure centre in a multi-ethnic area need to take to increase the involvement of Muslim women in its activities?

CASE STUDY 7.2 *Consumer behaviour: The package holiday*

In the late 1980s, there was widespread recognition that the British market for Mediterranean package holidays was changing. After the peak year of 1986 the total number of UK visitors, including business travellers, to Spain showed a slight decline, from 5.9 to 5.1 million by 1990. Within these figures there was a marked change in the proportion of independent and inclusive holidays, and a switch from Spain to France (see Table 7.1).

Table 7.1 Numbers of holiday visits to France and Spain by UK tourists, 1986 and 1989 (thousands)

	Independent		Inclusive		Total	
	1986	1990	1986	1990	1986	1990
Spain	1,481	1,821	4,076	2,816	5,557	4,637
France	2,548	3,123	1,234	1,871	3,782	4,994

Source: British Tourist Authority (1991).

Inclusive holidays to America quadrupled (from 111,000 to 472,000) in the same period, and Florida, rather than the Costa del Sol, became the place people dreamed of going in search of the sun. Long-haul holidays to the Far East, Australia and the Caribbean, showed significant growth, with the large mainstream tour operators offering many of these destinations for the first time.

The Mediterrean began to acquire a bad reputation in the British press: drunken and violent behaviour by young 'lager louts' in the streets of the resorts; overbooking and substandard accommodation; poor food hygiene and inadequate fire safety arrangements; clouds of algae in the sea and discarded hypodermic needles in the sand; and the resorts themselves overcrowded and overdeveloped with high rise hotels clustered all along the beach. So alarming was the situation to the tour operators that Charles Newbold, managing director of Thomson Holidays, the UK's largest tour operator, wondered, in print, 'if the package holiday as we know it is going out of fashion?'

What theories of consumer behaviour are relevant here? Here are some hypotheses:

Choosing the package holiday was originally an extended problem-solving decision, with high involvement on the part of the customers. As they became familiar with the regular holiday, the problem solving became more limited, particularly as the products themselves were increasingly homogeneous. There was little significant difference between the hotels, the resorts or the operators, and the holidays were sold as 'summer sun' rather than as distinctive destinations. These are the conditions that Krugman said created low-involvement decisions. The fact that bookings were increasingly being made nearer the date of travel, and on the basis of which company was offering the best 'late booking bargains', supports this view. When the purchase becomes routine, customers may change brands, or in this case destinations, in search of variety. The growth of new destinations – North Africa, Turkey, Cyprus and Florida, plus the long-haul destinations – is evidence of this.

The package holiday originally offered satisfaction of security and social needs. People could experience the sun and sights of a foreign country knowing that they would be in a group of similar people and with a tour rep to deal with any problems. Maslow's hierarchy suggests that once these needs are secured, the need for status and self-fulfilment come into play. Going to Spain no longer impressed one's reference group. The genuine innovators or allocentrics, the rich and the young backpackers, had already pioneered other more distant destinations, and once the first tour operators followed, the early adopters could impress their friends with slides from Turkey, the Gambia, the Maldives or Disneyland.

The need for self-development expressed itself in a growth in activity holidays, from windsurfing to rambling and painting. It was no longer enough just to sunbathe on the beach. Familiarity with foreign travel encouraged people to leave the organized tour behind and take an independent holiday in their own car (hence the increase in the number of holidays in France at the expense of Spain). Young people who had been taken on Spanish holidays since childhood needed to express their individuality by finding somewhere their parents had not been. The 'empty nester' generation preferred to look for new destinations and experiences while they still had the health and energy.

In Herzberg's terms, the basic elements of a holiday – accommodation, transport, beaches and tourist entertainment – had become dissatisfiers, taken for granted until something went wrong. There had to be something else – activities, exotic, high-status destinations – to motivate the choice. The converse of this is that when basic needs were not met, when the hotel was overbooked or unfinished, the beaches dirty or the streets unsafe, none of the higher needs mattered. Tourists very quickly desert destinations as a result of media reports of dangers to health or security.

Source: The material used in this case study first appeared in the author's article 'Homogeneous products: The future of established resorts', in W. Theobald (Ed.) (1994) *Tourism: The Next Decade*

QUESTIONS

1 How convincing do you find these explanations, in the light of your own and your family's holiday experiences?

2 What economic factors are at work behind the changes in package holidays? Are these in fact more significant than the behavioural explanations given?

3 What could the tourist resorts and the tour operators do to reverse the apparent decline? (What has happened since this case was written, and does it support or refute these hypotheses?)

Summary

Individuals' consumer behaviour, then, is influenced by, and modelled on the behaviour of other people with whom they are in regular contact Because of this, marketers are able to identify groups of people with similar characteristics who can be targeted by the same marketing campaign. This process, known as segmentation, is the subject of the next chapter.

Notes

1. Engel, J.F. Blackwell, R.D. and Miniard, P.W. (1990) *Consumer Behavior*, p. 27.
2. British Tourist Authority (1993) *Digest of Tourism Statistics*.
3. Kotler, P. (1994) *Marketing Management*, p. 195.
4. Fishbein, M. (1963) 'An investigation of the relationships between beliefs about an object and attitudes towards that object', *Human Relations*, 16, 233–40.
5. Howard, J.A. (1989) *Consumer Behaviour in Marketing Strategy*, p. 34.
6. Engel *et al.* (1990), *op. cit.*, p. 544.
7. *Ibid*, p. 28.
8. Krugman, H., 'The impact of television advertising: Learning without involvement', *Public Opinion Quarterly*, 29: 349–56.
9. Howard (1989), *op. cit.*, p. 28.
10. Engel *et al.* (1990), *op. cit.*, p. 273.
11. Bradshaw, J. (1972) 'The concept of social need', *New Society*, 30(3): 640–43.
12. Allied Dunbar (1992) *National Fitness Survey* (Summary), p. 5.
13. Quoted in Torkildsen, G. (1983) *Leisure and Recreation Management*, p. 212.
14. See Case Study 10.1.
15. Engel *et al.* (1990), *op. cit.* p. 252.
16. Marcuse, H. (1964) *One-Dimensional Man*.
17. Engel *et al.* (1990), *op.cit.*, p. 46.
18. Maslow, A. (1954) *Motivation and Personality*.
19. Torkildsen (1983), *op. cit.*, p. 211; For a detailed account of Maslow and research carried out in support of his theories, see Chisnall, P.M. (1985) *Marketing* pp. 39–45.
20. Herzberg, F. (1966) *Work and the Nature of Man*.
21. Lannon, J. and Cooper, P. (1983) 'Humanistic advertising', *International Journal of Advertising*, July.
22. Rapaport, R. and Rapaport, R.N. (1975) *Leisure and the Family Life Cycle*, p. 22.
23. McGuire, W.J. (1976) 'Some internal psychological factors influencing consumer choice', *Journal of Consumer Research* 2 (March), quoted in Engel *et al.* (1990) p. 363.
24. Kotler (1994), *op. cit.*, p. 186.
25. Chisnall (1985), *op. cit.*, p. 22.
26. De Bono, E. (1977) *Lateral Thinking*, Harmondsworth, Penguin, p. 27.
27. Engel *et al.* (1990), *op. cit.*, p. 398.
28. *Ibid*, p. 413.
29. Broadbent, S. and Jacobs, R. (1984) *Spending Advertising Money*, p. 339.
30. Festinger, L. (1985) *A Theory of Cognitive Dissonance*; for a full discussion of the concept, see Chisnall (1985), *op cit.*, pp. 26–28.
31. Rapaport and Rapaport (1975), *op. cit.*, p. 19.
32. Kotler (1994), *op. cit.*, p. 209.

33. Diamond, J., 'Making of a mega-myth', *The Guardian*, May 7 1993.
34. Hyman, H. (1942) 'The psychology of status', *Archives of Psychology* **38**.
35. Rogers, E.M. (1962) *Diffusion of Innovations*, p. 162.
36. Kotler (1994), *op. cit.*, p. 349.
37. Engel *et al.* (1990), *op. cit.*, p. 328.
38. Plog, S.C. (1974) 'Why destination areas rise and fall', vol. 14, No. 1, February, *Cornell Hotel and Restaurant Administration Quarterly*, pp. 13–16.

8   Segmentation

Why segment the market?

In Chapter 7 we saw that our choice of leisure products and activities are strongly influenced by the people with whom we live, work and socialize. Because of this, it is possible to target groups of people who share similar behaviour and attitudes towards a particular product, and can therefore be distinguished from the other groups making up the total market for the product. This process is known as segmentation, and comes between the two extremes of marketing strategy, mass marketing and customization.

Customization, creating a 'made-to-measure' product to suit each individual customer, is the ideal way of satisfying that customer's needs, but it is very time-consuming and labour-intensive. It is far more cost effective if the products are produced in large quantities on an automated production line, and everyone gets the same. The problem with this mass-market approach is that the standard product is not going to satisfy anyone perfectly.

Not everyone can afford their own swimming pool with private tuition. On the other hand, in the public baths, serious swimmers doing lengths are going to collide with toddlers learning to swim, and be jumped on by noisy teenagers. For this reason, centres nowadays divide their market up into segments and provide separate sessions for learners, senior citizens and length swimming. New 'fun pools' have been built to cater for those who just want to leap in and out of the water.

The core advantage of segmentation is that customers will be more satisfied with the product because it has been designed with their needs in mind. Their social needs are also satisfied because they will be mixing with people like themselves and avoiding other incompatible types (see Case Study 6.1: Club 18–30 in Chapter 6). Satisfied customers are more likely to come back and less likely to be lured away by competitors' offers. They may also be prepared to pay extra for the extra benefits and exclusivity. As we shall see in Chapter 12, the price can be set to match their sense of value and their ability to pay.

For the organization, if it knows exactly which segments it wishes to reach, it can select the media most likely to be read or seen by those consumers, and so spend less on general mass-market advertising. If it knows the lifestyles and attitudes of that segment and the benefits they are seeking from the product, the advertising message can be made more precisely persuasive.

As quoted in Chapter 4, Kotler said that the key to marketing strategy is segmentation, targeting and positioning. The first stage is to identify, through research, the segments into which the market falls. If you skilfully peel an orange it will divide into segments which are naturally separated by a thin layer of skin and can be handled cleanly. If you are less skilful you get juice everywhere and the orange becomes a shapeless mess. For effective marketing you need to find the natural segments that can be separately targeted. Viable segments should be:

- *measurable* in terms of size, purchasing power and characteristics;
- *substantial* enough to be worth targeting;
- *accessible* by marketing promotional and distribution channels;
- *differentiable* in terms of how they respond to marketing programmes; and
- *actionable* by the organization within the limits of its budget and resources.[1]

With this in mind, we shall now look at ways in which the market can be segmented.

Ways of segmenting the market

Geographic segmentation

For most leisure venues, finding out where their customers come from is probably the most important piece of research they can do. Most will come from a relatively local catchment area, and so advertising can be limited to a few local newspapers and radio stations. As the following examples show, the size of the catchment area will depend on the competition, the strength of the attraction and the distance people are prepared to travel.

A unique attraction like the Fleet Air Arm Museum at Yeovilton, which includes a Concorde prototype, found that people travelled up to 40 miles each way to see it. Allowing for differing road conditions, this probably represents the maximum distance people are likely to drive for a day out. Most ten-pin bowling centres have a catchment of less than six miles.

When the Pyramids Leisure Centre first opened in Portsmouth, it attracted people from all over the south of England to its leisure pool. As other towns developed their own flume rides and fun pools, the catchment area became more local.

Although Rugby League has a national audience on television, the major clubs are unable to grow as they are all concentrated in the same narrow area of northern England with very local catchments for 'live' spectators. That is why they are now considering mergers.

The Poole Arts Centre attracts a local audience for most of its plays and concerts, but a number of leading pop and comedy stars can draw people from anywhere in the South West to performances at Poole.

When Sheffield City Council built the Ponds Forge international swimming pool for the World Student Games in 1992, it closed several old-fashioned pools which had served local areas within the city. There is a general trend towards centralized, larger modern facilities at the expense of local neighbourhood provision in leisure, as in shopping centres and hospitals. The danger is that this denies access to those without cars, generally the poor and elderly.

Geographical segmentation is also important for airports and shipping routes. The tour operator Airtours began by specializing in tours departing from northern regional airports. This enabled it to undercut the operators based on Gatwick who charged supplements for departures from other airports. Once it had established a strong regional following, Airtours had the bargaining power to compete nationally, and is now the second largest British operator.

Demographic segmentation

Demographics, from the same Greek root as democracy, means the study of the characteristics of the population. It covers the external measurable characteristics of people, such as their age, gender, occupation, income, family status, education, race and nationality. Demographic segmentation can be carried out by means of straightforward quantitative research, and can be very useful in planning media campaigns. The demographic profile of the target market can be matched with that of the readership of newspapers and magazines to decide where to advertise. Demographic details alone have serious limitations, however, when it comes to deciding what to advertise and how, as will be seen from the following discussion of the types of demographic segmentation.

Occupation
The most commonly used way of defining a target market in the UK is the socio-economic grading system developed by the Joint Industry Committee for National Readership Surveys (JICNARS). This classifies people by the occupation of the head of the household into six groups: ABC1C2DE. Table 8.1

Table 8.1   The JICNARS classification of socio-economic grades

A	Upper middle class	Higher managerial, administrative or professional	Doctors, captains and above in the Forces; barristers, stockbrokers, senior managers and civil servants, directors of large companies	2.7%
B	Middle class	Intermediate managerial, administrative or professional	Accountants, head teachers and lecturers, architects, vicars, newspaper editors, engineers, middle managers	15.1%
C1	Lower middle class	Supervisory, clerical or junior managerial, administrative or professional	Junior managers, clerical workers, sales representatives, shop managers, nurses, teachers, students	23.9%
C2	Skilled working class	Skilled manual workers	Mechanical and electrical fitters, bricklayers, train and HGV drivers, dockers, miners, shop assistants, small traders, police constables	27.8%
D	Working class	Semi-skilled and unskilled workers	Labourers, machine operators, porters, bus conductors, cleaners, delivery drivers	17.8%
E	Those on the lowest level of subsistence	State pensioners or widows (no other earner) casual or lowest grade workers	Those on Social Security and other state benefits	12.7%

Source: Definitions from JICNARS (1982) *Social Grading in the National Readership Survey.* Examples from Market Research Society (1977) *Handbook for Researchers.* Percentages of adult population from JICNARS, *National Readership Survey 1990–91.*

shows the types of occupations that come into each group. Retired people on occupational pensions are classed according to their last job, housewives according to their husband's job. Owners of businesses can be anywhere from A to C2 depending on the size of the business, the numbers employed and the nature of their own work.

The classification is often used by practitioners and journalists in a very loose way, with 'ABC1' meaning simply the upper half of the market or the middle as opposed to the working class. The system was developed for media research and as such is a very useful tool. It should not be used however as a guide to income, consumption habits or lifestyles. Quinlan first pointed out the dangers of doing so:

> The difference in earnings between skilled and unskilled workers has been eroded. There are more C1C2DE than AB households in the top fifth of the British population in terms of income (manual workers may have more opportunity for overtime than their managers, for example).
>
> The poorer sections of society spend more on food, relatively and absolutely, than their wealthier neighbours.
>
> Even in the 1970s when the article was researched, C1C2 households represented a larger market for such apparently up-market products as brandy, colour TV, credit cards and property insurance.
>
> Children in working class homes are more likely to have expensive toys than children whose parents are rich. This may be because workers indulge their children while the middle class try to show that they are not spoiling theirs, or because heavy mortgages, school fees and life insurance leave the stereotypical AB with less disposable income.[2]

There is nevertheless a significant difference in leisure activities between the social classes. According to *Social Trends*, professionals, employers and managers were more likely to participate in outdoor sports than other groups, while the skilled manual and self-employed had the highest participation rates for cue sports and darts. Those in the professional group were more likely to play squash and golf.[3]

Torkildsen quotes a number of studies that indicate that the middle classes are more likely to use public libraries, or patronize drama, ballet and opera. Even swimming and the use of 'leisure pools' were shown to have an 'up-scale' profile.[4] He concludes that this is not a question of cost as free museums and libraries, subsidized theatre and evening classes, and low-cost activities like walking and camping also lack working class patronage.

The answer may lie in the cultural differences between the classes. Hanna believes that working class culture favours rewards through luck and chance, and a collective approach to leisure, in contrast to the competitive, achievement or status-driven individualism of the middle classes.[5] It is highly debatable whether such a cultural distinction is valid any longer, if it ever was.

Education
The *Target Group Index* includes 'terminal education age' as one of its variables. Whether an individual leaves school at 16, 18 or after higher education at 21 can indicate their ambition, intelligence, academic ability or curiosity about the world in which they live. Continuing in education may also increase their opportunity to practise sports, music or the arts. They may be more likely to speak a foreign language. Above all, they will be better qualified for professional or managerial careers.

For these kinds of reasons, studies show that those with a college education are likely to show above average participation in sports and arts activities both during their studies and afterwards.[6]

Gender
The differences between the sexes are obvious and are often used to create products for the different physical needs, roles and self-images of men and women. There is a wide difference between the extremes of masculinity and femininity, but, as Hofstede points out, these are as much cultural, learnt values as inherent characteristics.[7] Whole cultures can exhibit greater tendencies towards masculine values such as individual achievement and assertiveness, or feminine values of social cooperation and caring.

In their targeting of women, advertisers have in the past been guilty of portraying unreal stereotypes. Now Persil are using comedy star Robbie Coltrane and his grandmother to advertise washing-up liquid, instead of the idealized housewife and mother.

With three-quarters of British women of working age economically active (working at least part-time in paid jobs), the roles of housewife and mother have to be fitted into less time. As we saw in Chapter 6, this leaves less time for participation in sports and exercise. Nevertheless, a growing number of women are taking part in fitness activities, most notably in non-competitive, social forms such as aerobics and 'keep-fit' classes. In 1993, there were 13.5 million women taking part in fitness activities at least monthly, creating a market worth £700 million for the activities alone, not including the associated clothing, footwear and equipment.[8]

Age
The influence of age and family lifecycle stage on leisure demand was discussed in detail in Chapter 6, and some possible ways of segmenting the market by age were suggested there. Care should be again taken not to resort to stereotypes, of young people or senior citizens for example, which may seem patronizing or offensive to the people you are trying to attract (see Case Study 8.1: Targeting the new age).

Reebok has become wary of advertising their trainers with an image specifically aimed at the youth market. 'I've got players over the age of 60 at my tennis club, and just look at the numbers of veterans running in the

London Marathon', says UK marketing manager Gwyn Howells, who claims that Reebok has a greater proportion of its sales from older sports people than the rest of the trainer market.[9]

Lifestyle segmentation

Age, occupation, income, family status and education all help to describe and identify the characteristics of a market segment. It is tempting but, as we have seen, dangerous to use any of them in isolation to predict attitudes and behaviour. We all know from our own peer groups that people of the same age in the same college or office can behave in very different ways, yet we still fall into the trap of expecting people in other age groups or occupations to conform to stereotypes.

To get a more accurate and useful means of segmenting their markets, marketers have developed ways of dividing their customers into lifestyle groups. Kotler's definition of lifestyle is: 'a person's pattern of living in the world as expressed in that person's activities, interests and values'.[10] Or, to put it another way, the patterns in which she spends her time and money. Lifestyle is partly the result of the person's current circumstances (job, income, family), partly her background, parents and education, and partly the result of choices made according to her personality and aspirations. Whereas social grade or class defines what an individual *is* according to his work and income, lifestyle charts how she expresses what she *would like to be* through her leisure and expenditure behaviour.[11]

Lifestyle groups are researched by what is termed *psychographic* surveys. The technique is to ask a large number of questions about the respondents' attitudes and behaviour, usually by asking them to indicate on a five-point scale how strongly they agree or disagree with a statement. These questions are in a random order in order to reduce the chances of respondents being influenced by their earlier answers to be consistent rather than truthful. Some leisure-related examples from the *TGI* are given in Table 8.2. Demographic questions are also included. The results are analyzed by a computer technique called cluster analysis in order to identify clusters of people giving the same answers to a number of questions, and therefore sharing similar attitudes and behaviour.

Early work on lifestyles attempted to produce classifications into a number of universal and comprehensive lifestyle types. Plummer's AIO system used 36 major variables under the main headings of Activities, Interests, Opinions and Demographics.[12] Mitchell's VALS system analyzed Values and Lifestyles into nine groups from desperate survivors, through belongers, emulators and achievers, to societally conscious, and finally fully mature integrateds. This system is reminiscent of Maslow's in its idea that individuals can pass through a series of

Table 8.2   Examples of correlations between lifestyle statements and holiday destinations (TG1, 1985; BMRB). Numbers are indices, where 100 is the average for the whole sample.

'Agree strongly'	Holiday in last 12 months						
	France	Greece	Malta	Majorca	Scotland	Canada	Yugoslavia
Articles influence my choice of holiday	79	109	162	153	91	52	136
I prefer holidays off the beaten track	196	120	74	64	165	176	134
I like to go to familiar places on holiday	50	64	148	91	127	98	74
On holiday I only want to eat, drink and lie in the sun	55	114	128	125	59	65	89
TV programmes influence my choice of holiday	87	131	121	138	89	92	129
I try to take more than one holiday abroad each year	159	142	159	162	77	121	154
It's important my family thinks I'm doing well	72	95	125	106	105	80	86
I am happy with my standard of living	122	101	148	106	119	136	143
I am a workaholic	147	125	67	75	108	97	106
I can't bear untidiness	72	78	77	106	92	120	98
It's important to look well dressed	105	117	124	124	94	150	104
I have a very good sense of style	106	119	140	122	94	144	98
Fast food is all junk really	100	85	75	71	90	138	108
I try to include more fibre in my diet	132	93	66	76	130	136	125

stages from a need-driven stage, through outer-directed stages of belonging and emulating others, to a more inner-directed concern with self-development.[13]

The technique is now widely used to produce lifestyle and attitude groupings for specific product areas. For example, Air Canada identified four lifestyle groups among Canadians:

1   *Extravagant consumers*: predominantly female, higher than medium household incomes, include all age groups. An appealing vacation

would emphasize luxury, pampering and shopping for clothes (18% of the Canadian population).

2   *Nature people*: tend to be young, unmarried, well-educated. They want to go to new places to avoid routines, and to experience the universe generally without the usual concern for comfort (20%).

3   *Playsters*: primarily young males in active pursuit of sensual pleasure. A vacation for them would be inexpensive but swinging, modern and active, featuring no social values but fun (23%).

4   *Cautious homebodies*: older, less affluent, less well-educated. They want safety, and a predictable environment on their vacations (39%).

These groups were further analyzed for their propensity to take an air holiday. They were matched with vacation packages, such as Caribbean hotels for the extravagant consumers, and escorted coach tours of England for the homebodies. The next stage was to analyze an existing mailing list into the four types and mail them with details of the most suitable product.[14]

Closer to home, an unpublished study for Maison de la France divided the British holiday market into the following groups:

*   Disco, drinking, sun and sex
*   Britain abroad and no foreign muck
*   The far pavilions (long-haul travellers)
*   Outdoor, independent, adventurous
*   The middle class family abroad.

Geodemographic segmentation

Geodemographic analysis divides residential areas up according to the lifestyles of those who live there. Where we choose to live reflects our income, our family status, where we want our children to go to school, our social aspirations and our preference for city action or rural retreat (or the suburban compromise between the two). Therefore, people who live in similar neighbourhoods are likely to have similar behavioural, purchasing and lifestyle habits.

The first geodemographic system, CACI's ACORN (A Classification Of Residential Neighbourhoods), uses data from the UK census split into enumeration districts, neighbourhood areas of about 150 houses. ACORN identifies districts with clusters of common characteristics covering age, sex, socio-economic status and occupation, as well as the number of rooms in the house, the number of cars, and the means of travel to work. Each district is categorized into one of 38 neighbourhood types. These types are then assigned to every postcode in the UK, so that CACI can identify the demographic and behavioural characteristics from the address.

For example, DT1 2RD is category B 'Business people in better-off families, paying off mortgages and bringing up children', group 4 'Affluent executives, family areas', type 10 'Affluent working families with mortgages'. These have above average levels of 25–44 year-olds and children under 15, living in detached or semi-detached estates, likely to be in professional and managerial employment, highly educated, large proportion of working women, 60% owning two cars, above average incomes, and high expenditure on compact discs and videos. The proportion taking holidays is high, and winter holidays 2.3 times more popular than average. Far-flung destinations are especially popular. Pub-going is below average but wine bars are more popular than average. 'These are such active sporty people that it is easier to say which sports are NOT popular: fishing, bowls, bingo and darts have very low popularity while waterskiing and athletics are particularly popular.'

ACORN is used to analyze an organization's mailing list to produce a profile of the customers' age, affluence and location so that promotions can be targeted to suit the particular market. Having identified the main ACORN types of the existing customers, other similar postcode areas can be selected either for door-to-door leafleting or personalized mailings using names and addresses from the electoral rolls. It can also be used to identify suitable locations with the right types of customers for new shops or other premises.

ACORN is also used with the Target Group Index (see Chapter 5) to identify the residential areas with the highest concentrations of users of specific products and brands.[15]

There are now a number of other geodemographic systems on the market, such as Pinpoint and Mosaic. Geodemographic systems are widely used by the regional tourist boards and arts marketing organizations to enlarge and refine their mailing lists.

Behavioural segmentation

All the methods of segmentation discussed so far have focused on what type of person the customer is. It is often equally important to look at the relationship between the customer and the product, i.e. what the customer wants from the exchange.

Benefit segmentation

The example of swimming pools used at the start of this chapter is an example of benefit segmentation. Some customers will be swimming in order to keep fit, others to train for competitions, others will be learning to swim, and others will be there to play around in the water. These segments will not be confined to any one social class or age group, but each has different needs and expectations.

Occasion segmentation
On special occasions people are prepared to pay more for special treatment. Many restaurants now have special deals for children's birthday parties, while hotels and cruise lines have special honeymoon suites.

Status segmentation
Business people travel first-class and stay in five-star hotels as much for the status it confers on them as for the additional comfort. Hotels often cater for business guests during the week and target the leisure market at the weekends with lower prices and special activity packages.

County cricket clubs offer an ordinary membership package and a premium 'vice-president's grade' which allows them the best seats and other privileges, as well as appealing to their sense of status.

Usage segmentation
It is often found that 80% of the consumption of a product is by 20% of the users. It makes sense, therefore, to concentrate the marketing effort on the 20% who are heavy users of the product.

Mullin *et al.* segmented the supporters of a spectator sport as follows:[16]

> *Heavy*: season ticket holders
>
> *Medium*: regular single ticket buyer
>
> *Light*: occasional single ticket buyer
>
> *Defector*: former users in past 12 months
>
> *Media consumer*: follows the game in the press and TV
>
> *Non-aware*: interested in other sports
>
> *Uninterested*: not interested in any sport.

The marketer should attend to the needs of each segment and ensure that there are light, medium and heavy users for the product.

The heavy users supply the most revenue, and are also likely to recruit others through word-of-mouth recommendation. The organization needs to keep them loyal by good service and by rewards for continuing membership. There is a danger, however, if it becomes too dependent on season-ticket holders, members, or other heavy users, while light or occasional users are discouraged (at some county cricket grounds, light users are confined to the least desirable viewpoints, the majority of areas being permanently signed as 'members only'). If heavy users become defectors, for example, in protest at the loss of a star player, there will be no one to replace them.

Light or medium users may become the heavy users of the future, and it is easier to persuade them to come more often or to take out membership, than it is to find new customers from the non-aware. Media consumers can be persuaded to sample a live match by joint promotions and competitions in the media.

Non-aware and uninterested people are difficult to target for an established sport or activity, but offer a potential audience for a new venture. When the Sheffield Arena launched its ice hockey team, the Sheffield Steelers, it gave away thousands of free tickets to local schools to encourage children to come and bring their families. Students at the local colleges were given free tickets and were provided with a courtesy coach. At the first match there were 300 paying spectators and 1,000 free-ticket holders; at the third match 900 paying and 5,000 free. Not only were the free-ticket holders sampling the game and the American style razzamatazz that went with it, they were also helping to create the atmosphere that comes from a crowded stadium. The free-ticket promotion ran for nine matches. Four weeks after it ended, the match was a complete sell-out with 9,000 paying spectators compared with a national average of under 2,000.

Applying segmentation

Textbooks on marketing usually begin, as we have, with demographic segmentation. Middleton argues that in practice tourism organizations first segment their markets behaviourally, by purpose and benefit sought.[17] Applying his sequence to a leisure centre, the most immediately practical way of dividing the customers is by *purpose*, i.e. the activity for which they come. This will highlight areas of high and low demand, and enable the manager to plan the programme of activities, allocate rooms and staff, and to make plans for development. Within each activity, customers will be looking for different *benefits*. We have already discussed the different benefits sought by users of the swimming pool. Similarly, different facilities, programmes and promotions will be needed for those who use the fitness suite for training for a competitive sport and those who are there to lose weight. For each of these categories, the manager then needs to know their *usage* patterns – how frequently they come, whether they are regular users of the centre, or whether they also use competitors' facilities. From this, the centre must choose whether it is trying to attract new, non-aware customers, to increase usage by light users, or to win defectors from other centres.

It is only after defining the target market in this way that knowledge of their *demographic* characteristics becomes useful. Age and occupation can be a guide to how to reach them – through schools, businesses, housewives' or senior citizens' clubs, for example. For a national organization, demographics are, as explained earlier, a guide to which media to use. *Geographic* segmentation is equally important to a local centre as a guide to which local newspapers to use and where to distribute door-to-door publicity. Finally, *lifestyle* profiles can help to create the right promotional message and project the right image for the centre, so that potential customers will feel that using it will enhance their self-image and bring them into contact with the 'right' sort of people.

Targeting

Having identified the different segments of the market, the next step is to decide which to target. From the arguments in favour of segmentation given at the beginning of this chapter, it would seem logical to concentrate on meeting the needs of just one segment better than any other organization. This approach is known as *niche marketing*. As we have seen from the examples, though, many organizations draw their customers from a number of different segments. None of these segments is sufficient to sustain the business on its own, but together they make up a viable market. The organization could simply treat them as one undifferentiated market, but as we have seen, it is more effective to target each one separately with a modified marketing mix. This approach is known as *differentiated marketing*.

Niche marketing

Niche marketing is an effective competitive strategy for a small organization, the only viable option according to Porter.[18] A small business lacks the size to compete on the basis of lower costs and the resources to compete across the whole market. It must therefore select one segment of the market and offer a highly differentiated product. For example, the Poole Arts Centre cinema faced severe competition when the UCI chain opened a multi-screen cinema in the same town. UCI offered more seats and so could charge lower prices. The major distributors therefore favoured UCI with the latest popular releases. To compete, the Arts Centre had to concentrate on the 'art house' segment of the market – film enthusiasts with a taste for serious artistic or innovative films – and offer films that were not shown in the commercial cinema or second showings of successful films for those who missed them at the UCI. For example, when UCI were showing *The Flintstones* and *Jurassic Park*, the Arts Centre showed a rerun of *Much Ado About Nothing* and Alain Corneau's *Tous Les Matins du Monde*.

Niches are often spotted and developed by entrepreneurs targeting the innovator and early adopter types (see Chapter 7) who are dissatisfied with current mass-market products. Small independent operators first developed tours to Turkey, for example, for people who were tired of over-commercialized Spanish resorts. One problem with niches is that they only exist if the demand is large enough to sustain a small business venture, but not large enough to interest the major companies. Such a situation can be transitory. Within a few years of the specialist operators beginning tours to

Turkey, major companies like Intasun started to include the destination. The resulting rush to develop new hotels threatened to ruin the appeal of the resorts for the smaller companies' clients.[19]

Differentiated marketing

Another problem with niches is that concentrating on one segment of the market leaves the organization vulnerable if anything happens to reduce demand from that segment. As we have already said, demand for leisure activities is very volatile. A classic case is that of a very successful niche tour operator called Yugotours. Many restaurants and other leisure activities that catered for the expensive tastes of highly paid 'yuppies' in the City of London stock and financial markets ran into difficulties when the boom of the mid-1980s ended and many of their clients lost their jobs.

Catering for more than one segment spreads the risk. It also helps to overcome the problem of peaks and troughs in demand. For leisure centres, bowling, skating and similar activities, the peaks and troughs are daily. To overcome this they can target young professionals for early morning exercise before work; housewives, mothers and toddlers, or senior citizens during the day; school children in the late afternoon/early evening; and working couples or teenagers in the evenings. The hotel markets for business people in the week and leisure travellers at weekends has already been mentioned. Nightclubs also have to target different segments to fill quiet midweek nights.

Resorts and tour operators tend to have seasonal peaks. Beach resorts target senior citizens in the winter months. Alpine ski resorts repackage themselves as 'lakes and mountains' destinations in the summer, targeting walkers and those looking for relaxation and scenery.

Many large organizations need to fill their capacity with a mix of different segments at the same time. HF Holidays used to run its country 'guesthouses' solely for rambling holidays. Guests would have a choice of joining groups for strenuous, moderate or light walks. In response to declining numbers in the 1980s they diversified to offer a range of other activity holidays in the same centres as the walking ones – painting, bridge, country dancing, natural history, even murder and mystery. Marketing Manager Andrew Waller explained the new policy to the author as follows:

> In owning our own properties we can be likened to an airline, which has to work in a number of different markets and it is only the combination of these which produces a fill. Our requirement to fill our fixed bed capacity for as much of the year as possible has led us to follow a strategy of segmentation and new product development.

A problem with differentiated marketing is that each segment has different needs and different price sensitivities. A car ferry can be carrying coachloads of day excursionists who have paid ten pounds for a convivial day of drinking and duty-free shopping, alongside motorists who have driven up from their holiday in the South of France and have paid hundreds of pounds for the chance of a relaxing break in their journey. To solve the problems this caused, P&O Ferries now offer club class lounges where for a small supplement motorists can enjoy peace and quiet in reclining seats and be served with coffee and free newspapers.

The Multiplex cinema developed by UCI offers ten small theatres instead of the one large auditorium of the old style cinema. This enables them to offer a choice of films to cater for the family, teenage and adult segments and to respond to demand by showing popular films in more than one theatre if necessary, or by extending or shortening the film's run (i.e. the number of days it is shown.)

Differentiated marketing requires the company to develop a range of products and to have a segmented pricing policy. These will be discussed further in later chapters.

A return to customization?

Having said at the beginning of this chapter that creating a special product for each customer is prohibitively expensive because of the time and labour involved, it should be pointed out that computer technology is now reducing these costs and making a degree of customization possible in several areas of leisure.

One of these is health and fitness. A new customer has a detailed assessment of her state of fitness using electronic technology to measure pulse and respiratory rates, and body strength. A computer then generates a recommended programme of exercise on machines set to provide the right level of resistance or cardiovascular exercise. The customer can buy a swipe card for a certain amount of time on the machines and choose the length and frequency of the sessions to suit her other commitments. After the initial assessment the customer does not need individual supervision, and so staffing is kept to an economical level, one instructor oversees a room full of people following their customized programmes.

Another area is the growth of independent travel. The independent-minded traveller no longer has the choice of buying a package or working out her own itinerary and paying the full price for travel and accommodation. Companies now offer travel agents access to databases of accommodation, car-hire and seat-only fares on charter flights, so that from their computer terminal they can quickly put together an itinerary and make bookings to create a customized package for the client.

CASE STUDY 8.1   *Targeting the new age*

The 'new age' for the health and fitness industry means the over-40s market, which as we saw in Chapter 6, is one of the fastest expanding age groups in the UK and other European countries. The industry which had been very youth-oriented in the past, must learn to adapt to the needs of this new market, according to Dott Massimo Masarimo of Technogym.

How does the health and fitness industry perceive new age members? Recent over-50s promotions in certain clubs only attracted people over 60 because marketing campaigns did not understand the type of person they could attract. Consider the role models for this group: Mick Jagger, Jane Fonda and many other famous personalities are over 50. Fitness operators should see new age members as a much more flamboyant and potentially active social group. Maintaining a healthy lifestyle, looking good and feeling better are the key goals of these individuals. Increased leisure time will enable this group to take positive steps in its own lifestyle approach.

Marketing campaigns should promote exercise as a social and recreational experience. With high-tech machinery and qualified instructors, centres can offer preventive care to those who have never shown much interest in physical exercise.

Where then should operators start? One way is to focus on the needs of the individuals – you do not die if you have a weak bicep, but you can die if you have a weak heart.

Instructors can assess older users' capacity using modern technology to monitor their heart rate and set individual pulse rate targets according to their level of fitness. Avoiding over-exercise is an important consideration for older members. Fitness programmers can identify three target groups: people with minor problems, users with more severe medical problems, and those with high energy who successfully deny the ageing process.

As the industry begins to understand better the needs of this target group, it needs to look more closely at the types of exercise equipment needed for this age group. Machines need to be able to avoid overstretching those with physical problems, and ensure that good posture is kept throughout the exercises. Programmes that monitor aerobic performance and offer dietary advice can provide individuals with proof of the positive results of their exercise programme and encourage them to continue. New products such as walk aerobics, water-based exercise classes and seminars on subjects like lower back pain could be developed. Staff profiles may also change as centres recruit an older workforce to provide role models for new age members to emulate.

Source: Masarini, D.M. 'The new age', *Leisure Management*, Vol.14 No. 9, September 1994.

QUESTIONS

1 Using the classifications given in this chapter, how would you define the 'new age' segment in terms of demographics, lifestyle, and behaviour (including benefit and product usage)?

2 What modifications to their marketing mix (product, price, promotion, people, etc.) will health and fitness centres need to make to target this segment?

3 Suggest an appropriate promotional campaign to attract this segment to a local health and fitness centre.

4 Discuss the advantages and disadvantages of adopting a niche marketing approach to this segment.

Summary

Choosing the most suitable segments of the market as the target for a marketing effort is at the heart of marketing strategy. This choice determines the type of product that is created to meet the needs of the segment, the price that is set to match their ability and willingness to pay, the promotional message that matches their lifestyle aspirations and the benefits they are seeking, and the choice of media and distribution channels to reach them.

Modern segmentation techniques combine demographic facts about the customers with measurement of their lifestyle and their relationship with the product. Geodemographic systems can link these characteristics to specific neighbourhoods.

Competitive strategy influences the choice of target markets. Small businesses often begin by identifying a particular segment or niche which larger companies do not serve satisfactorily. Such niches can be transitory and over-concentration on one segment can leave an organization vulnerable to changes in demand and with unfilled capacity at times of the day, week or year. A differentiated strategy aimed at creating the optimum mix of business from a number of segments is therefore more commonly used. Technology is now enabling each segment or even individuals to receive the type of service most suited to their needs.

Notes

1. Kotler, P. (1994) *Marketing Management*, p. 280.
2. Quinlan, F. (1981) 'The use of social grade in marketing', *Quarterly Review of Marketing*, Autumn.
3. Central Statistical Office (1993) *Social Trends 23*, p. 147.
4. Torkildsen, G. (1983) *Leisure and Recreation Management*, pp. 231–31.
5. Hanna, M. (1975) *Leisure*.

6. Torkildsen (1983), *op. cit.*, p. 229.
7. Hofstede, G. (1980) *Culture's Consequences.*
8. Headland (1993) *Women Keeping Fit.*
9. Gwyther, M. 'Britain bracing for the age bomb', *Independent on Sunday*, 29 March 1992, p. 16.
10. Kotler (1994), *op. cit.*, p. 182.
11. See Veal, A. (1989) 'Leisure, lifestyle and status', *Leisure Studies* **8**, pp. 141-53. Veal, following Weber, sees lifestyle as primarily concerned with expressing *status* through consumption, but other more personal developmental needs may also be expressed.
12. Plummer, J.T. (1974) 'The concept and application of lifestyle segmentation', *Journal of Marketing*, January, p. 34.
13. Mitchell, A. (1985) *The Nine American Lifestyles.*
14. Burak, P. and Bennetts, A. (1985) 'Designing products for the leisure travel market', in Mill, R.C and Morrison A.M. (Eds) *The Tourism System*, pp. 82–97.
15. Publicity literature from CACI Information Systems, Avonmore Road, London.
16. Mullin, B., Hardy, S. and Sutton, W. (1993) *Sports Marketing*, p. 127.
17. Middleton, V. (1994) *Marketing for Travel and Tourism*, p. 76.
18. Porter, M. (1980) *Competitive Strategy.*
19. *Travel News*, 28 September 1989, p. 28.

9 Competitive strategy

Defining the competition
Industry structure
Competitive behaviour
Positioning
Case Study 9.1: Competition in tour operating
Summary

Markets consist of customers and the organizations competing for their custom. In the preceding chapters we have looked at how to analyze the customers, their behaviour and the segments into which they can be divided for effective targeting by a marketing plan. The other main strand of marketing planning concerns the competition.

Having segmented the market and chosen which segments to target, the organization must design its product, and the other elements of the marketing mix, in such a way that it will appeal to its target customers more than any of the alternatives available. It therefore needs to study its competitors, who can be defined broadly as those organizations offering similar benefits to the same customers.

Competition is the greatest incentive for an organization to improve its service to its customers. If it does not research their needs, and design its marketing mix in order to satisfy them, then someone else will. In this chapter we will show how to understand the nature of the competition and how to choose the right strategy to deal with it.

Defining the competition

Competition can come in several forms. First, there are the *direct competitors* who offer *similar products* to yours. Allied Leisure's MegaBowl centres are in direct competition with the First Leisure SuperBowl chain of centres. They are also in competition with other forms of entertainment that offer *similar benefits*, those of an active and sociable way of spending an evening, such as skating, dancing, cue games or laser-gun centres. These activities could be said to be the out-of-home sector of the leisure industry. An industry, according to Kotler, is 'a group of firms that offers a product or class of products that are *close substitutes* for each other. Close substitutes are products with a high cross-elasticity of demand. If the price of one product rises and causes the demand for another to rise, the two are close substitutes'.[1]

From the customers' viewpoint, however, bowling may also be a substitute to staying in and watching television, going to the cinema or the pub, so any form of leisure activity is *indirect competition*. On the widest definition, anything that competes for the *same disposable or discretionary income* may be seen as competition – for example clothes, magazines, records, cigarettes or home improvements.

MegaBowl need to ensure that the facilities, design features and atmosphere of their centres remain up-to-date and comparable to those not only of their direct rival but also of other entertainment venues. Their prices need to stay in line with those of other evenings-out, and to remain affordable by its customers, whether teenagers, young couples or families. Bowling went out of fashion in Britain after the 1960s boom because the centres were not refurbished and appeared dated, shabby and over-priced. The same problem re-emerged in the early 1990s when, as First Leisure's Chief Executive John Conlan admitted, the company had allowed the cost of bowling to rise to levels where an outing to the cinema looked like a cheap alternative.[2]

In addition to the existing competition, there is also the threat of potential competition from *new entrants*. If in a large town the existing bowling alley is always overcrowded at weekends or is shabby and unattractive, a rival firm may see the opportunity to enter the market.

In 1985 Sealink operated the only ferry service to the Channel Islands. When its new owner, James Sherwood, changed the timetable and introduced a high-priced premium service with cabins and restaurant meals included, a new company, Channel Island Ferries, immediately entered the route with a cheaper, basic service. The cheaper alternative was the one that survived.[3]

Organizations do not only compete for end-user customers. They also compete for control of the *distribution channel*. A tour operator needs to offer its customers competitive prices. To do this, it must negotiate rates with the hotels and airlines it uses. Large companies will use the volume of business they can offer as a bargaining weapon to negotiate better rates than their smaller rivals. Similarly, they will be able to negotiate more display space for their brochures in the racks of the travel agents.

Figure 9.1 shows the forces that determine the competitive environment in an industry, as summarized by Porter.

In analyzing the competition, the marketing manager needs to understand both the structure of the industry and the behaviour of the

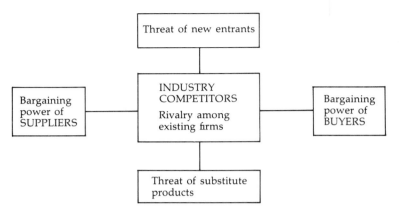

FIGURE 9.1   Forces driving industry competition.
Source: Porter (1980) *Competitive Strategy.*

competitors. The aim of the analysis should be to identify the organization's present and potential competitive advantages.

Industry structure

The structure of an industry is determined by:

- the number of competing brands;
- their respective shares of the market;
- the extent of horizontal integration, i.e. ownership of several brands by the same company;
- the extent of vertical integration, i.e. ownership of suppliers and distributors or retailers by the same company; and
- the barriers to new entrants.

These factors help to understand the relative strengths of the competing firms and the degree of control each can exert over the market. Markets can be defined in these terms as monopolies, free markets or oligopolies.

Monopoly

A monopoly is literally control by one. A firm with the monopoly of the supply of a product can in theory fix prices and determine the quality of service offered in a way that will maximize its profits. The customers have no alternative but to pay. In UK law any situation where one firm controls more than 25% of a market can be investigated by the Monopolies and Mergers Commission as a potential monopoly.

MegaBowl may have the only bowling centre in a town and so have a local *monopoly*. In theory this should mean that the company can charge high prices and offer minimal quality of service. However, although there is no direct competition, there are, as we have seen, many ways of getting similar benefits which compete for the customers' time and money. To take another example, British Rail has had a monopoly of rail services in Britain but has faced fierce competition from airlines, coaches, and private cars for the inter-city journey market. Pure monopolies, then, are difficult to establish in leisure. Because no leisure activity is essential, if a monopoly provider tries to exploit its position by raising prices, the customers can find a substitute or withdraw their custom completely.

Free market/pure competition

The opposite end of the spectrum is a free market where no one firm has the power to dictate terms and so prices are set by the balance between supply and demand, between what producers can afford to produce and what consumers can afford to pay. If prices are raised, consumption falls, leaving many consumers unable to satisfy their wants; new firms then enter the industry to take advantage of the unsatisfied demand and the competition restores prices to a level of equilibrium.[4]

This equilibrium depends on neither the producer nor the consumer having the power to dictate prices. In practice, this ideal is rarely found. Competition is restricted by various barriers to entry to a small number of firms who use their position to control prices.

Oligopoly

What is created under these conditions is an *oligopoly*, literally control by the few. Such conditions can be found in many sectors of leisure. For example, according to Haywood *et al.* five companies control 62.5% of the record market, six film distributors control 90% of film rentals, and three groups control 74% of daily press readership.[5]

Barriers to entry

In an oligopolistic market, the size and bargaining power of the large companies make it very difficult for a new competitor to enter the market. The established companies will be able to reduce prices to drive off the competitor, who will need considerable resources to survive the initial price war. The established companies will also use their influence to deny the newcomer equal access to distribution channels (see, for example, the British Airways/Virgin Atlantic dispute). In many sectors of leisure, the capital cost of the latest technological equipment also acts as an entry barrier, consolidating ownership in the hands of large companies who can afford to invest in, for example, ships, planes, or state of the art computerized white-knuckle rides.

Horizontal integration

Companies will offer a range of brands in the same market for a number of reasons. They may be targeting a range of customer segments, they may be exploiting gaps in the market or trying to prevent their rivals from doing so. They may have bought up competitors but wish to preserve the brand image and customer goodwill of the brands they have acquired.

In leisure, the volatility of individual product markets has led companies to acquire a diversity of leisure interests. Ladbrokes, for example, operate hotels and holidays, betting and gaming clubs, a DIY store chain, property and financial services. By diversifying in a range of markets, and countries, the companies are protected against sudden, unforeseen shifts in demand.[6]

Vertical integration

The main impulse towards vertical integration is to ensure a secure supply of materials and guaranteed distribution and retail outlets for the firm's products. Such integration is becoming increasingly marked in the travel business (see Case Study 9.1: Competition in tour operating).

In the home entertainment sector, the manufacturers of the equipment are acquiring the companies that produce the material that is played on it. Sony, for example, acquired Columbia Pictures and CBS Records, while Matsushita bought Universal Studios. Sony's anxiety to control the supply of material was formed by their experience with video systems. Sony's Betamax system was launched at the same time as their rivals' VHS system, and was generally considered to be technically superior in terms of picture quality. However, VHS sold better because customers could get a more attractive range of entertainment videos to play on it. Eventually Sony had to discontinue Betamax. The profits of the electronics companies depend on customers upgrading to the latest technical innovations (as with the move from vinyl records to cassettes to compact discs), so it was vital for Sony to ensure there would be a guaranteed source of attractive programmes for the next generation of innovations such as digital audio tape, CD video discs, and so on.[7]

These cases of Japanese/American integration have not proved entirely successful. Neither Sony or Matsushita made much money from the film industry, which is unpredictable and dependent on the popularity of each film. Sony had difficulties with the US managers they have appointed, and were sued by one of their leading record stars, George Michael. These cases do not invalidate the strategic logic of vertical integration, but warn companies to include human relations management and cultural differences in their assessment of the feasibility of the strategic options.

Competition and the public sector

Council-owned leisure centres could be said to have no direct competition in many cases, though private health clubs may compete for the more affluent segments of the market. Today in Britain, however, the management of the centre must compete for the contract to deliver the service specified by the local authority. The intention behind the legislation was to create competition between contractors but to date the contracts have either gone unopposed to the council's own management team or to a few private companies.[8] Nevertheless, the threat of new entrants is very real, and the current holders of the contract must demonstrate to the buyer of the service – in this case the local authority – that it can deliver the specified level of service at the contract price.

There is not yet (at the time of writing) any requirement for the extension of compulsory competitive tendering to publicly owned arts and entertainment centres. Such centres tend to have very little direct local competition. There is only a very small commercial sector with experience in operating venues, as opposed to mounting productions, and only one company, Apollo, of any size. It might be said, therefore, that the threat of new entrants is small. The main competition between venues is in negotiating with the suppliers, the theatre companies and the concert promoters, to get the most popular shows. The venues need to market themselves to the suppliers by offering the right facilities, the biggest audience potential and the best financial deal.

In both recreation and the arts, of course, the indirect competition is very strong. There is probably more potential for the centre in attracting local people away from their television sets than in competing for people from another centre's catchment area.

Competitive behaviour

The analysis of the structure of the industry will tell us what O'Shaughnessy calls the *capabilities* of our competitors. We also need to understand their behaviour, their *intentions*.[9] To some extent this could be determined by the structure of the industry and their place in it; a market leader has different concerns and strategic options from those of a challenger. However, how a firm responds to a given situation will vary according to its overall corporate objectives, e.g. the importance of the particular market in its overall strategy, and also according to the 'personality' of the firm – its attitude to risk taking for example.

In leisure, a local authority museum, a specialist collection run by a private enthusiast, and a commercial amusement park are in competition for the same 'day-out' family market. Each will have different profit and other objectives, different cost constraints, and different degrees of flexibility in its product, price and promotional tactics.

Writers on competitive strategy tend to use the language of warfare or of sport. There are therefore as many ways of dealing with competition as there are possible moves on a chess board or a rugby field. There is space here only to outline some of the basic choices.

Competition or cooperation?

The first choice is between what O'Shaughnessy calls *resolution by cooperation* and *resolution by competition*.[10] Outright battles for market share between two powerful competitors can be costly and damaging to both. News International's price cutting campaign in 1994 to increase the circulation of its *Sun* and *Times* newspapers succeeded at the cost of reducing the profits of the group dramatically. Such battles tend to be short-lived and are replaced by uneasy truces or, as O'Shaughnessy put it, peace through power. In the early 1980s a period of intense price competition between the two major cross-Channel ferry companies, Sealink and Townsend Thoresen, was followed by a period in which prices were allowed to rise in broadly similar ways, with only trivial differences within a complex price structure to give the impression of choice and to avoid accusations of a cartel. Advertising was kept at a high level but concentrated on building up brand loyalty as a barrier to new entrants.

Head-on competition or the blindside approach?

New companies entering a market will be more likely to succeed if they avoid head-on competition with established giants and instead adopt what Davidson called 'the blindside approach'.[11] This aims 'to side-step competition and carve out an unoccupied *niche* of one's own by aiming for a slightly different benefit' (a good example of the sporting metaphors mentioned earlier). Existing companies can stay ahead or move away from the competition by introducing regular enhancements or variations on the basic product.

The result is a differentiated market, where a range of products offer differing benefits, prices and quality to different segments. An example is the large number of small independent tour operators specializing in particular destinations and activities. As noted in Chapter 8, these companies survive because they have found segments large enough to sustain their businesses, but small enough not to interest the major operators.

Competitive options

As quoted earlier, Porter said that there were only three generic strategies for dealing with competition: low-cost leadership, differentiation and focus.[12]

Low-cost leadership is the simplest and most effective strategy but it requires large resources and strong management to sustain. It is generally the strategy of the leading companies in an oligopolistic market. It can also be used by a company from another sector or another country to break into an established market. Low-cost leadership may be short-lived, as it is easy for competitors to match a low price in an attempt to drive off the challenge. Low prices may make customers suspicious about the quality being offered, particularly if it is an unfamiliar brand. Such suspicions may be justified if the company has had to reduce the quality or cut out certain product features in order to reduce costs to pay for the price cut.

Differentiation takes longer to copy. An innovative technological breakthrough that meets a real customer need can take competitors a long time to imitate (it took PC computer firms a considerable time to acquire an operating system as user-friendly as that of the Apple Macintosh). A competitive advantage can be gained by a product that is newer, better, faster (or cheaper). The improvement can be in performance, durability, reliability or service features.[13]

Equally important in maintaining a difference when competitors catch up is the styling, the image and the presentation of the product. The theme pub or restaurant is an illustration of this. The food and drink may have the same basic ingredients, the building and location may be similar to many others, but the way it is presented, the decor, the music, the names given to the dishes, the style of the menus, signs and notices, and the costumes and personalities of the staff can give it a uniqueness that will stand out among its competitors.

There are many ways of differentiating a product. The secret of successful differentiation is to choose features and styling which are seen as relevant and attractive by the target market.

A *focusing* strategy concentrates on designing a product to meet the needs of one segment of the market better than the competition. The advantages and disadvantages of this were discussed in Chapter 8.

All three of these generic strategies are based on the organization creating a unique position for itself which distinguishes its offerings from those of its competitors, either by price, or product features, or the way in which it serves the needs of a particular segment. This process is known as positioning.

Positioning

In designing a new product or reviewing the marketing of an existing one, the key considerations should be the two Cs of marketing: *customers* and *competitors*. The aim is to create something that your customers will choose in preference to the alternatives offered by your competitors. They are more likely to do so if they have a clear idea of the advantages your product has over its competitors.

The process of identifying, creating and promoting these advantages is known as *product positioning*. The term was invented by Ries and Trout, who emphasized that 'it is not what you do to the product that matters as much as what you do to the mind of the prospect'.[14]

The Splashdown leisure pool at Tower Park faces competition from other swimming pools in the Bournemouth/Poole conurbation. But whereas its competitors, the pools at the Bournemouth International Centre and the Littledown Centre, attempt to cater for competitive and recreational swimmers as well as offering flume slides, Splashdown concentrates entirely on the excitement of the slides. It follows the classic advice on positioning:

- *Identify* the key benefits sought by your target customers.
- *Design* the product to deliver these benefits more effectively than your competitors.
- *Signal* these advantages to your customers.

Splashdown's brand name makes it immediately apparent what it offers. The slogan of the IceTrax and Splashdown joint promotional campaign – 'Fun with Ice and Water' – also emphasizes its positioning. In response, its competitors choose to emphasize other aspects of their centres where they have advantages.

In deciding where your product is positioned compared to your competitors in the minds of your customers, you will need to consider a number of criteria. What attributes of the product does the customer consider when choosing a brand? Which attributes does he consider your brand to be best for? (see Chapter 7, Consumer behaviour). The results of this research can be expressed as a perceptual map showing the positions of the competing brands visually.

Take, for example, cross-Channel ferries. Two of the most important attributes are speed and comfort. As Figure 9.2 shows, customers can choose between the speed of the Dover services and the comfort of the longer overnight crossings.

Figure 9.2 shows the relative positioning of typical ferry routes in the mid-1980s. Essentially, the longer the crossing, the more comfort was offered. In response to the threat of the Channel Tunnel, the companies operating the short crossings out of Dover – Sealink and P&O (S/P&O) – have been changing their positioning strategy to provide a more comfortable service which they see as a competitive advantage over the Tunnel, where passengers will remain in their cars. Another company, Hoverspeed, have chosen to position themselves directly against the Tunnel sector using high-speed

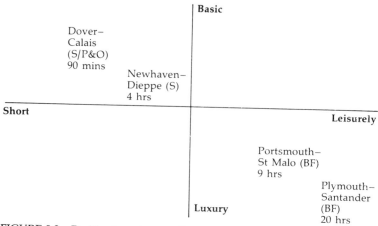

FIGURE 9.2   Positioning of cross-Channel ferries.

catamarans and hovercraft to compete with the Tunnel on speed, while retaining some of the advantages of surface travel.[15] Brittany Ferries (BF) on the longer, more comfortable routes in the western Channel see their position as more secure from competition from the Tunnel. However, they did see an opportunity for a new service on the five-hour Poole–Cherbourg route, offering a value-for-money service marketed under the brand name 'Les Routiers', associated with value-for-money transport cafes in France. This service occupied the empty basic/leisurely sector of the perceptual map (although the service has now been upgraded to match BF's other routes). The changed perceptual map is shown in Figure 9.3.

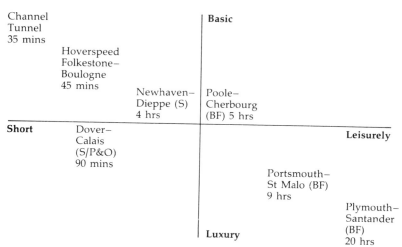

FIGURE 9.3   Positioning of cross-Channel travel in the 1990s.

A key decision in positioning a product is the *price/quality trade off*. The ferry companies have to decide how much extra customers are prepared to pay for the extra comfort they offer. With a choice of a comfortable ferry or a claustrophobic trip through the Tunnel at the same price, the customer may choose comfort. If the Tunnel is cheaper, his choice may change. The ferries therefore have to deliver an improved quality of service at a price which competes with the Tunnel. To do so they have had to renegotiate working practices to reduce labour costs and introduce larger ships to gain economies of scale. This crucial aspect of marketing is covered further in Chapter 12, Pricing, and Chapter 11, Customer service.

These simple examples are illustrations of how to identify a product-positioning opportunity. With sophisticated computer programmes a multivariate analysis could be made using a larger number of key criteria. An example of this technique applied to leisure parks in the East Midlands can be found in Hooley and Saunders' book on *Competitive Positioning*.[16]

Companies need to keep their positioning under constant review in order to respond to new threats and opportunities. Revising the positioning strategy could also be an effective way of reviving a declining product. Look for example how Lucozade sales have improved since it was repositioned from a drink for weak convalescents to a source of energy for athletes and 'ravers'.

CASE STUDY 9.1   *Competition in tour operating*

Each year up to 12 million British people take an overseas 'package' holiday, or inclusive tour to use the technical term. The number of inclusive holidays has remained static, while independent holidays abroad have increased from 8 million to 10 million between 1988 and 1992. 85–90% of the inclusive holidays are booked through travel agents. The summer market makes up some 8 million packages, of which 70% are short-haul beach holidays, mainly to the Mediterranean. Spain is the most popular destination. These beach holidays consist of a charter flight, transfers to a hotel, and optional excursions. As the hotels are very similar to each other and often take clients from several tour operators, the products offered by the main operators are homogeneous in character with little fundamental difference between brands.

Although there are an estimated 652 tour operators in the UK (CAA 1993), two-thirds of these holidays are sold by a group of five or six leading operators. The composition and balance of the group has changed over the years, but what has remained constant is that Thomson has retained market leadership with a 25–40% share (Table 9.1). Their rivals for the main summer beach market, particularly those on the edge of the leading group, have looked increasingly vulnerable; during the 1980s many well-known names were taken over or went out of business.

Table 9.1   **Market shares of the leading UK tour operators as %**

	1987	1989	1991	1993
Thomson	25	38	34	30
International Leisure Group (ILG)	13	19		
Horizon	7			
Redwing	4	7		
Owners Abroad	3	7.5	17	13
Airtours	3	6	13	18

Source: Industry estimates.

Those companies which have focused on particular market niches have generally been more resilient. The niches have included specific destinations, activities or age segments. Self-drive, self-catering holidays to France, skiing, and long-haul destinations have been profitable specialisms. The major operators have attempted to diversify into these sectors, impressed by the higher profit margins achieved by long-haul specialists such as Kuoni.

Vertical integration between charter airlines, tour operators and travel agencies (Table 9.2) has become increasingly important, but in Britain tour operators' experiences with hotel ownership has not encouraged them to develop further in this direction. Horizontal integration has also occurred as the major companies acquired small rivals or developed new brands targeted at particular market segments.

Table 9.2   **Vertical integration in the UK travel business (figures as at end 1992)**

Tour operator	Market share (%)	Charter airline	Market share (%)	Travel agency	Branches
Thomson	30	Britannia	28	Lunn Poly	528
Owners	17	Air 2000	12.5	Thomas Cook	389
Airtours	14	Airtours International	4.5	Pickfords	323
Cosmos	6	Monarch	12.5	Hogg Robinson	215
				(A.T. Mays)	(317)

Sources: Tourism Society meetings; Holloway (1990). *The Business of Tourism.*

The market leader

Thomson Holidays was formed in 1965 from a number of companies bought by Lord Thomson of Fleet, the newspaper proprietor. It formed part of his family's multinational holdings in oil, timber and publishing. The support of the Canadian-based parent company has given Thomson the advantage of

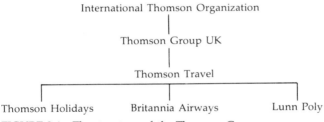

FIGURE 9.4   The structure of the Thomson Group.

strength and stability in competition with rivals that typically developed as entrepreneurial businesses focused on travel. From the start Thomson has owned Britannia Airways, which provides the majority of its charter flights. Lunn Poly, its travel agency subsidiary, has grown by acquisition and aggressive pricing to be the UK's largest travel agency chain. The structure of the organization is shown in Figure 9.4.

Thomson's strategy as market leader has been described by one of its executives as a virtuous circle (Figure 9.5). Thomson uses its high volume of business to negotiate low rates with its suppliers, the airlines, hotels, etc., which in turn allows it to offer low prices to its customers. This enables it to retain its cost leadership. As its prices are kept low by bargaining power it can also insist on a high standard of quality which is carefully monitored through Customer Satisfaction Questionnaires.

Thomson pioneered computerized reservations with direct access by travel agents. This not only ensures a high standard of service to agents and their customers, but also achieved economies of scale by reducing staff costs.

Thomson currently offers a range of 24 different brochures, thus appealing to a wide range of market segments, such as Summer Sun, Ski, Simply Greece, Lakes and Mountains, City Breaks, Young at Heart (i.e. over 60), Far & Away, A la Carte, etc. This wide range of products cushions it

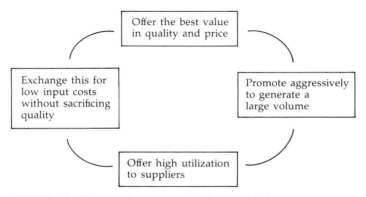

FIGURE 9.5   Thomson's strategy: the virtuous circle.

against fluctuations in demand for particular products and avoids allowing a rival to develop unchallenged in any significant sector.

The promotional strategy is aimed at creating a distinctive brand image for the whole company. Each brochure carries the Thomson brand and is designed to reflect on every page the primary colours of the Thomson logo: blue, red, yellow and white. The advertising messages convey quality and reassurance, celebrating the thousands of customers each year who 'Do It Again', or advising would-be adventurous travellers, 'If Thomson Do It, Do It. If Thomson Don't Do It, Don't Do It'.

Yet when its virtuous circle is threatened by a challenger taking away market share, Thomson has always reacted fiercely by reducing prices to drive off competition. In 1985, the challenge came from Intasun (part of Harry Goodman's International Leisure Group, ILG), which gained market share in a stagnant market. Thomson responded by reissuing brochures repeatedly to undercut its rivals. The resulting price war between 1986 and 1988 stimulated record demand but drove down industry profit margins (Table 9.3). The number three company, Horizon, ran into financial problems and was taken over by Thomson. By 1989, Thomson had increased its market share to 38%, but at the expense of a £15.9 million loss and 300 redundancies. The image of the industry was tarnished by press reports of overbooking, substandard accommodation, poor hygiene and trouble at resorts caused by 'lager louts' on cheap packages.

Table 9.3 Profitability of the 30 leading UK tour operators (CAA)

Year	Turnover (£m)	Profit (£m)	Profit as % turnover
1981	1,019.7	52.2	5.1
1985	1,841	60.7	3.3
1987	2,132	35.6	0.9
1989	3,048	−0.1	−0.003
1991	2,757.9	104.8	3.8

Source: Civil Aviation Authority.

In 1990 a truce emerged between Thomson and ILG. Thomson prepared a new 'flagship' product by financing the refurbishment of selected hotels in an attempt to reassert its quality image. The following year, ILG collapsed, primarily because of its problems in establishing Air Europe as a scheduled airline, but with the low profits of its tour operating base a contributory factor. Four new companies were formed by ILG managers, but only two have survived. The bulk of the business went to Thomson and its two main remaining rivals, Owners Abroad and Airtours.

Followers and challengers

Owners Abroad started as a charter seat broker for owners of villas in Spain, hence the name. It acquired a number of failing tour operations from British Airways in the 1980s in order to sell more seats for its airline Air 2000. It retained the existing brand names such as Falcon, Sunmed and Enterprise. It emerged from the fall of ILG as the number two operator with 17% of the market but was quick to deny any aspirations to challenge Thomson. 'We don't care what number we are as long as we are strong. We are building to our strengths. We will do more flights, self-catering, stick to what we know', tour operations director Dermot Blastland told the trade press in 1990.

Airtours began as a regional operator offering flights out of Manchester with keenly priced, no-frills products. In 1991 it expanded to a nationwide operator taking advantage of the gap left by Intasun and saw its share rise from 6 to 12% of the market. In 1992 and 1993 it acquired the regional operator and airline Aspro. It also bought into the travel agency side of the business by buying Pickfords and Hogg Robinson. This created the second largest chain of agencies – 548 branches compared to Lunn Poly's 630 and Thomas Cook's 389. Where Thomson had always run Lunn Poly as a separate business allowing space to other tour operators brochures, Airtours used the new 'Going Places' chain to give priority display space to its own products. Thomson therefore followed suit and both agencies competed for custom with low-deposit, money-off offers. By 1993 Airtours had risen to number two with 18% of the market at the expense of Owners Abroad (13%). In the three years from 1990 to 1993 its sales increased from £183m to £615m. Airtours then launched a take over bid for its rival in 1993.

To counter the threat, Owners had already formed an alliance with Thomas Cook to create its own preferred agency outlet. This meant that the three groupings were responsible for 60% of all tour operating and 40% of all travel agency business in 1993.

Thomas Cook had been acquired in 1992 by the German airline and tour operator LTU, which is controlled by the WestdeutscheLandBank. Cooks forestalled the Airtours bid by taking a 21.4% shareholding in Owners, thus linking it to one of the largest travel groupings in Europe. While Thomas Cook has expanded its branches in Germany as the travel agency arm of LTU, the German influence in the UK market has so far been indirect. In 1994 Owners rebranded all its products as 'First Choice'.

Ten years after embarking on a price war to defend its market leadership against Intasun, Thomson again faces a growing and aggressive challenger in Airtours. This time the challenger also has a powerful distribution network of its own, and the third major rival has a European dimension.[17]

Sources: This case study was compiled from a large number of sources, including trade press reports and talks by industry managers to the Tourism Society, and to Bournemouth University. All figures are industry estimates and are given for illustrative purposes only.

QUESTIONS

1 Is price leadership the only effective competitive strategy in this market?

2 What are the barriers to entry facing a new tour operator, and how could they be overcome?

3 If Airtours had succeeded in acquiring Owners Abroad, would this have created an unacceptable monopoly (or duopoly) in the package holiday market?

4 What indirect competition do the major UK tour operators face?

Summary

All organizations face some form of competition, direct or indirect. As leisure activities are not essential, the customer always has a choice of how he spends his time and money. The organization must therefore make him an offer that stands out from the alternatives available. It does that by creating a unique 'position' for the product which is different and better in ways that are important to the customer.

The process of positioning involves analyzing the needs of the customers using the methods described in Chapters 7 and 8 on Consumer Behaviour and Segmentation, and analyzing the nature of the competition in the ways described in this chapter. The choice of strategy will depend on two key sets of variables: the attractiveness of the market and the organization's competitive strengths.[18] Dahringer and Muelbacher suggest that the SWOT analysis should be used to compare the firm's distinctive competences with the critical factors for success in the industry or sector. From this it can determine its competitive advantages and make them the basis of its competitive strategy.[19]

Depending on the results of this analysis, the organization may choose a strategy of cooperation, cost leadership, of product differentiation or of focus on particular niches or segments.

To implement the strategy, a plan must be agreed involving all the elements of the marketing mix – product, price, promotion, distribution, and people. This will be the subject of Part 3 of this book.

Notes

1. Kotler, P. (1994) *Marketing Management*, p. 225.
2. John Conlan, in *The Guardian*, 19 January 1995.
3. Morgan, M. (1990) 'Moving ferries up market': *International Journal of Physical Distribution Management*, **20**(5).
4. See Gratton, C. and Taylor, P. (1988) *Economics of Leisure Services Management*, pp. 36–39.
5. Haywood, L.J., Kew, F.C. and Bramham, P. (1989) *Understanding Leisure*, p. 230.
6. *Ibid*, p. 228.
7. Terpstra, V. and Sarathy, R. (1994) *International Marketing*, p. 637.
8. *Leisure Management*, **13**(4), April 1993. See also Audit Commission (1993) *Realising the Benefits of Competition*.
9. O'Shaughnessy, J. (1992) *Competitive Marketing*, p. 129.
10. *Ibid*, p. 133.
11. Davidson, L. (1979) *Offensive Marketing*, p. 123.
12. Porter, M. (1980) *Competitive Strategy*, p. 34.
13. See Kotler (1994) *op. cit.*, pp. 293–306.
14. Ries, A. and Trout, J. (1982), *Positioning*.
15. Peisley, T. (1994) 'Ferries, short sea cruises and the Channel tunnel' *Travel and Tourism Analyst*, No. 4, pp. 5–23.
16. Hooley, G. and Saunders, J. (1993) *Competitive Positioning*, pp. 172–78.
17. Further reading:
    Bottomley, R.M. (1992) *The Travel Agent*.
    Holloway, C. (1994) *The Business of Tourism*.
    Hughes, E. (1994) *Travel Agents and Overseas Tour Operators*.
    Middleton, V. (with R. Astles) (1994) 'Marketing IT products: Thomson Sun hotels', *Marketing in Travel and Tourism*.
    'UK outbound', *EIU Travel and Tourism Analyst*, No. 3, 1993.
    'Who owns whom in the European travel trade?', *EIU Travel and Tourism Analyst*, No. 3, 1994.
18. See Hooley and Saunders (1993) *op. cit.*, p. 189 ff.
19. Dahringer, L.D. and Muelbacher, H. (1991) *International Marketing*, p. 279.

PART 3

The Leisure Marketing Mix

10 The leisure product

In this chapter we begin to look at the implementation of the marketing strategy through the various elements of the marketing mix. The key element is the product itself. Unless the product is right, the customer will not be satisfied, however attractive the price and however persuasive the promotion. The product is the means of delivering the desired benefit to the customer, or as Macdonald put it, the means of solving the customer's problem.[1]

This solution may involve a number of tangible and intangible elements, possibly services, facilities or equipment to be hired, rather than a manufactured product to be bought and used. Case Study 10.3, describing the leisure complex (significant word) at Tower Park, Poole, is used to illustrate some of the range of leisure products on offer in the 1990s, and is referred to throughout this chapter.

What is a product?

According to Kotler, a product is 'anything that might satisfy a need'.[2] This can include tangible goods and intangible services. Tennis rackets and tennis coaching, for example, are both products that need to be planned, produced

135

and promoted with a target market in mind. Marketing theories of product management therefore apply to a greater or lesser extent to both products and services, and the word 'product' is taken to refer to both unless specifically stated.

However, to the consumer, in this case the sportsman or woman, both the equipment and the coaching are only means to an end. What he or she is really buying is an experience, in this case a good game of tennis.

A product is sometimes said to have three elements:

- the *core benefit* that the customer is seeking;
- the *tangible elements* that deliver the benefit; and
- the *augmented product*, the additional features and services that distinguish the company's offer from others.[3]

The augmented product is the term used by Middleton to refer to the features, style and services which make the difference between the contractual product and the total experience of the customer in relation to the organization.[4]

If we visit Icetrax at Tower Park, Poole (see Case Study 10.3) for ice skating, the core benefit might be the enjoyment of physical exercise in the company of friends. The tangible elements include the ice rink, the skates for hire, and the ticket office. The augmented product could be the music and other effects which give Icetrax its distinctive style, plus the accessibility, the car parking, and the availability of other activities and catering facilities on the same site. When we decide where to go for a day or an evening out, it is the overall experience we consider.

This example shows that the total experience contains both tangible and intangible elements, and is more complex than the simple core/tangible/augmented distinction allows. Palmer demonstrates that a visit to the theatre involves a 'molecular' structure comprising the tangible elements – the box office system, the theatre building, the food and drink at the bar and the stage props and scenery, together with the service elements – the performance and the atmosphere created by the interaction between the actors and the audience.[5]

The resulting experience is *inseparable* from the moment of consumption; in other words, we cannot handle or test it before we pay for it. Indeed, we help to create the experience ourselves by taking part in the audience reaction. Nor can it be stored until a customer is found for it. A seat at tonight's show is highly *perishable*, i.e. an opportunity for revenue will be gone forever if it is not sold by tonight.

The experience of the customer is *subjective*, and can be strongly influenced by her *interaction with people*, both staff and other customers. Planning the level and the style of service to offer is therefore an essential part of the design of a leisure product.

Palmer analyzes the 'service product' into a core benefit and a number of secondary services:

- *Features*: added elements that differentiate the offering from its competitors.
- *Packaging*: bringing together a number of elements to create a comprehensive offer (as in a package holiday).
- *Styling*: a distinctive impression resulting from tangibles such as decor, and intangibles such as the way in which staff interact with customers.
- *Branding*: identifying the corporate image of the organization (see below).
- *Tangible evidence*: using the design of uniforms, signs, glasses or cups, programmes/brochures/menus, etc., to convey the brand image.
- *Process*: the service process and its effects on the customer, e.g. queuing, response times, etc.
- *Accessibility* and delivery.[6]

Out of these elements the manager must create a distinctive, desirable image and deliver a satisfying experience.

Another feature of leisure experiences is that they often *involve more than one organization* in creating them. Case Study 10.3 illustrates this well. Each company on the site is an independent business which has to run at a profit to survive. Each offers its own products to the public. The appeal of Tower Park, however, is created by the range of experiences on offer. The question of whether to spend their promotional budgets individually or on a corporate campaign for the whole park continues to be debated by the managements concerned.

Tower Park is just one attraction in the Borough of Poole, and while Poole jealously guards its identity as a distinct resort, in fact to the tourist it forms part of a single holiday destination with Bournemouth, the New Forest and the Dorset coast and countryside. The managements at Tower Park have a range of collaborative marketing options open, through the borough tourist office, the Southern regional tourist board, the English Tourist Board or, for overseas visitors, the British Tourist Authority. Which option they choose depends on their understanding of how their target customers reach a decision to visit, in other words, what they consider to be the product.

Leisure managers will inevitably have to focus mainly on the elements of the overall product experience over which they have direct control. They should not forget that their customers are often looking through different viewfinders (Figure 10.1).

FIGURE 10.1   The customer viewfinder. Which 'product' does the consumer evaluate? Different customers have different *product foci*, and advertising vehicles will be chosen accordingly:

- Splashdown: leaflets;
- Tower Park: corporate campaigns;
- Poole: visitor guides;
- southern England: the English Tourist Board's 'Southern England Holidays', and tour operator programmes;
- Great Britain: the British Tourist Authority/English Tourist Board publications.

Branding

One of the ways in which organizations signal their positioning and competitive advantage is by creating a distinctive brand image. Branding identifies the product and distinguishes it from those of the competitors by the use of brand names, logos, pack design, signing, merchandising and of course advertising.

A brand name gives the product an easily recognizable *identity*. It promises *reliability*. People prefer to buy from someone they recognize than from a stranger. The brand image says, 'We are a well-known firm with a professional approach to our business and a reputation to maintain. Trust us'.

A brand name also promises *consistency*. When you open a packet of Kelloggs Cornflakes or Heinz Baked Beans, you feel you know what you are getting. That is why people prefer to buy branded goods rather than loose products in brown bags. In the same way, the shop-front designs of Thomas Cook or Going Places travel agencies promise a consistent level of service and range of products. It saves the customer having to spend time checking the reputation and specializations of the agent before entering.

A brand image also conveys a *personality* with which the customer can develop a relationship. This may in some cases be associated with the owner or founder of the company – as with Richard Branson's Virgin group – or an invented character like Disney's Mickey Mouse. But brands do not have to be personified to convey a particular character. The Sega Megadrive CD computer games system markets itself to young people as a wild irreverent personality, 'the new rock 'n' roll', while the Philips' alternative aims its message at parents as an educational tool.[7] The personality enables the brand to be recognized at the point of sale and helps the customer form a habit of regular purchase.

In his book *Developing New Brands*, Stephen King says that a successful brand personality should be

- salient (easily recognized 'on the shelf'),
- relevant to people's needs and desires,
- coherent: content, price, packaging and image should all work together to produce the overall effect,
- a unique blend of appeals: to the reason, to the senses, and to the emotions.[8]

Branding is particularly important in leisure services. Where the core benefit is an experience, the promise of reliability and consistency, and the personality with which the customer identifies, have to be conveyed by the tangible elements, such as, the staff uniforms, the signposting and decor, the equipment and the stationery. Imprinting these with the brand logo and slogan can 'tangibilize the intangible'.

The process of turning a commodity into a brand can be clearly seen in Case Study 10.1: British Airways Leisure Travel class.[9]

CASE STUDY 10.1 *British Airways: Branding the leisure traveller*

Airline marketing has tended to concentrate on business travellers, wooing them with a range of extra services and benefits both in the aircraft and in the terminal. Leisure travellers, not on expense accounts, are usually labelled as 'economy class' and are left feeling very much inferior in the way they are treated.

Yet a British Airways study showed that economy class accounted for 75% of passengers carried (14 million per year) and 55% of revenue. Moreover, their numbers continued to grow despite the recession and political uncertainties which affected business class travel in the late 1980s.

Seeing an opportunity to increase their share of this market in 1990 BA launched two new brands.

Instead of the dismissive 'economy class' label, leisure passengers now bought 'World Traveller' or on European routes 'EuroTraveller' tickets. As BA put it, 'When people have paid £500 of their own money for a ticket, they want to feel they matter'. To show them they mattered, the World Traveller logo was shown on the ticket wallet, the check-in desk, the headrest of their seat and the travel rug and pillow.

The branding was not simply a question of sticking a new logo on the old product. Cabin crew were retrained to become more visible in the main cabin, spending more time with individual passengers. According to the promotional leaflet, improvements to the quality of service included:

- newly re-padded, firmer seats to make the flight more comfortable;
- World Traveller 'amenity packs', including socks, toothbrush and eye shades;
- higher quality electromagnetic headsets for the inflight entertainment;
- box games for children;
- new trays, place settings and stylish glasses for dining;
- complimentary hot towel, coffee and mints, plus between-meal snacks on longer flights;
- most important, the attentive service of the World Traveller cabin crew to make the flight as enjoyable as possible;
- finally, even a boiled sweet on descent!

The cost of the rebranding was estimated at £50 million, with a target of matching the 10% increase in business travel which resulted from BA's similar branding exercise 'Club World'.

The next chapter will look at how the organization can achieve a high quality of service by ensuring that they actually meet the expectations the branding and promotion have created. The role of the staff in this is vital.

Public sector organizations responsible for leisure and tourism marketing also have to create brands for their services or their geographical areas that are salient, coherent and relevant to the needs of their markets. This is more difficult because the organization has little or no control over the elements that make up a product called, for example, Dorset. It is relatively easy to create a brand by calling it 'Thomas Hardy Country'. It is extremely hard to deliver reliability or consistency of service to the visitors. Many local authorities now run tourism awareness and customer service courses for those in businesses which bring them into daily contact with visitors, but these cannot be made compulsory.

The product life cycle

Leisure managers also need to realize that all products have a limited life and that different marketing tactics are needed at different stages in their life. This is expressed by the concept of the product life cycle (Figure 10.2).

A new product will at first grow only slowly as customers gradually become aware of it, try it out and evaluate it. Then, if it is a good product meeting a need in an original way, it will go through a period of rapid growth. This success will however inspire competitors and imitators. Eventually, most potential users will have tried it and adopted it or a competitor's brand. At this stage, the sales level off to a relatively constant plateau. Finally, a new alternative is introduced, the existing product becomes out of fashion and sales decline.

This cycle can be completed quickly, as in the fads for yo-yos, frisbees and skateboards, or over many years. The British seaside holiday can be traced back to the example set by George III in the 1790s, and grew to be a mass market product with the advent first of rail transport and then of paid holidays. It probably reached its peak in the 1950s before declining in the face of competition from charter flights and cheap package holidays to the Mediterranean. According to Cooper, a graph of visitor arrivals in the Isle of Man between 1850 and 1990 shows clear stages of introduction, growth, maturity, stagnation and decline.[10] He uses Butler's classification of these stages in terms of tourism development: exploration, involvement in tourism, development, consolidation, stagnation and decline.[11]

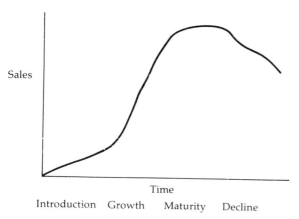

FIGURE 10.2   The product life cycle.

It is also important to distinguish between the life cycles of the *demand*, the *technology*, the *product form*, and the *brand*. Take for example the bicycle life cycle. The demand for personal mobility has grown with the growth of personal leisure time since the Industrial Revolution. Bicycle technology was first developed by Macmillan in 1839 and reached its modern form, with a metal frame, wire wheels and pneumatic tyres, by the end of the nineteenth century. Today the bicycle as a product class is at a mature stage, its growth being checked by the rise of the motor vehicle, but it is still finding viable niches for sport and recreation, and as local, young people's, or environmentally friendly transport. Within the product class, several forms of bicycle have risen and declined, for example the small-wheeled folding cycle, the racing bike, the BMX, and most recently the mountain bike. Individual brands like Muddy Fox will also have their own life cycle.

The lessons of the product life cycle for the leisure marketer

As we have seen, the growth, maturity, and decline of products takes place over widely varying timescales, so it is unwise to use the concept of the product life cycle to make detailed forecasts for a brand. There is no way of telling from a sales graph when introduction will become growth, when growth will flatten out into maturity, or when maturity will begin to decline.

Nevertheless, awareness of the characteristic shape of the product life cycle will protect managers against the myopia which assumes that their wonderful product will be successful for all time. They will begin to develop new products to add to their product range and in time will replace the current best-selling brand. And because they know that new products may have a slow introduction stage and take time to grow into their full sales potential, they will introduce new products while the current ones are still at the top of the curve rather than wait until they show signs of decline. Otherwise there may be a period where the old product's sales have slumped but the new product has not yet taken off. These two strategies are illustrated in Figure 10.3.

All managers need to monitor market trends for signs that their competitors are introducing new improved features or that their customers are becoming bored with the existing features. They should regard their businesses as a collection of assets – physical, financial, and human – to be used in whatever way best satisfies their customers profitably. At leisure complexes like Tower Park, the buildings are fundamentally just shells, spaces for leisure activities to take place. If the existing activities no longer attract people, they could be replaced with, for example, virtual reality games.

However, it would be equally wrong to assume that declining sales will inevitably continue. Ten-pin bowling was first introduced into Britain in 1960. By 1964, there were 150 centres. This growth in interest was short-lived

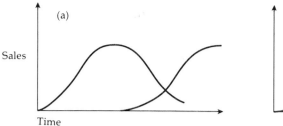
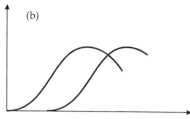

FIGURE 10.3   Two strategies for introducing new products. (a) New product introduced after current product begins to decline. (b) New product introduced while current product still at its peak of sales.

and by the end of 1967 only 50 centres were left. Only one new centre opened in the next 20 years. Then in 1988 a new cycle of growth, a new wave of popularity began. This can be attributed to several factors:

- *a new market*: a new generation of bowlers;
- *an improved image*: better facilities, more to do while waiting to bowl;
- *technological improvements*: new electronic scoreboards;
- *changing fashions*: a new vogue for American style in leisure.

With benefit of hindsight it can be argued that the 1960s bowling venues made their decline inevitable by not reinvesting in improved facilities once the initial boom began to fade. However, in the short term a better return was available by selling the city centre sites for office development.[12]

Product market strategies

Often, in public sector leisure and tourism marketing, closure is not an option for a declining product. You cannot close a tourist resort, and it could be politically unacceptable to close a leisure centre. Other *product market strategies* have to be used to revive the declining product. The choices are well-summarized in Ansoff's grid,[13] shown in Figure 10.4.

Taking a seaside resort as an example, the local tourism office may try *market penetration* tactics to improve its share of the current market by developing new creative advertising ideas or by devising low-cost packages with local hoteliers. The English Tourist Board have been running a campaign to promote the concept of 'The Great British Seaside' to win back UK holiday makers from taking their holidays abroad.

At the same time, the tourism office may be looking for new *market development*, by trying to attract overseas visitors or by targeting new market segments by age, activity or benefit (see Chapter 8).

	Current products	New products
Current markets	Market penetration	Product development
New markets	Market development	Diversification

FIGURE 10.4   Ansoff's product/market expansion grid (the lines on the grid are not as rigid in practice as the diagram suggests).

Often this may involve some kind of *product development*, such as designing new activity holiday packages or investing in new facilities. For example, in the 1980s Bournemouth Borough Council spent £9 million on building the Bournemouth International Centre to encourage business and conference tourism to compensate for the decline in the family holiday market.

Examples of *diversification* – finding new uses for your assets and resources – could be resorts where holiday accommodation has been converted to residential apartments for retired people, or for long-distance commuters, or where financial services are replacing tourism as the main industry.

CASE STUDY 10.2   *Beechdale Baths, Nottingham: Product development, diversification and branding*

Beechdale Baths in Nottingham, opened in 1970, provided a 33 metre main pool, teaching pool and diving tank. There was a cafeteria, and a gymnasium with swimming and diving teaching aids. In 1984 two squash courts were added. The following year the pool was divided into a 25 metre laned pool and a leisure pool area into which a 30 metre flume was added in 1989. Despite these modifications, Nottingham City Council were faced with a decline in casual swimming, poor financial results from the cafeteria, and a totally unused gymnasium area.

They identified a need for an indoor soft play facility for children under 10. This was designed as Hood's Hideaway, using the theme of Nottingham's local folk hero Robin Hood. The play area included the Sheriff's Castle, Robin's camp fire, an enchanted forest and a crystal cave. A separated theme eating area was designed, primarily for children's parties. In a simulated woodland setting a computerized sound system reproduced the sounds of arrows flying, a campfire crackling and a dragon's roar. The whole centre was refurbished, with a new reception area, improved cafeteria, new glazing and a closed-circuit security system.

To emphasize the change in image, the centre was renamed the Beechdale Swimming Centre and reopened by the Sheriff of Nottingham in

October 1993. In its first year it exceeded its sales targets and attracted 20 birthday parties a week.

Source: 'Merry times in Nottingham', *Recreation*, Oct./Nov. 1994.

Product range management

Most organizations do not rely on a single product for success, because, as we have seen, all products have a finite life and a prudent manager will be developing new ones before the old ones become obsolete or unfashionable. To make best use of their assets, a leisure organization will also need to appeal to a mix of different market segments, each of which requires a different 'bundle of benefits' (see for example the Venue nightclub in Case Study 10.3: Tower Park). Most leisure marketers will therefore be managing a range or portfolio of products.

One of the best known tools for managing a product range is the product portfolio matrix, devised by the Boston Consulting Group. This requires managers to analyze each product according to its market share and its growth,[14] as shown in the matrix in Figure 10.5.

Let us apply this matrix to the product range or programme of a theatre or arts centre. There will be a variety of activities and events, targeted at a mix of market segments at different times of the year. The management's aim will be to choose a programme that will best meet their commercial, artistic and community objectives taking the year as a whole.

Some elements of the programme will be tried and tested revenue earners and crowd pullers – for example, the Christmas pantomime season or the star-studded summer show. These are the *cash cows* which can be milked to produce the cash flow and profits which can be used to develop other parts of the programme.

Some shows will be more innovative and experimental, taking risks with new artists, writers or genres. They may be hugely successful or total flops, but a far-sighted management will take the risk in the hope of finding the new Andrew Lloyd Webber or Alan Ayckbourn. These shows are *problem*

| | | Market share | |
		High	Low
Growth	High	Stars	Problem children
	Low	Cash cows	Dogs

FIGURE 10.5   The Boston Consulting Group's product portfolio matrix.

children – no one knows quite how they will grow up! (A current criticism of British theatre managements is that they are unwilling to take the risk of putting on work by new writers and so are jeopardizing the long-term future of the industry.)

Some of the new shows will become *stars* – hit musicals, for example, which sell out months ahead. Others may fail. Close monitoring is needed and firm action taken to minimize losses.

The final section of the Boston matrix is for the shows that no longer have the same appeal they used to have. These are called *dogs* because they eat a lot, contribute very little and are best put out of their misery.

The theatre management may use such a portfolio matrix analysis to allocate its production and promotional budgets. It might be advisable to divert funds from well established shows (cash cows) to promote the stars with the best growth potential and to develop new shows (problem children) for the future.

This analysis has been linked by Barksdale and Harris with the

Level of utilization of facilities

		High	Low
Level of provision of facilities	High	Golf Cricket/football/rugby Beaches/seafront Parks and gardens Swimming pools Children's playgrounds (major sites)	Tennis courts Pavilions Children's playgrounds (minor sites)
	Low	Sports halls Countryside access	Croquet

FIGURE 10.6   Leisure provision analysis for Bournemouth Borough Council.

Level of utilization of facilities

		High	Low
Level of provision of facilities	High	Improve facilities Reinvest and develop Maximize usage	Find new markets Rationalize Find new uses
	Low	Improve existing facilities Build new facilities Identify and market under-used provision	Market more vigorously Sell

FIGURE 10.7   Strategic options for leisure provision for Bournemouth Borough Council.

product life cycle.[15] Problem children are at the introduction or early growth stage, stars are products that are definitely growing fast, cash cows have reached maturity, and dogs are products in decline.

An interesting application of portfolio analysis in the public sector is given in Figure 10.6. From this analysis, Bournemouth Borough Council leisure officers were able to review a number of options for the facilities in each category, as shown in Figure 10.7.

New product development

This chapter has suggested that new product development is the key to the long-term success of an organization. If so, where do the ideas come from? According to Jim Hennequin, who invented the system which animates the figures at Spitting Image's attractions and drives the Cinemotion's simulator seats, all he really does is find solutions to other people's problems: 'Invention only seems to work one way for all inventors. You're presented with a problem and you come up with a solution'.[16]

Very few products are invented in a sudden flash of inspiration. They are more likely to be a creative response to external and internal pressures, as shown in Figure 10.8.

Customer needs and expectations change with time and fashion, or because your competitors have brought out something new. Pressures to reduce labour costs or to increase throughput lead to new technological developments, often copied from abroad or modified from other sectors or

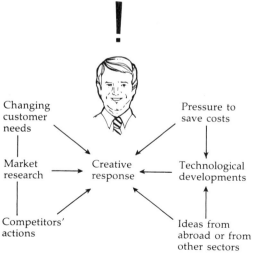

FIGURE 10.8   Sources of new product ideas.

industries. The successful organizations are usually those that anticipate and create change rather than those who follow it.

Ken Heathcote of the Fitness Association was a pioneer when he first opened a gym in a disused warehouse in Bolton in 1968. In those days there were no other fitness clubs in Bolton; now there are 20 in walking distance of his. At first, things were very quiet. The club gained momentum when he decided to provide a secondary facility – a sauna: 'Saunas were very new on the market. We built one ourselves with an imported boiler from Finland and it was an immediate success'. His career has been characterized by looking for new trends, investing in a facility and providing users with variety: 'You can't afford not to invest in new ideas. You have to have twenty or thirty balls in the air at one time'. He is convinced that virtual reality has a future in gyms. 'In years to come people will be able to get on a treadmill, put on their headsets and take part in an Indiana Jones adventure.'[17]

If you examine the leisure products on offer at Tower Park complex, most are based on simple pleasures that young people have always enjoyed – jumping into water, skating on ice, playing at soldiers, throwing things at targets. All have used modern technology to intensify the experience and to eliminate unsatisfactory elements.

Ten-pin bowling is based on the ancient game of skittles. The larger ball makes the crash of the pins more satisfying and increases the chances of success. The electronic scoreboard does the tedious maths for you and flashes your success to the whole hall. There is none of the drudgery of re-erecting the skittles and fetching your ball back. The design and branding of the centre links you to the glamour of American youth culture. The total, augmented, product is very different from the game still played in the back rooms of English pubs. The core benefit has been delivered in a new, more fashionable and exciting way.

Screening

Not all new product ideas succeed. It is important to minimize the risk of costly failure by systematic screening and testing. Tower Park Leisure Ltd (Case Study 10.3) began with a very different concept from the one they eventually developed after market research. The key questions to ask when screening product ideas are:

- Is there a market for it?
- Is it right for us?
- Can we make it profitable?

Is there a market for it?
Does the idea meet a need that is not adequately met by existing products? How would it compare with competitive offers (see 'positioning' in Chapter 9)? Who would use it, how often, on what occasions?

Is it right for us?

Is the product idea compatible with our company image, our strategic objectives? Does it complement our existing product range? Can we market it through our existing distribution channels and promotional literature? If not, is there another party who would be interested in developing it with us, or in operating it as a tenant or licensee?

Can we make it profitable?

Do we have the resources and expertise to produce the new product? What investment is needed? How large a market is there for it? What market price could we charge? What return on investment can we expect? What external factors could affect demand?

After the initial screening process, a detailed feasibility study would be commissioned, which might include testing the concept on a panel of potential customers.

The process of design and development would vary greatly depending on the nature of the product and the extent of the investment involved. It is important that the original marketing specification is kept to. There are always cost pressures and the danger that design and production people will substitute their own priorities for those of the customer. There are many examples of leisure facilities which are an unsatisfactory compromise between the needs of the users and what the budget allowed to be built.

Where possible, the new product should be test marketed on a small scale before full production starts. A tour to a new destination, for example, could be offered as an extra item in an established brochure, or a few departure dates offered through the local press in selected areas. If the tour proves popular and satisfactory, a full programme with its own brochure can then be developed.

CASE STUDY 10.3   *Tower Park, Poole*

What do you do with 74 acres of worked-out sand quarries on the edge of a windswept heath? The answer, for a group of Poole businessmen, was to create an innovative new leisure complex.

Their original idea was for a multipurpose regional stadium modelled on the Wembley Arena, to take advantage of the interest at the time in ice-related events, following the success of Torvill and Dean, and Robin Cousins. However, extensive research into the leisure market and a survey of the wants and expectations of the people of Bournemouth and Poole led to a very different concept.

Tower Park takes its name from a local landmark, a watertower which overlooks the site. The Tower Park leisure complex provides a variety of 'state-of-the-art' leisure and entertainment facilities on a single site. Access is probably the single most important selling point. A population of 420,000 in the Bournemouth/Poole/Christchurch conurbation can reach the site easily off the main Dorset Way dual carriageway linking Bournemouth and Poole. Free parking is provided for 650 cars.

Tower Park is a private-sector enterprise but it provides recreational benefits to local residents and enhances the attraction of the area to tourists. This helped to persuade Poole and Dorset councils to amend the structure and local plans for the area to allow the developers, Tower Park Leisure (Poole) Ltd (TPLP), to sell part of the site for a Tesco Superstore. This helped to fund the infrastructure and buildings for the leisure park.

A design competition was won by Faulkner Brown, well known for other innovative leisure buildings such as the Doncaster Dome. All the attractions are housed in a single sweep of buildings with an undercover walkway running along the front. The buildings cost around £15 million, financed by a loan from the European arm of an American bank.

Tower Park is unique in that while TPLP designed and built the complex, each attraction is operated as a separate commercial enterprise by companies who lease the buildings from TPLP. The 25-year leases were initially at minimum rents plus turnover-related increases phased in over the first five years, the companies therefore sharing the risk and potentially the profits.

The anchor tenants – the first to agree a major lease and give the project credibility – were United Cinemas International (UCI) whose multiplex cinemas have been a major factor in the revival of cinema-going. UCI offer choice – ten screens each with Dolby stereo sound and very comfortable seating. The benefits of the choice of films is partly the appeal to a range of audience segments, but also the knowledge that a trip to the cinema will not result in disappointment. If one film is full, there will be another popular film available in the same building. Tower Park offers the additional benefit of free parking right next to the cinema, unlike many traditional town centre cinemas. There are regular midnight showings for customers who have spent the evening elsewhere in the park.

Following UCI, the other main sites were soon taken. Tamarin Holdings operate Icetrax and Splashdown, and a Burger King franchise. The *Icetrax* differs from conventional rinks by being on two levels. The top circuit, with rails each side for novice skaters to cling to, runs outside the building at one point, thus giving skaters a change of scene and advertising their presence to passers-by. From this circuit skaters can slide down ice-ramps onto an open rink for more ambitious skating and ice-dancing to a CD disco interrupted by an erupting volcano! *Splashdown* has no swimming pool and offers an essentially fun experience with flumes, slides and tyre rides through whirlpools, rock canyons and waterfalls.

Another major tenant was Allied Leisure, who operate four businesses on the site. *The Venue* is one of the largest nightclubs on the south coast, with a total capacity of 1,800 people. There are two interconnected areas, catering for different tastes in music, or different moods during the night. This is now owned and operated by Rank Leisure along with *Collonades*, an American-style bar, which serves as a meeting point for the nightclub.

Allied still own *MegaBowl* which has 30 lanes with computerized scoreboards. Arcade games and satellite TV showing pop video channel MTV help to keep customers occupied while waiting to bowl and encourage them to stay longer in the building and spend more in the bars and cafe. It is one of a chain operated by Allied Leisure throughout the UK. Allied Leisure also own the Slots amusement arcade.

Inde Coope (Allied Breweries, no connection with Allied Leisure) run *Calendar's*, a cafe bar and restaurant, again with the American theme characteristic of Tower Park. Calendar's tends to cater for people who want to make the meal a main feature of the evening, and so complements rather than competes with Burger King. There is also a Pizza Hut, KFC, and now a Chiquitos Mexican restaurant on the site.

A number of small shop units are also let to traders – from banks to sweet shops – to offer a variety of services to Tower Park patrons.

The newest and most innovative attraction on Tower Park is *Quasar*. This is in essence a high-tech version of small boys' games of soldiers or cowboys, in which two teams creep around a darkened area shooting at each other and trying to capture their opponents' base. The difference here is that there can be no argument about who is 'dead'. Participants carry laser guns and breastplates which register every shot. At the end of a hectic 15 minutes, a print-out tells you how many hits you made and received. The same operator has now opened a Planet Kidz adventure play area for younger children.

Although each tenant markets its individual attractions, from the customer's viewpoint Tower Park can be seen as a single product – one experience combining several activities in one visit. None of the attractions is unique, but the ability to combine them on a site with easy access, free parking and a secure environment for children gives Tower Park a considerable advantage over its town centre competitors.

Tower Park attracts an estimated 2.5–3 million visitors a year (including 1 million to Tescos) which would place it near the top of the UK visitor attraction league. Unlike Alton Towers, for example, there is no single admission gate through which these visitors are counted. Its Burger King was one of the first to be sited outside a town centre and has become one of the most successful BK franchised units in the country. Table 10.1 gives estimated user numbers for each facility.

The concept has not been without problems, however. At peak times there is insufficient parking space. One option would be to build a multi-storey or underground car park, but financing this would require the introduction of parking charges, which would represent a major change in the marketing positioning of the site.

Table 10.1   Estimated users per annum of each facility at Tower Park

UCI Cinema	900,000
Icetrax/Splashdown/Burger King	700,000
The Venue/Collonades	445,000
Quasar/Planet Kidz	190,000
Calendar's	160,000
MegaBowl	145,000
KFC Express	150,000
Pizza Hut	130,000
Slots	80,000

Source: Managers' estimates, 1995.

The promotion of Tower Park as a 'corporate venue' was substantial before opening. The cartoon character Captain Sopwith and his Pup were used to brand the park and illustrate the range of activities it offered. Since then the tenant operators have preferred to use the bulk of their promotional budgets on their own campaigns for their individual attractions.

The fundamental problem for Tower Park has been the high capital cost of preparing and developing the site. High interest rates in 1990 and 1991, combined with the recession, forced the developers TPLP into receivership, despite the profitability of the tenants' operations, and the site now has new landlords, Park Leisure Ltd.

QUESTIONS

1   Analyze the products offered at Tower Park using the classifications discussed in this chapter.

2   How have new products been developed from the original core benefits?

3   What advantages do the new products have over earlier versions, from the customers' and the companies' viewpoints?

4   What other examples of this product development process can you find in contemporary leisure?

5   The flume slide pool was originally an innovative feature of a few holiday centres like Butlins and Center Parcs. It is now commonplace in leisure centres throughout the country. Describe this process in terms of the product life cycle and discuss the implications for leisure managers.

6   Should managers on the Tower Park site concentrate on marketing their own attractions, or should they combine resources to create a brand image for the site as a whole?

7   What stages of new product development did TPLP go through? How could they have avoided the problems they encountered?

8   Sian Johnson of Applied Leisure Marketing has identified 10 important contributory factors in the success of tourist attractions.[18] How does Tower Park rate in each of these areas?:

- Low land costs or rental, for example, where the landlord places a value on the visitor-generating ability of the attraction, or as the result of a planning gain (i.e. where the landlord agrees to provide land or buildings for leisure purposes in return for planning permission to develop the rest of the site).

- A write-off of a significant proportion of the initial capital costs through grants and sponsorship.

- A genuinely exciting and entertaining experience (over and above the cultural and educational value of the subject matter).

- An accurately defined and easy to reach target market.

- A location that is accessible to the target market, and ideally already used by them.

- A marketing budget large enough to reach the market.

- Efficient operation and staffing.

- Efficient use of space, using technology to speed throughput or to develop secondary points of sale throughout the site.

- A business plan that allows for the capital costs of replacing exhibits and experience techniques.

- Sources of supplementary revenue over and above admissions revenue, either by direct trading or by cross-subsidies from other users on the site.

9   Examine the Weymouth Diving Museum (Case Study 3.1 in Chapter 3) in terms of Sian Johnson's 10 factors.

Summary

A product is anything offered by an organization that might satisfy a want or need in its customers. It will have tangible elements, but what the customer is really buying is a benefit. In leisure this is usually an enjoyable or self-improving experience. In designing and marketing the product, managers have to consider the customer's total experience, including tangible and intangible elements, and also aspects not directly under the organization's control.

The theory of the product life cycle warns that products eventually experience declining sales unless they are redesigned or replaced. It is wise to develop new products while the current products are still at their peak of sales rather than wait until they decline. However, decline should not be thought of as irreversible. Product-market strategies open to the organization include increased market penetration and/or development of new markets for existing products, as well as new product development or diversification.

Most organizations develop a range of products rather than rely entirely on one for their profitability. The range needs to be reviewed and managed. Portfolio analysis using the Boston Matrix can help to decide when to allocate resources from established products to those with the greatest growth potential.

New product ideas are often a creative response to internal and external pressures. New leisure products have been developed by using new technology to deliver traditional leisure experiences in more satisfying ways. Screening and testing of new ideas can avoid costly failures.

The aim should be to create something which your customers will choose in preference to the alternatives offered by your competitors. Establishing a unique product position requires identifying the key benefits your customers want, designing the product to deliver them and signalling the advantages to the customers.

A strong, coherent brand image can help to signal these advantages as well as creating a personality which customers can recognize, respond to and rely on.

Notes

1. Macdonald, M. (1984) *Marketing Plans*, p. 79.
2. 'A product is anything that can be offered to a market for attention, acquisition, use or consumption that might satisfy a need', Kotler, P. (1994) *Marketing Management*, p. 445.
3. Kotler (1988), p. 432. In later editions he adds extra layers, including the generic, expected and potential product.
4. Middleton, V. (1994) *Marketing for Travel and Tourism*, Ch. 8, p. 90.
5. Palmer, A. (1994) *Principles of Service Marketing*, p. 8.
6. *Ibid*, p. 128.
7. Diamond, J. 'Making of a mega-myth', *The Guardian*, 7 May 1993, pp. 2.2–3.
8. King, S. (1984) *Developing New Brands*.
9. *Travel Weekly*, 1 November 1990, p. 1.
10. Cooper, C. (1992) 'The life cycle concept and tourism', in Johnson, P. and Thomas, B. (Eds) *Choice and Demand in Tourism*, p. 154.
11. Butler, R.W. (1980) 'The concept of a tourist area cycle of evolution: Implications for management of resources', *Canadian Geographer*, 24: 5–12.
12. Caie, G. (1991) 'Poised to strike', *Leisure Management*, 11(3): 63. Other interesting articles on the revival of ten-pin bowling in the UK can be found in *Leisure Management*, December 1991 and June 1993.
13. Ansoff, I. (1957) 'Strategies for diversification', *Harvard Business Review*, Sept./Oct., pp. 113–24.
14. See Lancaster, G. and Massingham, L. (1992) *Essentials of Marketing*, pp. 78–80.
15. Barksdale, H.C. and Harris, C.E. (1982) 'Portfolio analysis and the product life cycle', *Journal of Long Range Planning*, 15(6). They actually add to the menagerie

Infants (risky pioneering projects), Warhorses (high-share products with declining sales but still worthwhile cash generators), and Dodos (low-share and declining sales – facing extinction). See also Lancaster and Massingham, *op. cit.*, pp. 87–89.

16. *Leisure Week*, 13 January 1995, p. 10.
17. Seward, K. (1994) *Leisure Opportunities*, 25 July.
18. Johnson, S (1991) 'Attractive experiences', *Leisure Management*, 5: 42–45.

11 Designing and delivering customer service

Levels of service

In Chapter 9 we referred to the price/quality trade-off that is involved in most product positioning decisions. Put simply, the higher the price, the higher the quality of service the customers will expect. Conversely, the higher the quality, the more they will be prepared to pay.

In this colloquial usage of the word quality, we are more precisely referring to the *level of service*. What distinguishes a first-class air ticket from an economy class ticket is the level of service provided, e.g. the comfort of the seat, the leg room, the angle of reclining, the amount of attention from the cabin crew, the type of food, the complimentary extras, and so on. These features are specified in the publicity, and the customer chooses whether he wishes to pay extra for them.

In designing a new product or repositioning an existing one the organization has to decide what level of service to offer. This will depend on what level of service

- the target customers expect,
- the target customers are prepared to pay for,
- the competitors provide,
- the organization can afford to provide at the market price.

We will examine the role of price and costs in more detail in Chapter 12. What matters here is that the price/level of service decision affects the entire specification for the product. Customers of a budget hotel chain like Formule 1 will accept standardized rooms, no room service, self-service breakfast and no restaurant or bar facilities, because this is what is specified in the publicity, and because the price is much lower than a three-star hotel. For three-star prices they expect a great deal more.

It is possible for an organization to gain a competitive advantage by offering more features for the same price, or by offering a better quality service. The two are not the same thing.

Every organization aims or ought to aim to provide a high-quality service, whether they are the Ritz or Burger King. They provide different *levels* of service, but in their chosen terms both aim to provide *quality* of service.

Quality of service

Exact definitions of quality are difficult to arrive at. According to the dictionary, a product's qualities are its distinguishing characteristics.[1] In manufacturing, quality control means identifying, and removing from the production line, any products that do not possess these required characteristics, that do not conform to the specifications. The specifications are based on the requirements of the user, the customer. Quality, therefore, is judged by the customers, and in Palmer's words, 'occurs where an organization supplies goods or services to a specification which satisfies their needs'.[2]

The International Standards Organization defines quality as:

> The totality of features and characteristics of a product or service which bear on its ability to satisfy stated or implied needs.[3]

A quality service, therefore, is one that satisfies customer needs. A customer judges the quality of the service by the extent to which it meets his expectations. This is the basis of the approach used by Zeithaml *et al.* To them, a high-quality service is one where there is no gap between the expected service and the perceived service.[4] Customers will bring different expectations when eating at Burger King than when dining at the Ritz. They nevertheless expect quick, efficient service of hot food in pleasant, clean surroundings from BK, and if these are not provided they will take their custom elsewhere next time. Fast-food chains therefore take considerable care to ensure that their outlets provide a uniform quality of service.

Expectations

A customer's expectations are derived partly from personal needs, previous experience of similar products, and word-of-mouth recommendation from others. They are also derived from marketing communications such as brochures, advertisements and signing, and from the price. The marketer plays an important part in creating the expectations and therefore needs to be involved in ensuring that they are met.

As noted in the previous chapter, the branding of a product sums up the marketing message. The brand image influences expectations by promising consistency, reliability and a particular personality.

Perceptions

These promises have to be delivered by a service which is intangible, variable and dependent on the interactions of human beings. Not only can the service vary according to the performance of the staff, but it can be perceived differently according to the mood and preoccupations of the customer.

According to Zeithaml *et al.*, the five determinants of service quality that is, the five most important things customers expect from a quality service, are

- *Reliability*: the promised service is performed dependably and accurately.
- *Responsiveness*: the service is prompt and the staff are willing to help.
- *Assurance*: the staff are knowledgeable, courteous, and inspire confidence.
- *Empathy*: customers are given caring, individual attention.
- *Tangibles*: the physical facilities, equipment, personnel and communications (signs, documents, correspondence) create a good impression.[5]

Four out of these five determinants depend on the human element of the service. The tangible elements are the least important. British Rail, for example, has spent a great deal of time and money providing information for customers in the form of timetable posters, electronic train indicator boards, recorded announcements, and the like. But in a survey they found that 78% of customers chose to ask the station staff for this information. Indeed, most checked by asking twice of different people! Yet only 8% of those questioned regarded BR staff as helpful – a clear example of the gap between expectations and perceptions.[6]

The other thing to notice in Zeithaml's list is that the manner in which the service is performed – empathy, willingness to help, courtesy – is as important as how efficiently it is performed. Grönroos labels the former the functional quality, and the latter the technical quality of the service. The factors that affect consumers' judgement of quality are shown in Figure 11.1.

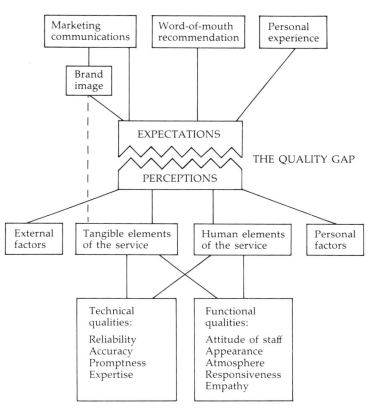

FIGURE 11.1   Quality: the fit between customer expectations and perceptions.
Sources: Based on Zeithaml *et al.* (1990) *Delivering Service Quality,* and Grönroos (1984) *Strategic Management and Marketing in the Service Sector.*

Delivering service quality

Stoll Moss Theatres, who manage 11 of London's West End theatres, have introduced a system of regular checks on the state of the theatres based on a fast-food franchise audit. They have realized the importance of the overall experience of theatre-going in generating repeat custom, and so have separated the active management of the theatre from the production management. Stoll Moss are aiming to create brand loyalty and have designed a logo showing a pair of hands applauding. Standard setting plays a part alongside staff training 'to remind people of the basics such as smiling and listening', and the development of a customer database.[8]

This example shows how leisure organizations are becoming more aware of the importance of delivering a quality service to their marketing strategy. To ensure that the customers receive the service they expect, managers need to pay attention to the functional quality as well as the technical quality. Both must meet the expectations created by marketing communications. Delivery of a quality service requires the commitment of everyone in the organization working together to achieve agreed objectives. This is the essence of the approach known as Total Quality Management. As the theatre example shows, there are a number of steps management can take towards improving service quality. The next section considers each step in turn, and then shows how they could form part of an approach to Total Quality in the organization.

Tangibilization

The tangible elements of the service create the first impressions. The decor, the design of the premises, the uniforms of the staff, the style of the signs, notices and menus, are all the first-time customer has to judge what service he is likely to get. The use of the brand logo on signs, print, equipment and uniforms reinforces the message of the advertising and establishes the professionalism of the organization. If the service experience is good they can also send the customer away with a positive impression of the organization, which may make him recommend it to others or return himself. If the service is unsatisfactory, however, the branding may imprint a negative image in his memory, and he may avoid the organization in the future.

Monitoring customer satisfaction

As discussed in Chapter 5, measures of customer satisfaction should form part of the management information system. As well as monitoring complaints and carrying out regular customer surveys, the organization can use customer panels, mystery shoppers or comparisons with competitors to discover both good and bad practices.

Setting standards

Many organizations now set standards of customer service against which their staff are judged. Examples of such standards include the maximum time a customer should have to wait to be served or to have telephone calls answered, the number of times a day toilets are inspected and cleaned, the percentage of right-time arrivals for transport services, the percentage of customers declaring themselves satisfied when filling in a questionnaire, and so on. Some companies use benchmarking to set the standards. A pub retailer chain may identify the houses which are performing best, and compare the others with them to analyze what improvements are needed.

Standard-setting communicates the top management's concern for customer service quality and sets priorities for managers and supervisors. I can provide the criteria for deciding whether to retain staff or contractors (as with Thomson's customer satisfaction questionnaires; Chapter 5). Local authorities specify service standards for the contractors managing their leisure centres, and can carry out regular inspections to check that they are being met, using a format set out in BS 6001. The standards may be published as a Customers' Charter, an approach adopted by the government for state-owned services such as health and education.

Whatever system is used, to be effective, standards must be based on research into what the customers expect. Zeithaml *et al.* suggest there is often a gap between what customers expect and what managers perceive their expectations to be. The standards must also be seen as worthwhile and achievable by the staff. Very often the achievement of a standard will have cost implications which the management may be unable or unwilling to accept. Improving the ratio of staff to customers will probably improve customer perceptions of the service, but it might also make the service uneconomic at the market price.

Service specification

To make the correct decisions and set the correct standards of service may require a detailed analysis of the tasks involved From this analysis, management, preferably in consultation with the staff, would agree a specification of how the task should be carried out in order to create customer satisfaction.

Such specifications cannot in themselves deliver what Grönroos called the functional quality of service, the manner in which it is provided. It is possible to specify what the telephone staff say, such as 'Good morning, thank you for calling Borsetshire Leisure, Mandy speaking, how can I help you?', but the words will sound hollow unless there is a genuine desire to be helpful to the customer. Specification can even adversely affect customer service if it reduces the role of the employee to carrying out a simple and repetitive part of the process with little contact or involvement with the overall result. Such 'de-skilled' employees can become bored and alienated, which will eventually show in their attitude to the customers. This is a major criticism of the so-called scientific management approach of Frederick Taylor and followers, who advocated a clear division of labour as the key to successful management.[9]

Quality systems

Nevertheless, task analysis and job specification has an important part to play in setting up a Quality Assurance System. Quality Systems are defined by the International Standards Organization as:

> all those planned and systematic actions necessary to provide adequate confidence that a product or service will satisfy given requirements of quality.[10]

Unlike quality control, which is concerned solely with inspection and detection of faults, Quality Assurance systems are designed to prevent rather than to cure customer service problems, the so-called Right First Time approach. They encompass the whole process of satisfying the customer, from the purchasing of supplies to the monitoring of the end results. The aim is to ensure that all employees are qualified, trained, and equipped to work to a single system with agreed objectives. The system has built-in procedures for inspecting and checking against agreed standards and for dealing with any defects that are identified. It therefore reduces the need for external supervision and checking by management.

British Standard 5750 (based on International Standard ISO 9000) provides a framework against which to measure an organization's quality system. It is written in terms appropriate to manufacturing but has been successfully adapted for leisure centres, colleges and other service industries. Organizations can apply to be registered as conforming to BS 5750, which can be an invaluable selling point when dealing with clients and customers.

BS 5750 requires the organization to produce comprehensive quality documentation. In the Oasis Leisure Centre, Swindon, the documentation consisted of

- the Quality Manual: outlining the overall quality policy of the centre;
- the operational procedures: setting the standards of service to be achieved;
- the work instructions: detailing how these standards should achieved; and
- records: monitoring the performance against standards.

The operational procedures identify the main factors that must be controlled to provide a satisfactory experience. In a leisure pool, these could include air and water temperature, lighting, water composition, admission procedures, information to users, cleanliness, supervision, equipment and maintenance. Responsibilities are allocated and procedures laid down, for example for dealing with undesirable behaviour or accidents.[11]

Critics of BS 5750 claim that it is unnecessarily bureaucratic, that it focuses on the system rather than the customer, and could stifle staff initiative. Peter Mills of the Oasis Centre claims that the exercise of drawing up the system in fact leads to simplification of existing systems of documentation, focuses attention on the customer experience, involves staff in the decision processes, and delegates greater responsibilities to them.[12]

A successful quality system requires all those involved in implementing it, management and staff, to be committed to good customer service. The design and implementation of the system should involve everyone in the organization.

Staff motivation

Involving staff in decision making and giving them responsibility is one way of motivating them to give good customer service. Quality systems encourage staff 'ownership of the problem' and 'empower' them to find solutions, to use two fashionable pieces of management jargon. This is part of the human relations approach to management, which stresses the social aspects of motivation, in contrast to the economic emphasis of the scientific management approach. Writers such as Mayo saw the importance of job satisfaction arising from workers identifying with the company, feeling that they belonged to a team and being fully involved in the work process.[13]

Customer care courses have played a central part in the strategy of firms which seek to gain a marketing advantage through improving service quality. The best known example is Jan Carlzon's repositioning of Scandinavian Airlines (SAS) in the early 1980s. He sent 10,000 front-line staff on service seminars as part of a campaign to improve the quality of service to business travellers.[14] The SAS course, 'The Human Factor', has since been used or copied by numerous other airlines and transport companies.

Such courses are not concerned simply with the techniques of customer service, how to smile and be polite. The aim is to create individuals with the self awareness and self-confidence that makes them want to be polite and helpful. Elements of the course might include:

- *Awareness*: what do they themselves think is good service when they are on the receiving end? What part do they play in creating an overall image of the company in the customers' minds?

- *Personal development*: their needs and goals for their work, recognizing and coping with stress, being assertive but not aggressive.

- *Techniques* for dealing with people: body language, transaction analysis, etc.

- *Role play* and case studies specific to the employee's work situation.

- *Company objectives* and the employee's part in them.

- *Company culture*: an opportunity to discuss management/employee attitudes to risk taking, creativity, responsibility, ownership of problems, etc.

The aim of such courses is to make staff understand better the ways in which they interact with their customers, and to give them the confidence to take responsibility for improving the service they provide. Such courses will only work if the management are also trained to create the working environment where a customer-centred approach can grow. Carlzon sent all his managers on a longer course to achieve this.

Quality circles

Quality circles provide a more permanent opportunity for staff to take responsibility for improving customer service. A quality circle consists of 6–8 people in the same work area meeting for an hour a week to solve quality problems in their work. Front-line staff who have regular contact with their customers can be brought together with operational staff whose work 'behind the scenes' affects service quality. By sitting down together, with a supervisor and a facilitator, they can become more aware of the problems and suggest solutions. To be successful, the issues raised at such meetings need to be taken up by management so that the circle members feel that their participation is producing worthwhile results.

Total Quality Management

All the elements we have so far discussed can form part of a Total Quality Management approach to the company. TQM is a means of organizing and involving everyone in an organization, in all activities, in all functions and at all levels. It recognizes that every staff member has an impact on the quality received by the customers, even though they may never meet them.[15] As

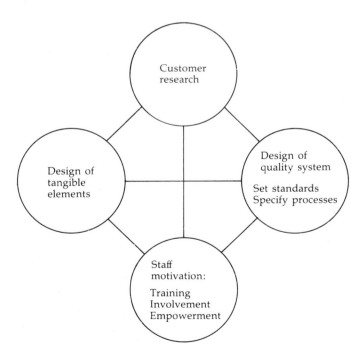

FIGURE 11.2   The key elements of Total Quality Management.

Mills says, it is not a mechanical process that senior management can set a match to and then stand back and watch: 'It requires real commitment, persistence and participation, it requires team education not merely staff training, and it requires a completely fresh look at the way we do things'.[16]

TQM is not merely concerned with making the customers happier; it is concerned to eliminate the costs of unsatisfactory customer service. These can include the loss of repeat business, but also the loss of potential business by failing to respond quickly enough to a market opportunity. It seeks to eliminate practices and procedures which do not add value to the product or contribute to satisfying the customer.

Readers may recall that unnecessary procedures were a symptom of operational orientation described in Chapter 3. TQM can be seen as the means of turning an organization towards a customer orientation.

Whatever system is adopted to achieve TQM, it should be apparent that the four key elements are the customers, the tangible elements, the systems and the staff. As Figure 11.2 shows, all four elements must be involved.

CASE STUDY 11.1   *British Airways: 'Putting People First'*

British Airways saw 'Putting People First' as a priority after the company was privatized in 1982. The company was making a pretax loss of £108 million, passenger miles were falling and staff were demoralized by the threat of redundancies.

First, BA carried out research into customer expectations, identifying the key dimensions of quality. This showed that interpersonal factors were twice as important as operational aspects. The airline needed to give equal attention to service and attention, and to timetable convenience and aircraft comfort. Attitude research among employees revealed that many were not aware of the part they could play in this. Accordingly, BA put all its staff through a 'Putting People First' course, covering personal development, handling their feelings, understanding and coping with stress, and being assertive.

BA then set up voluntary customer service teams within which staff discussed the results of the customer surveys and made recommendations for improving the service. These suggestions were then taken to management workshops where the CST leaders put forward their proposals for action. The results were built into staff training programmes and performance appraisals.

As a result of this process, BA were able to set marketplace performance indices, covering maximum waiting times, the number of check-in counters open, availability of duty-free stock, and so on. They also set up a systematic analysis of customer complaints. The tangible elements of the service were also changed with a new corporate livery, better ground facilities, and improved decor inside aircraft.

Having set up this quality system, BA made it the central theme of their advertising, with pictures of stewards and hostesses winging through space with engaging smiles and a whisky and soda for a weary executive reclining in 'the biggest business class seat in the air'.

By 1986, passenger numbers had increased to 19.7 million from 16.7 million in 1982, productivity per employee was up, as was turnover, and the airline reported a pretax profit of £195 million.

> *Sources:* Tank, A. (1987) 'Plain speaking' (a profile of BA marketing director Jim Harris), *Marketing*, 21 May, pp. 38–39.
> Moores, B. (Ed.) (1986) *Are They Being Served? Quality Consciousness in the Service Industries.*

CASE STUDY 11.2   *Holiday centres: Expectations and perceptions*

The invention of the holiday centre is usually credited to Billy Butlin. His holiday camps (the first one in 1936 was literally a campsite with tents) were set up to provide all-weather facilities for an all-in price. In response to the 1938 Act that entitled all workers to paid holidays, Butlin promised 'A Week's Holiday for a Week's Pay' with a package of accommodation, meals and organized entertainment. The Butlins camps reached the peak of their popularity after World War II.

By the 1970s, Butlins were in decline. The standard of accommodation in blocks of wooden 'chalets' compared unfavourably with that offered by overseas package holiday hotels, where the weather was better. The organized programmes of entertainment and games run by the ubiquitous redcoated staff, which had appealed to a generation used to the discipline and cameraderie of wartime, now appeared over-regimented, and the cheery morning calls over the camp public address system irritatingly intrusive. The success of the TV comedy series *Hi-di-hi!*, set in a 'Maplins' holiday camp of the 1950s showed the extent to which Butlins had become an outdated joke.

In the 1980s Butlins' remaining market share appeared threatened by plans by the Dutch company Center Parcs to open their first holiday village in the UK, encouraged by grants from the English Tourist Board. Center Parcs was founded by the owner of a chain of sports shops, with the aim of providing people with an escape from the bustle of urban life. Center Parcs are constructed among trees in a forest rather than in a seaside setting; the accommodation is in self-contained villas rather than rows of huts; the emphasis is on relaxation; and the centre of the site is a 'tropical water paradise under a space age dome'.

This concept was adapted to the British market under the direction of UK managing director Peter Moore: 'One of the most important things I brought was that Center Parcs had to be more than just a villa in a forest. We had to add another dimension to the peace and relaxation. I felt we needed to provide little dollops of excitement in water fun ... we needed to introduce sport and innovations such as the country club'. These extras, apart from the pool, were optional rather than included in the package price. The first British Center Parcs opened in Sherwood Forest in 1987.

Center Parcs aimed at a very different position in the market to Butlins, appealing to more affluent, individualistic customers with a yearning for nature and an interest in sport and fitness. Being considerably more expensive, it also had to offer a quality experience. 'Quality runs through our organization', claims Peter Moore. According to an interview with Catherine Larner, this means quality in facilities, quality in staff and quality in the environment. Only 7% of the 400 acre site is developed. 'We are paranoid about the environment. We want all our buildings to be invisible.'

Quality means designing villas which well-to-do women would admire as a second home; it means choosing Wedgwood crockery for the restaurant, and transporting plants from South Africa to create a living tropical paradise beneath the hardwoods of an English forest. 'If you think quality, you genuinely try to get into the mind of the guest and ask "what would my guest want?" Quality need not mean high investment – just making sure there is a fresh clean toilet roll in the loo or a crack in the window is replaced. It means not accepting mediocrity.'

The staff are at the centre of this emphasis on quality. Staff are recruited locally and are offered careers with potential. 'What we are trying to do is to persuade staff ... that they are leisure professionals, whose job is to give pleasure to other people. This doesn't cost a lot of money, it is just a question of attitude, recognition and training', says Peter Moore.

Center Parcs' emphasis on quality appears to have paid off, with year-round occupancy rates of 95% being maintained despite the recession. About 50% of the business comes from repeat customers or personal recommendations. The secret of success, according to Moore, is affordable quality.

Butlins' owners, Rank, responded to the threat of Center Parcs by consolidating the product on five sites, Minehead, Bognor Regis, Pwllheli, Skegness and Ayr, which received massive reinvestment in excess of £175 million between 1986 and 1989. Much of the old accommodation was replaced, new Sunsplash funpools (some of the first in the UK), white-knuckle fairground rides and themed cabaret bars were opened. The old camps were re-branded as Holiday Worlds. The redcoat uniforms were redesigned by top fashion designer Zandra Rhodes. A comprehensive programme of entertainment and activities is still provided, featuring big-name artistes, but the emphasis is now on the vast choice available to the guest. The new accommodation is increasingly self-catering in response to changing public demand.

As a result of this investment Butlins have regained their popularity and claim that 45% of its business is repeat. In 1990 Butlins was Rank's most profitable division, with pretax profit of £27 million, or £18 per visitor, well in excess of those of any overseas tour operators.

Butlins initially claimed that they were aiming their product 'up-market' and attracting an ABC1 clientele. Experience has shown that what they have done is to win back their traditional C1C2D customers from the overseas holiday. What their reinvestment has done is to provide what this type of customer now expects from a holiday, which is very different from what Butlins' original customers expected.

Source: This case study has been based partly on an interview with Peter Moore, *Leisure Management*, **9**, September 1994.

QUESTIONS

1 Butlins and Center Parcs offer very different types of holiday centres. In what sense can they both be said to provide quality products?

2 What elements of a quality system are illustrated by this case study?

Summary

As Case Study 11.1 shows, the quality of service can play an important part in the competitive strategy of the organization. There is a distinction between the level of service offered – the features included in the price package, and the quality of service – the extent to which it satisfies customer expectations. As the quality of service is judged by the customer according to the promises made by marketing communications and the brand image, it should be a major concern of the marketing as well as the operational management. A high-quality service can only be delivered when the whole company is committed to the concept and is working together in a coherent quality system.

Notes

1. The Shorter Oxford Dictionary defines quality as 'an attribute, property or characteristic (of something)'.
2. Palmer, A. (1994) *Principles of Service Marketing*, p. 173.
3. ISO 8402: 1986, 'Quality Vocabulary, International Standards Organisation'. quoted in Mills, P. (Ed.) (1992) *Quality in the Leisure Industry*, p. 2.

4. Zeithaml, V., Berry, L. and Parasuraman, A. (1990) *Delivering Quality Service.*

5. Adapted from Kotler, P. (1994) *Marketing Management*, p. 476.

6. Giblin, D. (1986) 'Customer care in British Rail', in Moores, B. (Ed.) *Are They Being Served?*, p. 57.

7. Grönroos, C. (1984) *Strategic Management and Marketing in the Service Sector.*

8. *Leisure Week*, 26 February 1993.

9. Taylor, F.D. (1964) *Scientific Management.*

10. See note 3 above.

11. BQA Leisure Services Quality Committee (1992) *Quality Assurance for Leisure Services.*

12. Mills, P (1992) *Quality in the Leisure Industry*, pp. 12–13.

13. Mayo, E. (1949) *The Social Problems of Industrial Civilisations.* See also the chapter on 'Managing the human element of the service encounter', in Palmer (1994), *op. cit.*, p. 197.

14. Kotler (1994), *op. cit.*, p. 25.

15. Palmer (1994), *op. cit.*, p. 188.

16. Mills (1992), *op. cit.*, p. 49.

12 Pricing

Price as part of a marketing strategy
The relationship between pricing and costs
Pricing and cost structure
Case Study 12.1: Pricing at EuroDisney
Trade pricing
Pricing tactics
Summary

The price an organization can charge for a product depends on what its customers are willing to pay. This is often termed the *value* the customers place on having the product. Value is determined by

- the importance to the customer of the benefit the product offers, and
- the alternatives available from direct and indirect competitors.

Leisure activities are optional and inessential, and many alternatives are available. Price, therefore, has a powerful influence on demand. If the price goes up, people can choose not to buy and so demand falls. If the price goes down, the activity becomes affordable to more people and so the demand increases.

This phenomenon, known to the economists as *price elasticity*, can be seen very clearly in tourism. The growth of tourism has often been the result of transport technology making new destinations affordable and accessible. This is the case both in the development of seaside resorts in the railway age of the nineteenth century and in the growth of the Mediterranean package holiday in the 1950s and 1960s as a result of the availability of charter flights by jet aircraft.[1]

The price sensitivity of the holiday market was clearly demonstrated in the mid-1980s. In 1985, Spanish hoteliers raised the prices charged to UK tour operators, and the result was an immediate fall in demand. In such situations, the marketer has two alternatives. One is to create and communicate a sense of the importance and uniqueness of the product so that the customer will be prepared to pay more for it. The tour operators had clearly failed to do this. The alternative is to reduce the price again to the level that the customer has come to expect. This, as we saw in Case Study 9.1 in Chapter 9, was what happened. Once the prices were cut, the sales of holidays rose again to record levels.

Case Study 9.1 illustrated the role price plays in competitive strategy; Thomson chose to cut prices in order to defend its market share, and the other companies were forced to follow. It also demonstrates how price decisions are made in response to market conditions – what the customer is prepared to pay and what competitors are charging – rather than on cost considerations. The market conditions forced the tour operators to reduce the costs, by computerization, redundancies and negotiating low rates from the hotels. Those who were unable to do so went out of business.

Price as part of a marketing strategy

Price, then, is a key element in an organization's marketing strategy. Porter's three generic competitive strategies all involve price decisions.[2] Low-cost leadership, as practised by Thomson in Case Study 9.1, self-evidently does. Differentiation will include price as part of the means of positioning the brand against its competition. Focus on particular market segments also has to take into account these segments' varying sensitivity to price levels.

Positioning by price/quality

Price decisions play an important part in the positioning process, both in creating competitive advantages and in signalling the advantages to the customers. The price at which a product is offered creates expectations of its quality. In developing a new hotel, a decision must be made at an early stage as to whether it is to be five-star, three-star or budget. The hotel is then designed and operated to deliver a particular level of service at a particular price range.

The price range is determined by the prices charged by other hotels offering similar services. Within the broad range the new hotel will still need to differentiate itself by variations in the amenities, style and comparative prices. The hotel may decide to undercut the prices offered by rivals in the same price range or to charge slightly more, depending on its competitive strategy. These options are known as *penetration* and *skimming* pricing.

Penetration

Both strategies may be used by a new health club opening in an area where there is established competition. The low-price strategy may be aimed at penetrating the market quickly by winning customers from the other clubs.

As we have said, price is a very effective short-term technique. The difficulty may come later when the new club attempts to raise prices in order to improve its profitability.

Skimming

The alternative of opening with prices higher than the competition may be appropriate if the new club provides new facilities that are not available elsewhere. A high price will help to communicate the superiority of the services offered, and also enable the club to recoup its investment more quickly. This strategy, known as skimming (as in skimming the cream off the top of the milk), is often used with electronic goods where the 'innovators' segment of the market are prepared to pay high prices for the latest equipment.[3] Nintendo's *Game Boy* was introduced in the UK at around £70 when a hand-held console was a new concept, and later reduced to £40 after it became established.

Harvesting

As new versions of products such as the hand-held games console come onto the market, the prices of the older models are reduced to ensure that they are sold before they become obsolete. This strategy is known as harvesting – gathering in the profits while they can still be made. The development costs will have been recovered during the skimming stage, so the company can now afford to reduce its prices.

Segmentation by price

The price/quality decision will be related to the market segment to be targeted. If a health club charges higher membership fees than its competitors, this implies not only that the club offers better facilities but also that it caters to a more affluent, 'better class' of members. That segment may be prepared to pay extra for the benefits of exclusivity.

Alternatively, the club may charge below the market price in order to tap potential demand from those who are interested in health and fitness but feel unable to afford the prices charged by other clubs.

Price discrimination

As we saw in Chapter 8, most organizations need to practise differentiated marketing, which aims to attract a different mix of customer segments at different times in order to gain the best possible revenue. Pricing is an important tool in achieving this.

For example, a nightclub will be busiest, and most profitable, at weekends when everyone wants to go out for the night. It can charge high prices that young professional people can afford. Such people constitute the 'core segment' of the club's business and the facilities would be designed with them in mind. At other times of the week, these core customers are less likely to come in great numbers, and so, if the club is to stay open and cover its overheads, it must seek other sources of custom.

One option would be simply to charge lower prices in midweek, but this might draw 'core' business away from the weekends and reduce the overall revenue. If, on the other hand, the reductions were available only to holders of student cards, this would attract new customers who could not afford the weekend prices, and the overall revenue would increase.

This is an example of selective or *discriminatory pricing*, where different groups are charged different prices for the same product or service. The aim is to gain new business by reduced rates without affecting the revenue from existing customers. The reductions are therefore only available under carefully defined conditions. These can be by category of customer, by time or date of use or of booking, depending on the market. British Rail's range of fares aimed at leisure travellers only apply to journeys started after 10 a.m. so as to exclude commuters and business travellers who have to travel earlier and so have little alternative but to pay the full price. There are further reductions for senior citizens, young persons and families travelling with children, but these are available only to holders of the appropriate railcard. BR have also copied the airlines in offering 'advanced purchase excursion' (APEX) fares for tickets booked in advance.

This type of pricing policy recognizes that the value of a product depends on its importance to the customer. For instance, people are prepared to pay more for a train, flight or ferry ticket for their main summer holiday than they are for the same journey for a short break or day excursion. The latter are more optional, often taken on impulse and booked at the last moment. A low price, especially if advertised as a bargain, can persuade them that they can afford to go. In the summer when there is an excess of demand over supply, people will accept a high price rather than forgo their 'essential' annual holiday with all its benefits of escape, relaxation, status and discovery.

Hotels, ships, airlines all apply price discrimination, often with complex price grids to ensure that the maximum possible revenue is achieved on each occasion. Computer reservations systems enable management to reserve space for high revenue-yielding business or release it for lower yield optional business according to demand. Unsold seats or beds can be offered as 'late availability bargains' to a network of agents linked to the central reservation system. This process of *yield management* is central to the profitable management of tourism businesses, yield being the actual revenue achieved (as distinct from the brochure price or 'rack rate').[4]

The relationship between pricing and costs

Readers may be surprised that we have not begun this chapter by considering the cost of providing the service. This is deliberate, if provocative. As we have already said, the price an organization can charge for a leisure activity depends ultimately on how much the customers are prepared to pay for it. This in turn depends on how much they value its importance to them, how much of their disposable income they can afford to spend on it, and how much is charged by their competitors for similar or substitute activities.

If the organization can provide the activity at that price and make a profit, it will do so. If not, it will either find ways of reducing its costs, or get out of the business. Levitt quotes the car manufacturer Henry Ford, who expressed this very clearly:

> You will note that the reduction in price comes first. We have never considered any costs as fixed. Therefore we first reduce the price to the point where we believe more sales will result. Then we go ahead and try to make the price. We do not bother about the costs. The new price forces the costs down and forces everybody in the place to the highest point of efficiency.[5]

Ford was not saying that the costs do not matter. It is essential to understand the nature of the costs, to control them and to reduce them where possible. But the organization's costs should not determine the price. The market does that.

The competitive nature of the leisure and tourism industries today forces companies to take a similar approach to that of Henry Ford. The cross-Channel ferry services between Britain and France, as we saw in Chapter 9, have been preparing to meet the competition from the Channel Tunnel which opened in 1994. The strategy has been to invest in improved on-board facilities in order to position themselves as a more comfortable and enjoyable alternative to the Shuttle. They also need to match or undercut the Tunnel fares, and so cannot increase prices to pay for their investment. Instead they have had to reduce their labour costs, often by protracted and bitter disputes with the unions.

Compulsory competitive tendering (CCT) legislation is intended to produce the same downward pressure on costs in local authority leisure services. Private contractors and direct service organizations tender to deliver a specified level of service for an agreed contract fee, often with a maximum level specified for the prices it can charge the public. The threat of losing the contract to a lower bid forces the existing direct service organization to examine and reduce its costs. The successful contractor has to

ontinue to control costs in order to deliver the service and achieve
rofitability within the terms of the contract.

ubsidized prices

here may be circumstances where the costs are such that it is impossible to
eliver the service required at a price the users are prepared to pay, but it
ould be socially and politically unacceptable to discontinue the service. It
en becomes a political decision whether to grant a subsidy to make up the
ifference between the cost of providing the facilities and the market price.
he subsidy can be seen as a price paid by the whole community for the
alue of the facility to the whole community.

Subsidies may be used to enable specific disadvantaged groups to
ave access to the facility at prices they can afford, or to retain the facility as
 whole for the social, cultural and economic benefit of the community.
porting and cultural facilities may be seen as one of the means of attracting
urists and persuading companies to move their offices and factories to an
rea. Galleries and museums have traditionally been provided as educational
sources for the public.

Critics of subsidy argue that this leads to inefficiency and lack of
ntrol over costs (such as the fees paid to star performers by state subsidized
pera houses) . On the other hand, the negotiations between the company and
e provider of the subsidy can be used as a way of forcing the company to
stify its level of expenditure in the same way as CCT does in other areas.

ponsorship

lany arts and sports organizations seek sponsorship as a means of bridging
e gap between the revenue from ticket sales and the costs of providing the
rvice. Again the sponsorship is a price paid by the sponsors for the value
ey derive from being associated with the event or facility. This value will
e discussed in Chapter 21.

ricing and cost structure

lthough the market is the final arbiter, the organization's pricing strategy
oes need to take into account the nature of the costs it incurs, particularly
e proportion of fixed and variable costs.

ixed costs

ome types of leisure organizations have a high level of *fixed costs*, i.e. costs
at are incurred regardless of the number of units produced and sold. A

health club, for example, has to pay the rates, rents, heating and lighting of its premises and to depreciate the costs of its equipment whether anyone uses it or not. A zoo has to house, clean and feed its animals whether anyone comes to look at them or not. In the short term, at any rate, an elephant is fixed cost! In such cases, there are few costs that vary in proportion to the number of visitors. They may employ a few temporary staff at peak period and need more guide books and souvenirs to sell, but otherwise the costs are fixed.

The objective of the pricing policy is to ensure that the overall revenue exceeds the fixed costs of running the establishment during a given period of time (month, season, year). A simple *cost plus* formula,

$$\text{Price} = \frac{\text{total operating costs}}{\text{forecast no. of visitors}} + \text{profit margin},$$

may serve as a guide to pricing but is too simplistic to achieve the optimum result. Instead, the organization will use the price discrimination method described earlier to stimulate demand at quiet times and maximize the revenue from busy times. Some segments will pay above the average yield required and others below. It is the mix of price segments taken together that must produce a profit over the period.

Variable costs

In other cases, the majority of the costs are *variable*, i.e. the costs vary per unit produced or per customer served. A coach hire company's costs will vary according to the distance (which determines the fuel consumption) and the hours the driver has to work. In such a case, a price for each hiring can be calculated from:

- the total variable cost: fuel, wages, etc.,
- a proportion of the fixed costs (coach depreciation and maintenance plus office overheads) based on the expected workload of the company, and
- a margin for profit.

Nevertheless, the price has to be competitive or the hirer will go elsewhere. When the National Bus Company was privatized in the 1980s, the new independent companies looked to enter the private hire market but had to renegotiate lower wage rates with their drivers to compete effectively.

Break-even point

A coach tour contains a mixture of fixed and variable costs. The company's overheads and the costs of owning and maintaining the coach remain whether it goes anywhere or not. Once a decision is taken to run the tour the costs of fuel, drivers' wages and expenses also become fixed. In addition there are the variable costs per passenger of accommodation and meals (assuming that the company can cancel its bookings without penalty). Figure 12.1 illustrates this. The fixed costs are £1,000. The variable costs are £50 per person for accommodation, etc. A 50-seat coach will have a maximum cost of £3,500 if it is full, which works out at £70 per passenger. How much should the company charge? To help to decide, the chart can be used to calculate the *break-even point*, that is, the point at which the revenue covers the costs. A price of £75 would mean that the tour would break even when 40 seats were sold. A price of £100 would mean a break-even point at 20 seats. Which price the company chooses will depend on the likely demand and the competition.

Marginal costing

The tour price might have to be set over 18 months in advance in order to include it in the season's brochure. What seemed an attractive price and a reasonable forecast of demand then may become unrealistic as a result of political or economic changes unforeseeable at the time, or as a result of the actions of a competitor. The operator may find he is unable to sell enough seats to reach the break-even point.

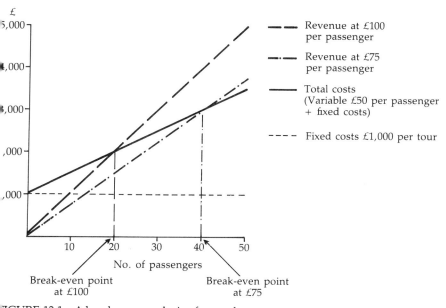

FIGURE 12.1   A break-even analysis of a coach tour.

In this situation, the *marginal cost* of carrying each addition‹
passenger becomes relevant. This is the additional cost of one extra unit, i
this case £50. Figure 12.2 illustrates how this is used to determine what pric
reduction to make in order to sell spare capacity. The price was set at £10‹
but only 15 seats were sold at this price. Rather than run the tour at a los
the unsold capacity was offered at £65. The marginal priced seats covered th
variable costs and made a contribution of £15 each to the fixed costs, as
result of which the tour broke even at 32 passengers and made a small prof
if the coach was full. Obviously, the lower price would have to be promote
differently, restricted to a particular group or sold through different channe
as part of a different package, since passengers who paid £100 would l
justifiably angry if they found themselves sitting next to someone who pai
£65 for exactly the same holiday.

This is a simplified example of a practice which is regularly used i
tour operating where the need to sell off unsold capacity cheap is almo‹
inevitable given the volatility of demand and the long timescales involved i
planning a tour. To avoid direct comparison, the various elements of th
tours – flights, hotels, duration, etc. – are repackaged to create a differei
and cheaper 'late-booking offer'. In theory, a distinction should be draw
between the strategic factors that determine the brochure price and th
tactical reasons for price reductions. In practice, the reductions are a
integral part of tour operating strategy, 'a near certainty if supply exceec
demand', as Middleton puts it.[6]

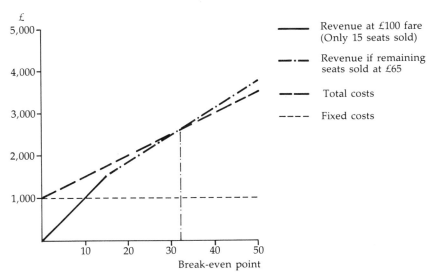

FIGURE 12.2   The break-even point of the coach tour with marginal pricing.

Entry pricing and secondary sources of revenue

Sometimes leisure organizations will offer prices at below even the marginal cost of the operation. Cross-Channel ferries in conjunction with national newspapers often have special day excursion fares, which are below the passenger taxes they have to pay the port authorities. This is done because once the passengers are on board ship they spend heavily in the bars, restaurants and duty-free shops. This practice is known as setting a *low entry price* in order to encourage *secondary spend*.

This secondary spend is an important factor in the profitability of most hotels, tourist attractions and leisure centres. The layout of the building and the route taken by visitors can be designed so that everyone has to pass through the gift shop and near the refreshment areas.

Low entry pricing is used by computer games manufacturers like Sega. Their MegaDrive games computer console is priced at £80, which is more affordable than a full personal computer. Children can save up for it or get it as a present. Once they have the MegaDrive, they then have to pay £40 each time they want to buy a new game.

CASE STUDY 12.1 *Pricing at EuroDisney*

One of the causes of the financial difficulties of EuroDisney in its first years of operation was the failure to get the combination of entry prices and secondary spend right.

The prices for admission to EuroDisney were set higher than those of their European competitors (Table 12.1) as it was assumed that Disney's unique reputation and the scale of the attraction made comparison irrelevant. There were few concessions and no seasonal reductions. It was also assumed that secondary spending would be at similar levels to the US

Table 12.1 Visitors to leading European theme parks, 1992

Theme park	Country	Admission charge (£)	Visitor numbers (millions)
Alton Towers	UK	14	2.6
Thorpe Park	UK	11	1.3
Chessington	UK	13	1.5
Total all UK parks			10.8
Futurescope	France	15	1.9
Asterix	France	17	1.7
De Efteling	Netherlands	11	2.7
Legoland	Denmark	9.50	1.3
EuroDisney	*France*	*28*	*11 target*

parks. As most Americans travel to the parks by car, Disney did not realize the importance of coach and tour operators in the European travel market, and so made little concession to the trade either in pricing, booking systems or facilities for coach drivers.

In reality, changes in the exchange rate of the franc against other European currencies, coupled with a Europe-wide recession, made EuroDisney prices seem expensive. Disney's publicity increased the public interest in theme parks, but many people chose to visit cheaper parks such as Asterix or Alton Towers, both of which enjoyed increased visitor numbers. Keenly priced packages to Florida made a visit to Disney World seem comparable in price to EuroDisney, which did not enjoy the same climate (Table 12.2).

Table 12.2 Prices of inclusive tours to EuroDisney, Paris, and Disney World, Florida; prices for a family of four, 1992

	EuroDisney		Disney World	
	Total	Per day	Total	Per day
Outside resort				
Airtours	£636 b&b 7 nights	£91	£1,696 room 14 nights	£121
Thomson	£700 b&b 3 nights	£233	£1,848 room 14 nights	£132
Inside resort				
British Airways Holidays	£938 b&b 3 nights	£313	£2,898 room 7 nights	£414

Source: Travel News, 9 April 1992.

Only by offering special price reductions to local Paris residents (combined rail and admission tickets at below the normal admission price) did EuroDisney achieve its target of 11 million visitors in the first 12 months. This brought its own problems, with long queues on busy days, which did not create a sense of good value for money.

Although the admissions target in 1991/2 was met, the secondary spend was well below forecast. Having paid what appeared to be a high price to get into the park, visitors were reluctant to spend much more on food, souvenirs and merchandise. Many people walked considerable distances back to the car parks for a picnic rather than pay what they feared would be high prices in the catering outlets (visitors are forbidden to bring food or drink into the Magic Kingdom). As with the entry price, Disney's calculation of what customers would consider a value for money price turned out to be wrong, and per visitor spend was 25% down on their budget.

There were other factors contributing to the financial problems of EuroDisney (such as their inability to repay the capital costs by selling the resort hotels, and the high royalty charges to the US parent company), but the failure to get the right price structure and the resulting loss of secondary spend were major ones (in 1993, admission fees only amounted to 50% of the total revenue).

The management subsequently introduced a more flexible pricing policy with three seasonal bands and a variety of group, trade and age reductions. Prices of food and merchandise were also reduced. However, the initial perception that the park was overpriced persisted, and visitor numbers fell from 9.8 million in the first year to just 8.8 million in 1993/4 (see Table 12.3). The company reported a loss of 5.3 billion francs.

Table 12.3 EuroDisney results

	1992/3	1993/4
Visitor numbers[a]	9.8 million	8.8 million
Hotel occupancy		
October–March	37%	48%
April–September	72%	71%
Total	55%	60%
Expenditure per room	FFr 1,025	FFr 882
Total revenue	FFr 4.90 billion	FFr 4.15 billion
Theme park[b]		FFr 2.20 billion
Hotels		FFr 1.6 billion
Other (corporate deals and sponsorship)		FFr 0.32 billion

[a] During the 12 months to 30 September 1994.
[b] Theme park revenue is 50% admission fees, and the rest from car parks, food and merchandise.
Source: The Times, 4 November 1994.

In December 1994, EuroDisney announced a cut in its main season price for 1995 from 250 francs (about £30) to 195 francs (£23). This amounted to a 22% reduction on the entry price, and was estimated to equate to 5% of the company's revenue. It was aiming for a 700,000 increase in attendance as a result. 'Our prices were simply too high for the market, particularly with the economic recession in Europe at the present', said Steve Burke, the chief operating officer.

Analysts pointed out that the entry price cut probably had the effect of cutting the *overall* cost of visiting EuroDisney (including travel, overnight stay, food, drink and merchandise) by about 5%. 'The impact on customer thinking of a 5% change in the overall cost of a visit is unlikely, in our opinion, to generate a significantly higher rate of admissions', said Nigel Reed of Paribas Capital Markets.

Source: The Guardian, 15 December 1994 and numerous other press reports.

Inclusive charges or pay as you play?

Disney (see Case Study 12.1), along with British holiday centre operators like Butlins and Pontins, charge an inclusive price for admission and the use of all the rides, entertainment and activities. This is designed to create a sense of value for money in the customer's mind as well as saving the labour cost of collecting money on each ride.

Center Parcs holiday centres, aimed at higher socio-economic groups, charge extra for many of the sporting facilities on the basis that not everyone will want to use all of them.

Many health and fitness clubs operate on a membership basis, as do most private golf, tennis and squash clubs. For an annual fee, members can use the facilities, and the bar and restaurant, as often as they like. As well as reducing the cost and inconvenience of paying each time, it gives members a sense of belonging and exclusivity and encourages them to make good use of the facilities, while giving the club a guaranteed income in advance.

The disadvantage of inclusive charges is that a potential member has to make an immediate commitment and pay a considerable sum of money, which will deter those who are only casual visitors. They are more likely to be attracted to a centre where they can try out an activity on a 'pay as you play' basis. Similarly, in travel it may be better to quote a lower fare for the journey and then charge extra for meals, entertainment and sleeping accommodation, than to charge a higher inclusive fare.[7]

A middle way between membership and 'pay as you play' could be to offer a price for a course of instruction or programme of exercise which may or may not lead on to further commitment. The Littledown Centre in Bournemouth, while operating a general pay as you play policy, encourages regulars to buy a reduced price monthly pre-payment ticket. For the cardiovascular exercise machines customers can buy an electronic swipe card for a given length of time which allows them to use the machine as often and for whatever length of session suits them until the card runs out.

Joining fees

Many clubs, societies and professional bodies charge a joining fee on top of the first year's subscription. It is sometimes justified as a way of covering administration costs, but is really a means of discouraging people from letting their membership lapse in future years, or from switching between clubs, since if they subsequently apply to rejoin they will have to pay the joining fee again. It also enables the club to waive the fee as a sales promotion! That people are prepared to pay joining fees is an expression of the value they place on membership.

Trade pricing

As well as a published price structure for the public, leisure and tourism organizations have another set of prices which are available only to those in the travel trade. This may be seen as another form of discriminatory pricing.

Bulk purchase pricing

To encourage group visits, there will probably be a *group rate*. This may be a single price for parties of more than a specified number, or a sliding scale of reductions according to the size of the group. A ratio of free places to paying customers may be offered as well as or instead of the group reductions.

These group rates would be available to any group organizer, such as voluntary leaders of social clubs, scouts, guides, and the like. Commercial group organizers such as coach companies and tour operators are likely to be given further reductions designed to encourage them to develop, and promote, a programme of visits. An example is the *ITX* (inclusive tour excursion) rate offered by airlines and ferry companies. This will be for an agreed allocation of seats on an agreed number of dates, often with additional reductions subject to the agreed target being exceeded. The tour operator often pays a deposit to secure the allocation of seats, and becomes liable for the full rate on any seats not released back by an agreed date. The transport company has the benefit of selling a large number of seats in one transaction, but has to be careful not to allocate too much space to ITX business. Over-dependence on reduced-rate business will reduce the overall revenue yield, and pass control of the marketing of the service to third parties, making it difficult for the carrier to increase prices when needed.

Coach group visits to attractions are often arranged not by the company but by the drivers, who will choose the attractions which offer them the best incentives. These may include meals, a set fee, or a percentage of the amount spent by the passengers in the gift shop. The costs of these incentives will have to be built into the prices charged to the passengers.

Commission to agents

If the organization decides to use retail agents to sell its tickets, it will have to negotiate a percentage commission to pay on each sale the agent makes. Such agents include travel agents and theatrical agencies, the latter often dealing with sporting events as well as plays, films, shows and concerts. In travel, the standard commission is 10%, but with the supply of tour products exceeding the display space available, agents are often able to negotiate 'over-rides' of an extra 2.5 or 5% from operators. This may be subject to their achieving an agreed sales target. Free or reduced-rate holidays for the agency staff may also be offered as incentives to reach sales targets. The relationship between operators and agents will be discussed in Chapter 13. Whatever is agreed, the cost of paying commission has to be allowed for in the budget and included in the tour price.

Pricing tactics

This chapter has concentrated so far on the strategic decisions that are taken to create a price structure for the organization. This structure may be altered for short-term tactical reasons in response to fluctuations in demand or competitors' actions.

According to Holloway and Plant, tactical discounting can be divided into regular discounting (for early booking or payment, for bulk purchase, or to clear unsold capacity) and special sales promotions offering money off for a limited period.[8] There is, however, a danger in regarding discounting as merely a tactical issue. If the price is regularly discounted, customers come to expect the reduction and may then be reluctant to pay the full price. The reduction is then in effect part of the pricing structure. For this reason, trade, bulk and seasonal prices should be planned and budgeted for at the same time as the full 'brochure' price, as we have indicated in this chapter.

Discounting unsold capacity can also become expected, as happened a long time ago with the January sales in the shops, and is in danger of happening with 'late savers' and the like in the travel agencies. Customers delay buying at the full price in the near-certain hope of getting a bargain later. To minimize the loss of full-price revenue, the discounts should be carefully limited in time and conditions, in other words, treated as sales promotions. We will examine the tactics of sales promotion in Chapter 17.

Psychological pricing

If the price must match the customers' perceived value of the product on offer, then the way the price is presented has to be judged carefully. A simple and common example of psychological pricing is the use of £49.99 instead of £50 in the hope that this will be perceived as less expensive. In contrast, any discount offered has to be large enough to be seen as a worthwhile bargain, a concept sometimes labelled the JND (just noticeable difference). Then there is the question of what price the discount has been deducted from. In some cases the full price may be deliberately set high to allow retailers or salesmen to offer what appear to be generous discounts at the right psychological moment in the negotiations.

The headline price, the one quoted in large type on the advertisement, in the window, or on the cover of the brochure, is often the cheapest on offer, allowing the claim 'from only £29', even though the average price may be considerably more. Headline prices usually ignore the extra costs which the consumer has to pay to obtain the whole experience. With a computer this could include delivery and installation, the software, a printer and perhaps a joystick for playing games. With a holiday, it might include transport to the airport, insurance, excursions and, of course, the holiday spending money. Some package prices recognize this and quote an all-inclusive price to emphasize the competitiveness of the offer. Discriminatory prices may be disguised by repackaging, including more or fewer elements in order to avoid direct comparison.

The presentation of prices must comply with consumer protection legislation such as the Trades Descriptions Act, the Unfair Contract Terms Act and the Misleading Advertising Terms Act as well as voluntary codes of practice covering advertising and sales promotion. The essence of these is that the customer must be made aware of the full cost and terms of the offer before purchase.

Summary

Price is ultimately determined by the market; in other words, by what the consumer is prepared to pay, how important and necessary the purchase is, and what the alternatives offered by competitors would cost. This is particularly true in leisure where no activity or product can be regarded as essential and demand is therefore directly affected by price. Price plays a central role in marketing strategy, as a means of obtaining competitive advantage and of communicating the positioning of the product in terms of its quality and its target markets. The first pricing decision is therefore which broad range to choose – for example, between budget, three-star and five-star standards of service.

Within this range, the prices may be above or below those of competitors according to the objectives of the company and the stage of the product life cycle. There is also likely to be a range of prices aimed at different market segments, in a discriminatory price structure designed to achieve the optimum revenue yield on each occasion.

This revenue yield has to make a profit over the costs of the operation (taking into account any subsidy or sponsorship revenue provided in return for the wider social, cultural or economic value of the service). The organization needs to know the fixed variable and marginal costs of its activities in order to determine the overall revenue target for the various elements of its price structure. Ultimately, the organization has to deliver the service at the market price, reducing costs if necessary in order to do so, or get out of the market.

Discounting, often regarded as a short-term tactic, has become an inescapable part of many sectors of leisure and tourism, and therefore needs to be considered in the pricing strategy. The way prices are presented must take account of consumer psychology, balancing the consumer's desire for a bargain with their understanding of the overall cost of the total experience they are purchasing.

Notes

1. For an account of the development of package tourism see Renshaw, M.B. (1992) *The Travel Agent*, pp. 57 ff.
2. Porter, M.E. (1980) *Competitive Strategy*, p. 34.
3. Baker, M. (1985) *Marketing: An Introductory Text*, p. 256.
4. Middleton, V. (1994) *Marketing in Travel and Tourism*, p. 95.
5. Ford, H. (1923) *My Life and Work*, Levitt, T. (1960) 'Marketing myopia', *Harvard Business Review*.
6. Middleton (1994) *op. cit.*, p. 95.
7. See Morgan, M. (1990) 'Moving ferries up market', *International Journal of Physical Distribution Management*, 20(5), for an example of a high inclusive price which acted as a deterrent.
8. Holloway, C. and Plant, R. (1992) *Marketing for Tourism*, p. 94.

13 Place: Getting your product to the market, or vice versa

Product, promotion and price are relatively self-explanatory elements of the marketing mix, which all happen to start with the letter P. To find the fourth element of his now-famous 'four Ps', McCarthy had to be a little ingenious. 'Place' in his terminology does not simply stand for the place where the product is sold, but for 'the whole process of making the product available and accessible to potential customers'.[1] This process very often involves intermediaries who provide a distribution channel by which the product is moved from the manufacturer to the consumer.

Distribution is not the most glamorous part of marketing, but it is arguably the most important. All the rest of the marketing effort to persuade customers to buy is wasted if they cannot find the product on sale, if the telephone lines are always busy, or if the retailers recommend a competitor's product. Like drainage channels, distribution channels can be taken for granted until there is a blockage and the sewage comes back up the plughole into the sink.

Distribution channels

Figure 13.1 shows the standard distribution channel of manufacturer, wholesaler and retailer, and some leisure and tourism examples. It could be argued that in tourism the tour operators are manufacturers and the accommodation, transport and attractions are the supplies of raw materials.

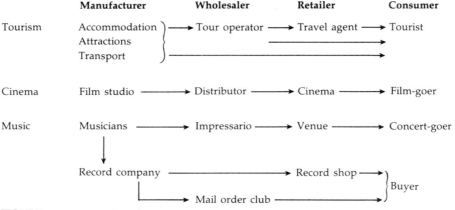

FIGURE 13.1   Examples of distribution channels in leisure.

What really matters is that the product, the experience which the tourist pays for, is the end result of the work of a chain of different organizations. This is sometimes called the value-added chain. Each organization adds extra value. Each depends on the others, and all impact on the quality of the end product. The relationships within the chain need to be marketed as carefully as the relationship with the final customer.

In some fields of leisure, the channels are less obvious. (This may be why Leadley, in his book *Leisure Marketing*, aimed at ILAM members in public sector leisure centres, does not cover place or distribution at all.) Marketing channels can convey not only the product itself but also information, promotional material, reservations and payments.[2] A manager of a leisure organization must concern himself with three key questions:

- Where can potential customers get information?
- Where can they make bookings and buy tickets?
- How accessible is the location where the experience is enjoyed?

Let us illustrate this by the example of a small leisure attraction – a local museum.

Information channels could involve distribution of leaflets to tourist information centres, hotels, pubs and cafes, either by the organization itself or through a distribution agency. Normally these outlets do not sell tickets, but they may need to be motivated by offers of complimentary tickets or reciprocal arrangements.

Sales outlets could include coach operators and tour operators, or their drivers and resort representatives, who might expect to receive commission for the business they bring to the attraction.

Telephone enquiry and reservation systems would be needed even by a small attraction. Potential customers will want to know about opening hours and prices before travelling, and school groups, for example, may want to book guided tours and talks. An attraction's reservation system would probably be a simple diary, but in other leisure sectors a more complex system would be needed. Major museums such as the Pompidou Centre now offer pre-booking for popular exhibitions to allow customers to avoid queuing by agreeing to come at specific times.

Payment systems. Groups may want to pay in advance or on account. People today are used to paying for everything by credit card. The attraction that insists on individual cash payments is inconveniencing its customers and may lose business as a result.

Access to the museum is also important. Customers need to be able to find the museum, park their cars and coaches, or get close using public transport. They will want to enter it without undue queuing, especially if the queue is in the open air. In a busy city location this may be difficult to achieve, but at least customers can be given advice on parking and public transport in the publicity leaflet. Good signing can not only help customers who have decided to visit but also attract other passers-by. The Abbotsbury sub-tropical gardens enjoyed an increase in visitors from 55,000 to 80,000 a year after a signpost was erected at the junction with the main coastal tourist route near their site.

Location. The location of the museum will determine its catchment area and the ease of access. Often, museums are located in historic buildings in the heart of conservation areas and therefore have little choice but to market the existing location as effectively as possible. Other organizations are less tied. Supermarkets are moving out of town centres to sites with ample car parking near major road systems, and other retailers such as travel agents have to follow them. The neighbourhood analysis systems described in Chapter 8 can identify the sites with the best catchment area of their target customers.

Leisure centres are showing similar trends. Doncaster Council opened its new leisure centre, the Dome, on an out-of-town site where it has been joined by a Warners Multiplex cinema, a bowling centre and fast-food outlets (see also Case Study 10.3: Tower Park, Poole). Southampton Football Club are proposing to move from their traditional city centre ground, the Dell, to a larger site with better road access, where the football stadium will form part of a community leisure complex. While these kind of moves may be in the short-term interest of the organizations and their car-owning customers, there are longer-term issues for the state of city centres and the environment.

The use of intermediaries

The simplest form of distribution is to sell direct to the customer, a single level channel. For a leisure centre or health club with a purely local market this may be the best or indeed the only choice.

Once a decision is made to target people beyond the immediate catchment area, the organization will have to consider finding other sales outlets. Nightclubs in small towns in Dorset and Somerset sell tickets through local coach companies who bring people in from 20 or 30 miles around. For a tour operator or a West End theatre, having an efficient system of information distribution, agency sales, telephone bookings and payments is essential to survival. The purpose of such a 'multi-level' channel is, as Middleton put it, 'to extend the number of points of sale or access away from the location where the service is performed'.[3]

Middleton also identifies a second function which is to 'facilitate the purchase of the product (e.g. tickets) in advance'. In the case of the night-club, advance purchase reassures customers travelling from a distance that they will not be turned away at the door because the club is full when they get there. It also helps the organizers anticipate the demand for coaches and plan accordingly. People who apply in advance for a fully-booked date can be offered alternatives. If they just turn up, they will go away disappointed.

If the purchase is made well in advance, as in the case of a package holiday, the company has the use of the money to earn interest. Some tour companies have relied heavily on this interest to supplement their narrow profit margins.

Choosing the channel

The target market

The choice of distribution channel depends on the target markets the organization wishes to reach. As we said in Chapter 7, the organization needs to research and understand the decision process of their consumers, part of which is the information-search stage.[4] The questions the organization needs to ask are:

- *Where do customers normally look for information on this type of product?* Do they visit the travel agent or the tourist information centre, or look at the holiday pages of the Sunday papers, the leaflets in the hotel lobby, or the 'what's on' page of the Friday night local paper? Wherever they look, that is where the publicity material needs to be.

- *When and where do customers make the decision?* Is there a conscious search, an extended problem-solving process, or is the decision taken on impulse? In the latter case, well-placed publicity and an attractive, well-signed exterior will be important.

- *Who influences the decision?* Do customers come into the travel agency already knowing what they want to buy or do they take the advice of the agent? Once on holiday do they decide individually what to do each day, or do they take excursions pre-arranged by the tour company? Is the excursion decided in advance by the tour company or is it left to the coach driver to take passengers to the attractions which give him the best commission?

The comparative costs of using the channels

The use of intermediaries or agents has clear benefits for the producer, but it also creates additional costs, which must be paid for out of the sales revenue from the customers. The costs involved in both options need to be compared before the decision is made. Table 13.1 shows a comparison of direct selling and using agents (assuming both methods need a computer reservation system and reservations staff).

The direct selling tour operator Tjaereborg used the advertising slogan 'Cut the cost of your holiday. Cut out the travel agent'. They also put a poster in the arrivals area at Gatwick Airport which read 'If you haven't been with Tjaereborg, we hope you enjoyed your holiday. You certainly paid too much for it'. Other tour operators build the cost of paying 10–15% commission to agents into the price of the holiday. Broadbent demonstrates that this cost exceeds the additional advertising costs needed to sell direct to the public, and enabled Tjaereborg to charge lower prices.[5]

Nevertheless, as mentioned in Chapter 9, nearly 90% of overseas package holidays from the UK are bought through travel agents.

The value added by the channel members

The extra costs must therefore be justified either in terms of the additional business the organization will gain or the additional value the customers will gain. Welburn suggests a number of reasons why this should be so.[6] To the

Table 13.1 Comparative costs of direct and agency distribution

Additional costs of direct selling	Additional costs of using agents
Consumer advertising	Trade advertising
Consumer promotions	Trade promotions
Staff to respond to customer enquiries and requests	Sales representatives to visit agencies
	Computer links to central reservations systems
Postage to customers	Bulk supplies of brochures
Wastage of brochures in direct mailing	Wastage of brochures not racked
	Educational and incentive trips
	Commission

producer, in this case the tour operator, the use of an intermediary such as
travel agent offers:

- *Wider coverage*: brochures displayed in up to 7,000 high street shops.
- *Local selling*: the travel agent talks to the customer face to face an
  can choose the best product, and the most effective sales message, fo
  each individual.
- *Advance purchase*: if the customer books in advance through a
  agent, the operator gets the money earlier and can earn interest on i
  In other sectors, such as sportswear, the retailer pays for his stoc
  when he orders it rather than when he sells it.
- *Stockholding*: the brochures are held in the travel agency, th
  sportswear in the sports shop, rather than taking up storage space i
  the producer's premises.
- *Lower administrative costs*: the travel agent deals with questions an
  problems that would otherwise involve the operator in addition.
  work. Direct selling operators employ enquiry staff specifically t
  provide after-sales reassurance.

To the final customer, using a travel agent or local retailer has the followir
advantages:

- *Local purchase*: it is more convenient to book the holiday during
  regular shopping trip, and all the elements of the holiday (insuranc
  passports, currency, the journey to the airport) can be bought at th
  same time – an example of what is known as 'one-stop-shopping'.
- *Local reputation*: it is reassuring to know that if anything went wron;
  there would be someone responsible with a local reputation t
  maintain who would therefore have an interest in settling the clai
  amicably. The brand of the retailer may be better known than that c
  the producer.
- *Comparison*: customers can collect several brochures at one visit an
  choose the one that best suits their needs.
- *Demonstration*: in a sports shop, the customer can try out th
  equipment. A travel agent will be able to give expert advice, look u
  information on the resort, or show a video.

Middleton points out that the biggest drawback to direct selling methods i
travel lies in their limited capacity to secure last-minute bookings. One of th
major roles of the travel agent has become that of a late-booking centre. Th
latest bargains on unsold capacity are available to them on computer link
with the tour operators, and a selection are advertised in the windows. Th
public know where to look for a cheap, short-notice holiday. The addition.
sales this gains for the operator may be crucial to profitability. To achieve th

me result by a mailshot or press campaign would be slower, more xpensive and difficult to target.

he bargaining power of the channel members

ne producer can only gain the advantages listed above if his product is splayed and recommended by the retailer. He must market and sell his roduct to the retailer before he can reach the public. Trade marketing, like onsumer marketing, begins with understanding the needs of the customer, this case the retailer. What a retailer needs are:

Iaximum profits per shelf space
his will be achieved by stocking products that sell well and which give a igh profit margin to the retailer. In travel, this means products that offer igher rates of commission. While the standard rate is 10%, many operators fer 12.5% or more to agents who achieve agreed sales targets.

atisfied customers
his means choosing the right products for the local market. It also means loosing reputable brands with proven records of reliability and quality.

tress-free staff
he retailer expects regular supplies of the product (or brochures), simple ccounting procedures, prompt payment, and no complaints from istomers. The producer should also offer training (e.g. familiarization isits) and incentives for reaching sales targets.

orporate identity
hops today are carefully designed to create a unified brand image for the etailer. Producers' displays will only be acceptable if they harmonize with iis image. There is a growing trend towards retailers' own brands. ainsbury's brand offers as credible a guarantee of consistency, reliability nd quality as any manufacturer's brand. Thomas Cook sell holidays which re packaged by other operators but are sold under their own brand name.

ravel agency chains have lists of preferred operators whose products are iven display space. Often the branches are told exactly where on the shelves ach brochure should be displayed. In the 1980s Pickfords Travel had a 'gold st' of preferred operators. To be included on this list, the operator had to:

- offer a value for money product,
- appoint and support all Pickfords' branches,
- offer additional commission or a promotional support package, and
- offer a year-round range of products.

While Pickfords consulted every level of the company, counter staff opinio was more likely to get an existing operator removed (for poor-qualit service) than a new one added. The final decision was made by fou directors of the company. Justifying their policy, a director said, 'This allow our counter staff to develop a far higher level of product knowledge. If yo sell everything, you end up knowing nothing.'[7]

It will be obvious from this example that it will be the majc companies, with a record of high-volume sales, well-known and truste brand-names and the resources to offer incentives, who will dominate th preferred lists. Indeed, as we saw in Chapter 9, the main multiple trav agencies are each owned by or allied to a major tour operator. A sma specialist operator would find it difficult to gain space in these agencies. I distribution options would be to use the independent agents whose policy is 1 offer a wider choice than the multiples, or to use direct marketing methods.

The tour operators also have their needs, especially the need to mak effective use of expensive brochures. The leading long-haul operator Kuor produce over a million copies of their main Worldwide brochure at a cost c £1.50 each. They carefully monitor the performance of their agents in tern of the ratio of brochures received to bookings made, and use this as th basis of the allocation for the next year:

- 14 top performing agencies achieve a ratio of 32:1 and are sent 2(brochures.
- 1,000 agents achieve 40:1 and are sent 50 brochures.
- The remaining 2,000 appointed agents average 90:1 and are sent 1 brochures.

Kuoni do not supply brochures to every ABTA agent (of which there a over 7,000 in the UK). They operate a *selective* distribution system rather tha an *intensive* one. In Germany until recently tour operators distributed on a *exclusive* basis to agencies belonging to the same group of companies an stocked only their products.

Control of the distribution channels

In choosing the channel, the producer must decide whether using th retailers involves an unacceptable loss of control over how the product marketed. This control can affect the product itself or the promotional an distribution mix. Films made in Britain have to use American stars or aday the script to make it accessible to an international audience throug American-owned distributors. Travel agents expect to be given exclusiv rights to sell the products and take strong exception to the operator usir other methods such as direct response advertising or deals with credit car companies.

Theatres selling tickets to coach operators and short-break operators must balance the benefits of having someone else promote and sell their shows for them with the risks of allocating too many seats at reduced prices for speculative bookings. If the operator fails to sell the allocation, the theatre may be landed with unsold tickets when it is too late to resell them. Also, if the theatre becomes too dependent on the operators, they may use their bargaining power to hold down prices, and reduce the overall revenue yield of the theatre. As we saw in previous chapters, this is what has happened in the relationship between Mediterranean hotels and the major tour operators.

Trends in distribution

The trends described above in travel are found in most retail sectors today:

- ownership is concentrated, with vertical and horizontal integration;
- the decision on what to stock is taken centrally;
- stocking is selective, with fewer brands and increasing tendency towards own-label brands.

The effect is retailer-led channels which favour own-brand products and high-mark-up mass market brands. An example of this would be the British cinema where five major chains (MGM, Warner, UCI, Odeon and Showcase) own 61% of all screens and receive 85% of the box-office revenue. Most have links with the big Hollywood studios or favour the mass-market Hollywood blockbuster films for their commercial appeal. As a result, small-budget British films find it difficult to reach an audience. Only 38% of British films made in 1992 went on general release, 29% went on the alternative art-house circuit and 33% were not screened at all.[8]

The logistics of the physical distribution of goods to retailers is a major concern to the manufacturers of tangible goods. The whole system is organized to minimize the storage of the goods, which instead move from the farm or factory through central depots to the supermarkets just in time to restock the shelves with fresh produce. These *just-in-time* systems depend on computerized monitoring of sales and stock levels. In service industries the speed and efficiency of the distribution process is achieved through electronic distribution of information.

As we saw in Chapter 12, tour operators and transport companies juggle the allocation of places and the prices charged to different market segments in order to achieve the optimum revenue yield. This inventory and yield management can be carried out with greater precision if the reservations computers are linked directly to computer terminals on the travel agents' counters, so that each transaction is instantly recorded. The link can be through the telephone system, or by faster and therefore cheaper systems such as the Istel network originally developed by the Midland Bank to link its branches, but which is now widely used by travel companies.

The major world airlines are combining to develop worldwide computer reservations systems (CRS) or global distribution systems (GDS). These offer the travel agent access not only to the CRS of the airlines themselves, but also to international hotel chains and car hire companies. Major cruise lines and tour operators have also linked with the GDS, making them as important in leisure as in business tourism. The travel agency's terminal is a full personal computer (PC) which can also be used for office management purposes. Other applications include automatic ticketing and invoicing, and video pictures of the hotels and resorts. The leading GDS systems are:

> *Amadeus*: Air France, Lufthansa, Iberia, SAS. Claims 60% of European CRS business.
>
> *Galileo*: British Airways, KLM, Alitalia, Swiss Air, Olympic, United, US Air. Dominant (80%) in UK, 30% of US and 40% of European markets.
>
> *Sabre*: American Airlines. 45% of US market. Some 500 UK outlets.
>
> *Worldspan*: Delta/TWA/North West Airlines, and ABACUS group of seven airlines. Links with American Express. 15% of US market. 500 UK terminals.[9]

The development of electronic distribution has a number of implications:

- The cost creates a *barrier to entry* to the travel industry, which strengthens the positions of the major companies.
- Smaller organizations have little alternative but to use the systems owned and controlled by major international companies, with consequent *loss of control*. There need to be safeguards that the owners do not use their position to manipulate the system to channel bookings towards their own flights, to spy on their rivals' business or to poach their customers (cf. the current dispute between Virgin Atlantic and British Airways).
- The systems are potentially open to *wider use* by non-travel organizations and individuals. Businesses with large travel budgets may choose to make their bookings direct rather than through a travel agent. It is also technically possible for operators and hotels to be booked direct by individuals with a PC and modem in their own homes. Major hotel chains now have sites on the Internet which make electronic brochures and booking forms available to millions of users.

How quickly direct booking via computer becomes common practice will depend on how many households acquire the equipment for other purposes, such as working from home or shopping for other more frequent goods and services. No one is going to acquire the equipment simply to book the annual holiday. Many people will still prefer to entrust their booking to the advice and expertise of a reputable travel agent rather than to sift through a mass of offers on their computer screen at home. The travel agents will, however, need to market their 'added value' convincingly to retain their customers.

CASE STUDY 13.1   *Distribution channels in sport*

If distribution is taken to encompass the whole process of making the product available and accessible to potential customers, then the distribution system whereby spectator sports are made available to a live and a media audience is more complex than the classic producer–wholesaler–retailer model. A suggested model is shown in Figure 13.2.

For a sport to thrive there must be a substantial number of players at the grassroots level, playing for enjoyment and recreation in local clubs, or at school. Without them there would be nowhere for the stars of the future to learn the game, and no one to buy the equipment and other merchandise associated with the game, or to attend the big matches. Once the sport is established it will be possible to market it to a wider audience, particularly on TV, and to export it to other countries; but unless there is a solid base of dedicated support the initial interest will soon wither, as has happened so far with attempts to export soccer to the US, American football to Europe, or Rugby League to Wales.

If a sport wishes to attract paying spectators, it needs to consider their needs as well as those of the players. Spectator sport offers benefits closer to entertainment than to recreation. The core benefit is the excitement that comes from not knowing what will happen next – what Rottenberg calls 'uncertainty of outcome'.[10] A sporting contest fulfils the same basic human need as the telling of a story in a book, film or play. Just as the author of a novel attempts to make the story more exciting by making the reader identify with the characters and by emphasizing the wider significance of the outcome, so too does the sports industry. The single match is made more significant by being part of a series, a league championship or knock-out cup competition. On the result depends promotion or relegation, or the Cup. This adds value to the match, thereby increasing the demand for tickets.

If the match is the product for which the spectators pay, then the distribution system includes the players, the team or club, the tournament organizers and the sport's governing body.

The players are economic units in themselves. They supply the spectators' need for heroes (and villains), sporting role-models and lifestyle symbols. They enhance the appeal of the contest and the value this adds is expressed in the appearance fees, prize money, and transfer fees they earn.

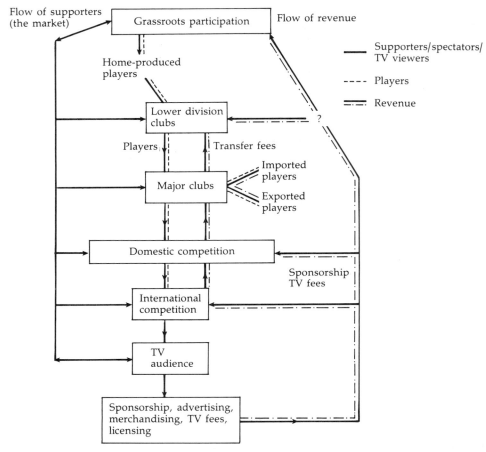

FIGURE 13.2   The distribution and value-added chain in a spectator sport. Grassroots participation and TV watching sustain each other. Grassroots participation is the source of supply for professional players. Revenue from sponsors, etc., depends on the TV audience. This revenue goes back into the international and domestic competitions, mainly to major clubs. The major clubs get players either from the lower clubs or from abroad. The lower clubs depend on transfer fees to survive.

Even in individual sports like tennis, athletics or motor-racing, they need the team managers and tournament organizers to create the occasion to give significance to their performance, just as the organizers need them to draw the crowds. This symbiotic relationship sometimes results in tension, as seen in the relationship between Nigel Mansell and the Williams team, John McEnroe and the Wimbledon tournament, or the industrial dispute between the star players and American baseball clubs. As in all distribution channels the needs and wants of each member have to be met to the satisfaction of all.

In team games, the domestic competition between leading clubs is the basis of commercial spectator sport. It is the clubs who employ the players and develop their abilities. The club offers its supporters the satisfaction of their need to belong to something that gives them a sense of identity, as is celebrated in most football chants. The success or failure of their team provides a continuing soap-opera-like story, and forms a regular topic of social conversation. In exchange, the club receives revenue from admissions, from catering at matches and from sales of merchandise in the team's colours. At the top level, Manchester United earn 30% of their revenue from merchandising that exploits their brand image – scarves, replica kit, etc.[11] (see Table 13.2).

Table 13.2   Manchester United FC, annual accounts 1991/2 and 1993/4

	1991/2	1993/4
Average match attendance	35,000	43,000
Sales	£20.1 million	£43.8 million
Pre-tax profits	£5.1 million	£10.8 million
Transfer reserve fund (net transfer spending 1992/3: £3.99m)		£4.8 million
Net assets (£million)		
Excluding players (12)	14.7	15.4
Valuation of players	24	20 (12)
Sources of income (£000)		
Gate receipts	11,142	17,920
Television	1,843	3,959
Sponsorship and advertising	2,756	4,693
Merchandising, etc.	2,705	14,232
Catering and conferences	1,699	3,011

Increasingly, this revenue is supplemented by income from sponsors and advertisers who support the club as a means of reaching a target market and of associating their brand name with the emotional values of the game and the team. The star players are particularly effective as advertising symbols that are instantly recognizable and attractive, and so can command large fees.

The revenue-earning potential of the club depends on its success on the field. Well-established clubs like Manchester United and Tottenham Hotspur can survive short-term failure because of the brand loyalty of their fans, but they need to remain in the top division to retain this in the long term. Success in the domestic competition also brings extra earning potential by gaining a place in European competitions. To remain at the top of the game, the clubs revitalize their 'product' by buying new players. These come mainly from the lower-division clubs who depend for their financial survival on developing young players and then selling them on at higher prices to the bigger clubs, a clear example of a value-added chain.

While Blackburn Rovers have bought their success in the Premier Division by spending £6.84 million net in 1991/2, Crewe Alexandra generated nearly half a million pounds in net transfer income.[12] AFC Bournemouth in 1991/2 only remained solvent by selling players to higher clubs (Table 13.3).

Table 13.3   AFC Bournemouth annual accounts 1991/2

Average match attendance	4,454
Annual turnover	£876,000
(season tickets and gate receipts)	
Other operating income	£501,000
(donations, advertising sponsorship, etc.)	
Net operating deficit	(£276,000)
Net transfer income 1992/3	£671,000[12]

The other main source of income for the sport comes from television. The attractions of sport that we have identified can draw a large TV audience at comparatively low cost to the station. This in turn enables the station to attract advertisers, and also sponsorship for the broadcast, the team and the players (Ryan Giggs is sponsored by Nike; his team, Manchester United, are sponsored by Sharp, and play in the Premiership sponsored by Carling, which is shown on BSkyB satellite television in broadcasts sponsored by Ford).[13] Satellite TV stations like BSkyB try to outbid the public terrestrial channels for major sports coverage, such as Premiership football, international cricket and Rugby Union, in order to attract subscribers to their 'pay-to-view' channels.

The TV audience is attracted mainly by international sport – cricket test matches, rugby's Five Nations Championship, Golf Open Championships and the Ryder Cup, Wimbledon tennis, etc. These are also the main sources of income for the governing bodies (each international match at Cardiff Arms Park brings the Welsh Rugby Union £6 million).

Particularly in team sports, the national teams draw their players from the grassroots through the distribution chain of the domestic club competition. Even in (nominally) amateur games like Rugby Union, players need to get taken on by the major clubs (Bath, Cardiff, etc.) in order to be noticed by the national selectors. In individual sports, too, promising tennis players and golfers need to be encouraged and coached by local clubs and then compete successfully in domestic championships in order to emerge on the international circuit.

The TV audience are the end-users of the distribution chain that starts with the youngsters playing in the local park. It is the TV audience that generates the profit on which the survival of the game depends.

As in all distribution chains, there are conflicts of interest and battles for control. The system encourages consolidation. The successful clubs attract the best players, both because they can pay the highest fees and because they provide the best chance of international recognition. This increases the chances of the same clubs always winning, e.g. Bath in Rugby Union, Wigan in Rugby League, Liverpool in football in the 1970s. This can reduce the 'uncertainty of outcome', and studies in America have shown that overall gate receipts in a league are higher when there is a close contest by several teams for the leadership than when one dominates.[14]

The market for players, and audiences, is becoming international. Jurgen Klinsmann joined Tottenham Hotspur for £2 million and Paul Gascoigne went to Lazio for a similar sum. These kinds of movements of top stars enhance the appeal of the top clubs and raise the standards of competition. There has been a tendency, however, for clubs to import foreign players of lesser reputation as a cheaper option to buying and developing domestic players, according to Gordon Taylor of the Professional Footballers' Association. 'The vast majority [of foreign players] have not made the grade and have been no better than our home-grown players. Millions of pounds have been lost into thin foreign air, and if this continues it may cause our natural full-time breeding clubs, those such as Crewe Alexandra, to collapse. On average the yearly transfer turnover is a credit balance of some £5–10 million to the lower division clubs. If this goes abroad it is a serious loss.'[15]

The other effect of imports in reducing the market for domestic products is to reduce the opportunity for international success. Football and cricket teams that rely on foreign stars for success and spectator appeal reduce the chances of native players developing to international standard and so weaken the strength of the national team, on which the financial success of the sports depend. Football may follow cricket in introducing 'protectionist' measures to limit the number of imported players in teams in domestic competitions.

Control of the distribution channel is contested between the clubs who want to retain their star players for domestic games, and the national governing bodies who want them released for training and playing for the national side.

The dependence of the sports on television and advertising revenue also gives the media interests bargaining strength which can be used to influence the way the game is marketed. The times of matches are set to suit the TV channels (Lennox Lewis fought Frank Bruno in Cardiff at one in the morning in order to suit American TV schedules; experiments have been made with football and rugby matches played in quarters to increase the opportunities for advertising breaks). The rules of the game are modified to increase spectator appeal (the sixth tackle rule in Rugby League; the fielding restrictions in one-day cricket; even a proposal after the 1990 World Cup in Italy to widen the soccer goal posts to increase the number of goals scored).

The way the game is presented is changed to make it more attractive (coloured clothing and name bands in one-day cricket on the initiative of Australian TV channel owner Kerry Packer). One of the most dramatic examples of a sport changing to meet the demands of a TV audience is the £75 million deal struck between Rupert Murdoch's satellite TV empire and the British Rugby League. Not only will the new league be formed by amalgamating some of the best known teams in the game, to the horror of supporters and traditionalists, but the whole competition will switch from winter to summer.

Most important of all is the question of how the money generated is channelled back into the sport. The TV revenues generally go to the sports governing bodies, who then make grants to the domestic game. The domestic competition is subsidized to varying extents in each sport. Somerset County Cricket Club received 46% of its income from the Test and County Cricket Board as their share of the profits made by Test and other international matches.[16] Manchester United earn 16% of their income from television and sponsorship – the amount they receive from Sky TV depending directly on their position in the league (see Table 13.2). Newport Rugby Club in South Wales earn 8% of their revenue from television and Heineken's sponsorship of the Welsh league competition, and another 18% from direct sponsorship and advertising.[17] In England, the Rugby Football Union is using £5 million income from Sky TV to make grants to clubs for improvements to their grounds. Some of the leading clubs are arguing that it should have been divided *pro rata* between the top clubs without conditions.[18] The leading rugby players, who devote increasingly large proportions of their time to the game, are also asking whether they should receive some direct benefit from the money their efforts generate. (At the time of writing, professionalism as a principle had been accepted by the Rugby Unions, but how it will apply to players below international level was very unclear.)

Some of this money then filters back into the grassroots through transfer fees, youth teams and other development activities undertaken by the clubs. The Lawn Tennis Association uses the profits from the Wimbledon championships to fund its development programmes and centres.

However, the grassroots facilities are threatened by cut-backs in local authority spending, the sale of playing fields for housing and other development, and the decline of sport in schools as teachers are less eager to work unpaid overtime to run sports teams after school and at weekends. The future of spectator sports depends on amateur clubs at the grassroots level encouraging participation and interest. The question must be asked whether some of the money spent on star players would in the longer term be better spent at a lower level of the distribution chain.

The model proposed in Figure 13.2 could be adapted to other sectors of leisure. Similar relationships between grassroots participation, local and national commercial venue managers/promoters, regulatory bodies, media companies and sponsors exist in the arts and entertainment industries, with similar flows of spectators/consumers, artists/performers, and revenue.

QUESTIONS

1   Identify the stages in the distribution chain for a particular sport. What value is added by each stage? Show how these stages are interdependent.

2   Use this analysis to discuss current concerns in that sport, e.g.

   ● Should county cricket have fewer one-day matches?

   ● Should there be a limit on the number of foreign players in football's Premiership teams, or in Rugby Union's Courage League One?

   ● To what extent can Rugby Union become a professional sport at club level?

   ● What are the implications of the decisions of the European Court of Justice that the present system of transfer fees for footballers is illegal?

3   Make a similar analysis of the distribution and value-added system in a field of the arts, e.g. music, painting, theatre and film, or publishing. How far do similar concerns as those identified for sport exist in this field? (e.g. concentration of outlets, over-dependence on imported talent, over-commercialization, lack of reinvestment at the grassroots, etc.).

Summary

Distribution is a vital but often neglected part of leisure marketing. Once an organization decides to target markets outside its immediate local catchment area it will need to consider using intermediaries, such as retailers or agents.

The choice of distribution channel will depend on the target market, the comparative cost of the channels and the value added by the channel members. Larger organizations can use their purchasing power to dictate terms to smaller members of the distribution channel and gain preferential treatment in retail outlets. Smaller organizations may therefore need to find alternative channels, such as direct selling, to reach their potential customers.

The concepts of distribution and issues such as control of distribution channels can be applied to analyze the relationships between performers, event promoters, sponsors and the media in sport, entertainment and the arts.

The trend in the high street towards retailer-led channels with a selection policy favouring high-yield mass market brands is mirrored by the increasing dominance in the film industry of the major cinema chains with links to US distributors and studios and by the growing influence of global TV magnates, such as Rupert Murdoch and Kerry Packer, on the organization of professional sport.

This last example also demonstrates the growing importance of distribution systems based on the electronic transmission of information and entertainment rather than the physical movement of goods or people. Leisure opportunities will be increasingly bought and consumed by people in their own homes without the need to traipse to the shop or venue.

Notes

1. Kotler, P. (1994) *Marketing Management*, p. 530.
2. *Ibid*, p. 527.
3. Middleton, V. (1994) *Marketing for Travel and Tourism*, p. 203.
4. Engel, J.F. Blackwell R.D. and Miniard P.W. (1990) *Consumer Behaviour*, p. 27 (see also Chapter 6 of this book).
5. Broadbent, S. (1984) *Twenty Advertising Case Histories*.
6. Welburn, H. (1987) 'Travel selling and distribution', *Travel and Tourism Analyst*, July, pp. 3–15.
7. *Travel Agency*, February 1986.
8. British Film Institute, *Film and TV Handbook 1995*.
9. Middleton (1994), *op. cit.*, p. 209.
10. Rottenberg, S. (1956), 'The baseball players' labour market', *Journal of Political Economy*, **63**, p. 243, quoted in Gratton, C. and Taylor, P. (1985) *Sport and Recreation: An Economic Analysis*. See also Cooke, A. (1994) *The Economics of Leisure and Sport*, p. 206.
11. *The Guardian*, 7 April 1994.
12. Boon, G. (1993) *Survey of Football Club Accounts*.
13. Carter, M. (1995) 'Sports sponsors play for a bigger stake in the game', *The Independent on Sunday*, 15 January.
14. Sloane, P. (1980) *Sport in the Market*. See also Corry, D. and Williamson, P. (1994) *A Game without Vision: The Crisis of English Football*.
15. *The Guardian*, 5 August 1994, p. 21.
16. Somerset County Cricket Club, *Annual Report 1994*.
17. Newport Athletic Club, *Annual Report 1993/4*.
18. Armstrong, R. (1994) 'Clubs upset as RFU keeps tight grip on £5m Sky cash', *The Guardian*, 29 November 1994, p. 23.

PART 4

The Promotional Mix in Leisure

14 Promotion

The promotional mix

Promotion is the final element of the marketing mix. If the product has been designed to meet the needs of the target market, priced competitively and made available in the right places, then it should be relatively easy to devise an effective promotional campaign. If not, then no amount of clever promotion can compensate.

To promote, according to the dictionary, means to encourage or advance something. Promotional activities include any actions designed *to encourage or advance the sales of the product or service* (the same techniques can of course also be used to encourage and advance non-commercial objectives such as health awareness, participation in sport, or the popularity of a political party).

Promotion achieves these objectives by communicating a message about the product to the target market. The marketer can choose from a number of means of communicating the message – advertising, sales promotion, publicity, personal selling and direct marketing – which form the *promotional mix* of the campaign. The message must then be carried to the prospective customers, either in person or through the media. The choice of media is sometimes referred to as the *communications mix*.

The promotional and communications mix decisions will be determined by the overall marketing strategy, as illustrated in Figure 14.1.

FIGURE 14.1   The relationship between promotion and marketing strategy.

Communications theory

If the message is to have the desired effect, it must be expressed in terms that the target audience will understand and respond to. Schramm's model (Figure 14.2) shows the elements of the communications process in terms of a TV transmission.[1] The picture is encoded into radio waves, transmitted through the air and decoded by the receiver.

This process takes place in face-to-face communication, such as a college lecture. The sender, the lecturer, chooses, from his comprehensive knowledge of the subject, words that will convey the subject in terms that his students will understand and relate to. This is the encoding process. The students do not write down every word he says, but try to pick out the key phrases for their notes. They are decoding the message. A good lecturer will watch his students to make sure they are listening, and, if necessary, slow his delivery to let them finish writing before he introduces the next topic. He is responding to feedback.

In a similar way, the advertiser chooses words and images that express the advantages of the product in ways that the particular audience will find interesting and memorable. To continue the radio analogy, the advertisement must be 'on the same wavelength' as the audience. A salesman talking face to face with a client can watch and listen to the client's reactions and modify his sales message accordingly. Non-personal communications such as advertising cannot receive such instantaneous

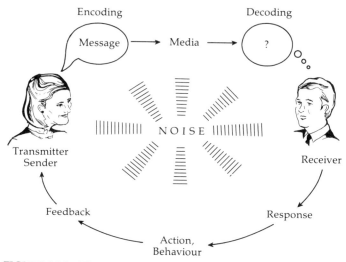

Encoding

Message

Media

Decoding

?

N O I S E

Transmitter
Sender

Receiver

Feedback

Response

Action,
Behaviour

FIGURE 14.2   The communication process.
Source: After Schramm (1961) *The Process and Effect of Mass Communication.*

feedback and so the advertiser must ensure, by research, planning and testing, that the message has been encoded correctly.

Using this model as a guide, we shall now look at each stage of the process. The discussion will use the word advertisement but the same principles apply to other forms of marketing communication.

The receiver

The receiver will decode the message by comparing it with what he already knows. If the message is totally unfamiliar or at variance with his existing knowledge and attitudes, he will reject it or ignore it – an effect known as cognitive dissonance (see Chapter 7). To avoid this danger, the advertiser must have a good understanding of the target market segment and design the message to appeal to their needs, preoccupations, interests, and attitudes. As we saw in Chapter 7, these will vary according to their age, sex, family status, lifestyle and cultural aspirations.

The message will also need to take into account the receiver's previous experience of the product category and of the particular brand. Rossiter and Percy divide the target market for a promotional campaign into four types:[2]

- New category users,
- Other brand users,

- Brand loyals,
- Brand switchers.

This division of the market is similar to the example of user segmentation given in Chapter 8. The message must be different for each type of user. A campaign for a health club, for example, may have as its objectives any of the following:

- to make non-users aware of the benefits of exercise;
- to make people who belong to another club aware of the superior facilities on offer;
- to change their attitudes to the club and its facilities;
- to persuade existing members to renew their subscriptions or to come more often.

Changing attitudes is more difficult, as discussed in Chapter 7, because of our resistance to ideas that do not fit into our existing experience and thought patterns. Rather than challenging them directly, advertisers have to appear to reinforce existing attitudes and then introduce an element of surprise that makes the receiver pause to think.

The response

How advertising works

Every day we receive hundreds or even thousands of promotional messages – mailshots in our morning post, adverts in our newspaper, posters we pass on the way to work, window displays in the shops, leaflets thrust at us in the street, and commercials on the radio and television as we try to relax in the evening. Research (quoted by Baker) proves that we remember only a small percentage of these messages.[3] Our minds screen out the vast majority of them as irrelevant and uninteresting. This process, known as selective perception, was described in Chapter 7.

The first task of an advertisement, then, is to attract *attention*. It can do so by design features such as size, colour, or position, by images or slogans that are unusual or intriguing, or by using a dramatic story or humour to entertain the viewer or reader. These features are designed to make the receiver notice the advertisement and so gain awareness of the product.

Even if the advertisement succeeds in gaining attention, it will not succeed in its objectives unless it also engages the receiver's *interest*. As Simon Broadbent says, the advertiser does not want the reader to say, 'What a good ad!', he wants her to say, 'What a good product!'[4] It must offer a solution to her problems, or satisfy her needs. The characters and situations depicted must be ones that she can identify with or aspire to. Otherwise she will mentally screen it out and forget it.

Advertisements must therefore contain relevant information. However, this is not likely to be enough to result in a sale except in the case of an already highly involved customer who is actively seeking to buy that type of product (see Chapter 5). Classified advertisements might work simply by informing those who are already looking that a certain item is for sale. Display advertisements also seek to persuade uncommitted readers of the benefits of the product. They appeal to the emotions in an attempt to create *desire* for the product. How they do this we shall discuss later.

Finally, the advertisement must create a response from the receiver. Interest and desire must be turned into *action*. It should say how and where the product can be obtained, or include a coupon, address or phone number for further information. It may also include an incentive for the customer to buy now, from that producer or dealer (rather than later from someone else) by means of some kind of sales promotion (see Chapter 17).

What we have described follows the *AIDA model* (attention, interest, desire and action) of the effects of advertising, first proposed by Strong.[5] Though undoubtedly over-simplistic, it is a memorable and useful checklist of the aims of advertising, and provides a good framework for other more complex theories.

All the models have as their basis the assumption that an effective advertisement makes the receiver *think* about the product, *feel* positively towards it, and *do* something to purchase it. Lavidge and Steiner labelled these the cognitive, affective and conative stages of the response.[6] The *cognitive* stage involves the rational conscious part of the brain, the *affective* stage involves the emotions, and the *conative* stage a resulting change in behaviour. To clarify the processes in each stage, Lavidge and Steiner distinguished between simple awareness and real knowledge of the product, and graded the affective response from mere liking, through preference, to conviction.

Rogers, looking at the role of advertising in the adoption of new products, argued that the effect of advertising is to interest the consumer enough to *evaluate* the merits of the product and then to give it a *trial* before adopting it.[7] This model is apt for the process by which someone decides to take up a new form of leisure activity. Broadbent, writing as a practising advertising agent, went further and said that it is often the trial and not the advertisement that convinces the customer to change her attitude to a product.[8]

The relationship between these models is shown in Figure 14.3. They are known as *hierarchies of effect models*, as they assume a progression from one stage to the next.

The PIECE process of Engel *et al.* has been included in the figure to demonstrate that these models have some validity as attempts to describe the

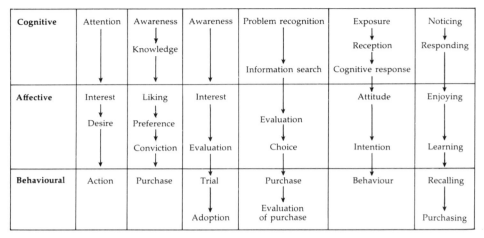

Cognitive	Attention	Awareness	Awareness	Problem recognition	Exposure	Noticing
	↓	↓ Knowledge ↓	↓	↓ Information search ↓	↓ Reception ↓ Cognitive response	↓ Responding ↓
Affective	Interest ↓ Desire ↓	Liking ↓ Preference ↓ Conviction ↓	Interest ↓ Evaluation ↓	↓ Evaluation ↓ Choice	Attitude ↓ Intention	Enjoying ↓ Learning
Behavioural	Action	Purchase	Trial ↓ Adoption	Purchase ↓ Evaluation of purchase	Behaviour	Recalling ↓ Purchasing

FIGURE 14.3   Hierarchical models of the response to advertising.
Source: Based on Kotler (1994) *Marketing Management,* p. 602.

changing mental states of a customer involved in an extended problem-solving process (see Chapter 7). In routine or impulse purchases of low-involvement products, the order may be reversed – the customer tries the activity, enjoys it and then decides to find out more about it – or the emotional and rational responses occur simultaneously.

The other weakness of these models is that they assume that the advertisement will result directly in a response. This is of course nonsense. Very rarely do we see an advertisement and immediately cut it out or write down the details, let alone rush out to buy the product. More often we forget about it until something reminds us of it. This can be a recognition of a need: 'Where shall we go tonight?' – 'What about that new place that was advertised in the *Echo*?'; or the sight of the logo on a packet on the shelves or the sign over the entrance: 'That's the one that's been in the adverts. Let's try it!'

Modern advertising practitioners see their task as creating a memorable image for the brand that will come to mind at the moment when the consumer has to choose between that brand and its rivals. If at that moment she remembers the message of the advertisement, it has succeeded. 'What ultimately counts isn't whether the consumer can remember the brand when shown the ad, but whether she remembers the ad when shown the brand', as the advertising research agency Millward Brown puts it.[9]

The final column in Figure 14.3 is a summary of contemporary thinking on the way advertising works. First, the advertisement must be noticed among all competing messages. The consumer must react to it, cognitively or emotionally. Most advertisements aim to entertain, as the process of enjoying makes learning more likely. The consumer's memory of the advertisement is then triggered by packaging, signing or point-of-sale display. Having recalled the advertisement and the enjoyment of it, the consumer is more likely to choose it from the alternatives on offer. In this model the cognitive and affective stages may happen simultaneously in response to the entertainment.

Learning and remembering

The way in which we learn and remember messages is therefore a key to the way advertising works. Learning by rote, or *repetition*, is a technique used in advertising as much as in an infants' school. A phrase, made easily memorizable by rhyme, alliteration, puns, music and other devices, is repeated again and again on TV or radio.

Another technique used in schools is *conditioning*. The child's good behaviour is reinforced by praise and bad behaviour is deterred by verbal or physical punishment. There are two types of conditioning used in promotion. One is *operant conditioning*, which reinforces customers' purchasing behaviour by extra benefits for heavy users, such as membership privileges or bulk discounts. For customers of services, staff can reinforce their decision to buy by treating them as valued customers and good friends. After-sales service, or simple tactics such as sending Christmas and birthday cards, can also help to condition them to think favourably of the organization.

The other form is *classical conditioning*. In this, the advertisement takes a natural emotional response to a stimulus, for example a cuddly young puppy, and links it with a product, for example a roll of toilet paper. After seeing the advertisement a few times, the customer becomes conditioned to associate the brand of paper with the lovable softness of the dog.

Returning to the analogy with schools, students are often given work which enables them to learn by solving a problem or completing an investigation for themselves. This is known as *cognitive processing*. The mental effort of working out the answer embeds the process in the memory. The more elaborate the process, the greater will be the learning, according to Engel *et al.*[10] Advertisers use this by setting the viewer or reader a little puzzle to solve in the form of a play on words, an unusual juxtaposition of images or a joke. Getting the joke involves the viewer in the advertisement and increases the likelihood that it will be remembered.

The message

As we saw in Chapter 9, companies spend considerable time and thought on their competitive strategy and brand positioning in order to give their brand a real advantage over its rivals. The advertisement has to convey the competitive strategy and brand positioning to potential customers in the 30 seconds of a radio or TV commercial, or the shorter time during which they glance at a press advertisement or billboard. With 100 words or less, the advertisement must create awareness, interest, desire and action, and implant the idea of the product in the memory. How can it gain the maximum impact in this short time? What should the message of the advertisement be?

Rosser Reeve said that the advertisement should concentrate on putting across the *unique sales proposition* (USP) of the brand. 'Each advertisement should say to each reader: "Buy *this* product, and you will get *this specific benefit"'*. The proposition should be one that the competition cannot or does not offer, and it should be so strong that it can move millions.[11] The problem with this prescription is that genuine USPs are very hard to find in a competitive free market. Most package holidays, most leisure centres and health clubs offer broadly similar facilities. Listing minor differences can make for boring advertisements. Only when there is something new to offer – a new destination, a new ride, a new activity – is the USP approach used effectively in isolation. Even then, the advantage may be short-lived. When Butlins relaunched their holiday camps, their Sunsplash fun pools with flume rides were a unique feature and a focus for their advertising. Now most urban dwellers in Britain have several fun pools within reach for a day out, Butlins' uniqueness lies not in any single feature but in the range of activities included in the price. Their advertising therefore seeks to convey an overall image of the centres under the brand name of Holiday Worlds, slogans such as 'The Excitement Continues', and a series of colourful action pictures.

As we have said in Chapter 10, in leisure what people are buying is an experience. They are therefore more likely to be persuaded by the kind of advertisement which creates an impression of the experience, one that appeals to the emotions rather than one that lists rational reasons to take part. The advertisement should aim to create what Ogilvy called a *brand image* or personality:

> Build sharply defined personalities for [the client's] brands and stick to them year after year. It is the total personality of the brand rather than any trivial product difference which decides the ultimate position in the market.[12]

The image is encapsulated in pictures and slogans, but should also be reinforced by the packaging, the signing and tangible appearance of the product, and by the style of service given. Each year different variations of the theme are used, but the image remains the same. This approach sees advertising as a continuing investment rather than a quick fix.

Wilmshurst points out that the two approaches are not mutually exclusive: a product may be advertised on the strength of a USP and may also have a strong brand image.[13] Both should reflect the positioning (Chapter 9) strategy of the brand because what matters is how the brand is perceived by the customer in comparison with the competitors.

The sender

The receiver's response will depend on how much trust she has in the source of the message – its credibility. That is why a personal recommendation from a friend who has sampled the product is the most effective form of advertising. Clubs and societies offer incentives to encourage members to persuade their friends to join. The next most credible source is a report by a journalist.

Advertising messages meet with an automatic scepticism which the advertiser seeks to overcome by putting the message in the mouth of a credible source. This can be a well-known personality, or an actor who appears to be someone with whom the target audience can identify. Celebrity endorsement is a common tactic in advertising for sports equipment. Testimonials from previous customers or seals of approval by trade associations, such as ABTA, can also help to establish credibility.

The image of the company is also important. A well-known reputable company will be trusted more than an unknown one, or one with a bad reputation. It is the role of public relations to ensure that the company maintains a good corporate image, as we shall discuss in Chapter 18.

Although most people have a healthy awareness of the intentions of advertising, this need not be a barrier to receiving the message. As Lannon and Cooper say, we know we are being sold to, we expect advertising to exaggerate, sing praises, and transform products.[14] We are not passive victims of manipulation. Instead we enjoy advertising as entertainment. Our disbelief is disarmed by adverts that do not take a direct hard selling approach, but amuse us and invite us to share the joke. Often in modern British advertising the joke is at the expense of the advertisement itself. We don't take it seriously, but when we come to the point of deciding which product to buy, we remember the joke and we remember the brand being advertised.

Feedback: Measuring the success of advertising

Lord Leverhulme, the founder of the Lever Brothers soap empire, is reported to have said, 'Half my advertising budget is wasted. The trouble is, I don't know which half'.

Today, advertising campaigns are tested and monitored very carefully to check whether the money has been well spent. There is still, however, considerable debate within the industry over exactly what should be tested, reflecting the parallel debate over how advertising works.

Ultimately, all promotional activity has to be justified by its effect on sales. For new products with genuinely unique selling points, or for special offers and incentives, it should be possible to plot the effect of the campaign on the sales graph. Even so, the rise in sales could be partly due to external factors, such as the weather – a key factor in many leisure activities – or a change in the fortunes of a competitor. Market share is probably a better guide than total sales.

For campaigns which are designed to develop a brand personality, the advertising industry argues that the effect on sales is long-term and cumulative. A more immediate measure is therefore needed to assess whether the campaign is having an effect. Various measures have been used:

- *Recall* – of the advertisement, the brand name, or the sales message.
- *Attitude* towards the brand, compared to its competitors.
- *Brand personality* – 'if the product were a person how would you describe it?'
- *Understanding* of the message of the advertisement.
- *Intention to purchase.*

These can be monitored before and after the campaign, or by a continuous tracking process, to isolate the effects of the campaign. Campaigns are often pre-tested on sample audiences in situations designed to replicate the way in which they would normally look at the advertisements. An audience may be invited to preview a film or TV programme. Before the showing they are asked to fill in a form giving their choice of free gifts from a list of brands including the one under test. After the showing they are asked about the programme and also about the adverts, to see what they remembered. Finally, they are offered a second set of gifts from the same list, to test whether their choice has been affected by the advertisement. This process, known as persuasion-shift testing, is criticized as not mirroring the way purchase decisions are made and as not being a true test of the brand image type of advertising.

Millward Brown, for example, offer tests to determine whether the viewer has remembered not just the story line of the advertisement or the brand but the sales message that links the two. This will show whether, when they reach the point of decision to buy, they will be reminded of why they should choose the advertised brand. 'What matters is not whether a commercial is enjoyable but whether it advertises the brand enjoyably. It's crucial that the elements in the commercial that convey the message and link it to the brand aren't overshadowed by other things. It's a matter of … whether the creative idea will really stick to the brand'.[15]

Promotional strategies in leisure

Theories of marketing communications have been developed largely in relation to the advertising of fast-moving consumer goods with well known brand names. In leisure, examples of the promotion of brand personalities can be found in large companies such as Nike and Reebok, or Sega and Nintendo. The majority of leisure organizations have much smaller budgets and different promotional objectives.

Very often the objective is to *communicate* the benefits not of a single product but *a programme of events or activities*. The advertisement serves to inform the public of what is on at the local cinema, theatre or leisure centre, in the hope that the name of the show, film or activity will be a sufficiently good selling point to draw them in (this can make it difficult to sell less well known shows and artistes). A large amount of the promotions budget must necessarily go on informative advertisements.

The task of creating interest and desire for the particular event has to be performed by other elements of the promotional mix. More detail of the performance can be conveyed by obtaining press or local radio publicity, or by distributing leaflets to regular users, libraries and tourist information centres. The Riviera Leisure and Conference Centre in Torquay, for example, spends most of its advertising budget on local press adverts for events, but also tries to send out a press release every week. This is partly to add publicity for the events but also to counteract local criticism of the cost of the centre to the local council-taxpayer.

Nevertheless, the venue needs a brand image in order to encourage the public to think of it as a possible choice for an evening's entertainment. With a limited budget this can only be done by careful and imaginative design of logos, advertisements, print, and the premises themselves. Even an advertisement which is simply a list of dates and performances can be branded with the identity of the venue. The Riviera also insists that the organizers of events at the centre use the correct name and logo on their own publicity material.

Small budgets can be spread further by cooperative advertising. The Riviera runs regular 'readers' offers' with the local evening paper, such as a chance to be a lifeguard for a day. To enter such competitions, the reader has to send in three coupons from the paper. The centre also cooperates with other attractions in the area, the Paignton Zoo, the Show Caves, Model Village and Torbay Steam Railway, to produce and distribute a 'five star attractions' leaflet aimed at day trippers and summer visitors to the area.

The smaller and less well-known the organization, the more the public will need to be reassured that it is a competent, reputable and professional operation that can be trusted with their money. The credibility of the organization will be judged by the appearance of the stationery, the

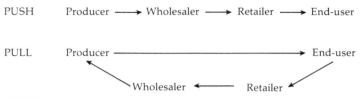

FIGURE 14.4   Push and pull promotional strategies.

way the phone is answered, and the appearance of the staff and premises. A good brand identity will help to create a good impression.

Some programmes, particularly those of tour operators, are too complex to be explained in a short advertisement. The media advertisement's objective is therefore *to persuade the potential customer to send for a brochure*. It is the brochure that has to sell the holiday and establish the credibility and personality of the company. The design and production of the brochure will therefore be the largest item in the company's marketing budget. Often the media advertisement will be a small space in the holiday section of a weekend paper, using the destination and the price as selling points with a simple design to catch the eye and identify the company. Nevertheless, to design a small ad that stands out amongst all its competitors on such a page is arguably a greater challenge than designing a double-page spread.

Another factor in the promotional strategy will be the position of the organization in the distribution channel. Does the retailer, i.e. the travel agent or the venue, carry out its own promotion for the product, or does the producer, i.e. the tour operator or the show impressario, have to promote the product in order to bring the public into the retailer's office to buy it? This is known as the choice between *push and pull strategies* (Figure 14.4).

The choice of strategy will depend on the degree of influence each player has on the consumer's decision process, and the relative power of the producer's and the retailer's brand names. In most cases there will be a combination of the two strategies, with each player in the channel marketing itself to the others and providing support for joint promotions. For example, while the Tourist Boards of Jersey and Guernsey advertise direct to the public, they also provide pictures and art work for the brochures of tour operators, airlines and ferries serving the islands, and work together with them on promotional roadshows and familiarization visits for travel agents.

Integrated marketing communications

Recent thinking on marketing communications has stressed the importance of what Schultz called the integrated marketing communications (IMC) approach.[16] Because of the increasing number of promotions competing for the individual's attention resulting from the fragmentation of the audience, the growing number of advertising media and the increasing sophistication of the consumer, promotional success depends on a strong message being delivered as often as possible. Rather than regarding the promotional mix as made up of separate campaigns using separate methods (devised often by different agencies), the IMC approach sees them as different methods of delivering the same message, each reinforcing the others.

Summary

The ways in which the promotional objectives of the organization are achieved will depend on the the target market. All promotion involves communication with people who interpret, or decode, the advertisement according to their own needs, preoccupations, attitudes and experience.

The advertiser needs to 'get on the same wavelength' as potential customers by using language and imagery that they can relate to. He must also establish his credibility as a believable and trustworthy source of information.

Many theories of how advertising works are hierarchical models that assume the potential customer moves through a number of stages from unawareness of the product through to action to purchase it. While these are useful in understanding the elements of thought, feeling and behaviour involved, particularly in an extended problem-solving decision, they do not represent the way the customer uses advertising in everyday decisions.

Some advertising does attempt to create an immediate response, by emphasizing the unique selling points of the product. More often, however, the task of the campaign is to make the customer remember the brand and recall it at the moment, perhaps much later, when the decision is made. It does so by creating a memorable brand image, appealing to the emotions as well as to reason. Advertising often needs to entertain in order to be noticed and remembered.

Some forms of promotion are designed to have an immediate effect on sales. Others can be argued to be a longer-term investment, and their effectiveness has to be measured in terms of changes in the customers' awareness, attitude, intention to purchase or knowledge of the product's attributes.

Leisure organizations often have different promotional objectives to a consumer goods producer. They may have to communicate a programme of events rather than a single product. They may have a complex offer which cannot be fully explained in an advertisement and so have to persuade the customer to send for a brochure. The promotional strategy also needs to take into account the relationships within the distribution channel as well as with the end customers.

Having summarized the elements of the marketing communications process, the next chapters examine in more detail the different forms of promotion, which form part of an integrated marketing communications approach.

Notes

1. Schramm, W. (1961) *The Process and Effect of Mass Communication.*
2. Rossiter, J. and Percy, L. (1987) *Advertising and Promotion Management*, p. 83.
3. Baker, M. (1985) *Marketing*, p. 274. He says that the average consumer is exposed to 1,500 messages a day but only receives nine.
4. Broadbent, S and Jacobs, B. (1984) *Spending Advertising Money*, p. 339.
5. Strong, E.K. (1925) *The Psychology of Selling*, p. 9.
6. Lavidge, R. and Steiner, G. (1961) 'A model for productive measurement of advertising effectiveness', *International Journal of Marketing*, October.
7. Rogers, E.M. (1962) *The Diffusion of Innovations*, pp. 79–86.
8. Broadbent and Jacobs (1984), *op. cit.*, pp. 43–44.
9. Publicity brochure, Millward Brown, Leamington Spa.
10. Engel *et al.* (1990) *Consumer Behaviour*, p. 398.
11. Reeves, R. (1961) *Reality in Advertising*.
12. Ogilvy, D. (1963) *Confessions of an Advertising Man*.
13. Wilmshurst, J. (1992) *The Fundamentals of Advertising*, p. 136.
14. Lannon, J. and Cooper, P. (1993) 'Humanistic advertising', *International Journal of Advertising*, July, quoted in Wilmshurst (1993) *op. cit.*, p. 204.
15. Publicity brochure, Millward Brown, Leamington Spa.
16. Schultz, D. (1992) *Integrated Marketing Communications*, London, NTC Business Books.

15 Advertising

Setting the advertising objectives
Setting the advertising budget
Using an advertising agency
Media selection
Handling and evaluating responses to advertising
Summary

In Chapter 14 we looked at the theories of marketing communication, including advertising. This chapter is concerned with how a leisure marketer uses advertising in practice.

Advertising is defined as 'any paid form of nonpersonal promotion by an identified sponsor'.[1] This differentiates it from personal selling, and from publicity gained by PR activity, which is not directly paid for. The definitions sometimes add 'in a public medium' to distinguish it from promotional literature and direct mail.

Media advertising is a very effective form of promotion as it reaches a wide audience more cost effectively than personal selling; it allows complete control over the message, unlike publicity; and it is harder to ignore than direct mail. Even if we do not concentrate on it, advertising is part of everyday life and we absorb its messages while watching TV, listening to the radio or glancing through a paper.

Setting the advertising objectives

Before planning the campaign, the organization needs to be clear on what the advertising is intended to achieve.

The ultimate objective is to reach a *sales target* which will give the desired level of profit over the costs of the operation. For this to happen the advertisements must be seen by the right *target market* and achieve a sufficient *response rate* in terms of the proportion of the total audience who buy the product or request further information.

To create this response the advertisement must have an effect on the way the potential customers think, feel and act towards the product. This effect will depend on their previous relationship to the product. Rossiter and Percy suggest that the *communications objectives* could include:[2]

- *Category need*: creating a need for the product category.
- *Brand awareness*: getting the brand better known.
- *Brand attitude*: reinforcing or changing attitudes to the brand.
- *Brand purchase intention*: encouraging action to purchase.
- *Purchase facilitation*: telling the customer how easy it is to purchase the product.

From these objectives will come the choice of the message, the creative design of the advertisement, and the selection of the media. They will also determine the budget needed.

Setting the advertising budget

Ideally, the advertising budget should be calculated on the basis of the objectives as set out above. The media plan must reach sufficient numbers in the target market to produce the size of response that will achieve the sales target. Using this *objective and task* method requires considerable experience of response rates and media costs, plus considerable confidence in the accuracy of the predictions.

Cautious managers, particularly those with financial responsibility, would prefer to base the advertising budget on what they know from previous experience they can afford to spend. This involves a certain *percentage of sales*, actual or forecast, being allocated to promotion. The actual percentage will vary according to the stage of the product life cycle – new products require higher advertising spending to launch them into the market – and the competitiveness of the industry. Wilmshurst quotes a survey in 1973 that showed a range from less than 1% to over 14%, with three-quarters of firms spending under 8%.[3]

In a survey of 52 UK companies Mitchell found that 40% used objective and task methods, and 27% used a percentage of future sales to decide their advertising budgets. The remainder used a variety of other methods.[4]

Another factor in setting the budget is the level needed to achieve *competitive parity* or 'equal share-of-voice'. It is unwise to spend significantly less than your competitors if you are aiming for a similar share of the same market. Media Expenditure Analysis Ltd (MEAL) can provide figures on the value of the advertising placed by a competing company in the national marketplace, while smaller companies should be able to calculate for themselves the amount being spent by their local competitors.

All three methods have their weaknesses taken singly. The objective and task calculation could produce a higher figure than the company can afford. The percentage of sales approach can lead to the budget being cut because of declining sales, leading into a downward spiral. Basing the budget on those of your competitors assumes that you share the same objectives and the same level of financial resources. None of the methods takes into account the fact that different creative ideas can produce very different responses for the same money.

Broadbent says that in practice companies tend to use a combination of all three plus the lessons of previous years in deciding the budget.[5] The exact figure will depend on how adventurous an approach the corporate culture or the individual manager is prepared to take.

Using an advertising agency

What an advertising agency does

Except for the most routine classified advertising the organization is likely to use the services of an advertising agency. The benefits offered by an agency include:

Research

The agency will have access to omnibus research reports such as the *Target Group Index* which small companies cannot afford to purchase. Agencies may also carry out primary research to help plan the campaign. They will have experience of likely response rates.

Creative design

Devising effective and memorable advertising requires flair and imagination. Those possessing these qualities are likely to work for advertising agencies. Using an amateur artist who happens to be a manager, or a lifeguard, or somebody's wife, is unlikely to produce good results.

Production

The agent produces the advertisement in a form known as finished artwork that can be printed without further processing by the publication. They will also produce, or get specialists to produce, the commercials for TV and radio. Very few companies are likely to have the facilities to perform these technical services in-house.

Media scheduling

From its previous experience, and from the research data, the agency will know which media will give the best coverage of the target market. The

choice of media is increasing, and without expert advice an inexperience
marketing manager can easily be persuaded by space salesmen to spen
money on inappropriate publications.

Media buying
Because they are regular buyers, advertising agencies can obtain discoun
from the media which are not available to other buyers. They may also b
able to obtain sought-after positions (e.g. the Christmas/New Year T
guides) that are not released to casual buyers. TV commercial slots are sol
and resold in a complicated system called pre-empting, which requires a
expert buyer to get the best deal.

Design services
As well as media advertising, agencies can design and produce promotion
literature, window displays and other point-of-sale material, write pres
releases and handle publicity events connected with the campaign. The LM
agency in Portsmouth even designed the exhibition area known as Th
Submarine Experience for the Royal Naval Submarine Museum at Gosport.
      Agencies that offer this full range of services are known as Fu
Service Agencies.

A local leisure or tourism organization may feel that it does not need all o
these services. It may only advertise in the local paper, which provide
simple design and layout for the advertisements at no extra cost. Not havin
a professionally designed logo and corporate image would be a fals
economy, but it may not be essential to use the other services offered b
agencies. To meet these needs there are many agencies specializing in on
aspect of promotion, e.g. design, media buying, sales promotion, publ
relations, and so on. It may seem that using an agency is a luxury for a sma
leisure business, but there are many who specialize in small account
According to White, 'for the majority (of agencies), a typical client is likel
to be spending £40,000–£50,000 or less, and many clients – most advertiser
in fact – are spending less than £15,000 on media advertising'.[6]

How an agency is paid

Traditionally, agencies earned their money from the commission allowed a
a discount by the media. They would charge the client the full rate, e.g
£1,000, but the space would actually cost them 15% less, £850. The media tha
allow commission to agents – press, TV, cinema, radio and poster sites
were known as 'above-the-line' media because of the way the accounts wer
presented.
      Other services provided by the agency, such as the production o
promotional leaflets, display material or events, would be charged to th

ient on a cost plus profit margin basis. Because these would appear as a
parate item on the accounts they are known as 'below-the-line' work.
riginally, the cost of designing and producing the 'above-the-line'
dvertisements was covered by the commission from the media, but as
esign technology becomes more sophisticated, the cost of the artwork is
ow usually charged as a separate item or the whole service is supplied for a
egotiated fee.[7]

hoosing an agency

hoosing an advertising agency needs care. The agent should have a good
ack record in the product area, and be of a size compatible with the
ganization. A local leisure company would be better advised to choose a
cal agency, or a leisure specialist, rather than a large national agency to
hom the company would be a minor account not meriting the attention of
e top people. Saatchi and Saatchi, for example, would normally have
nsidered the Club 18–30 account too small, but took it for the opportunity
gave to gain publicity by a daring campaign (with jokey references to the
in, sand and sex image of the Club).[8]

Where possible, a number of agencies should be invited to 'pitch' for
e account by producing outline proposals for the campaign. Today,
owever, agencies are less keen to spend too much time producing proposals
hich may not be accepted, particularly for small accounts.

riefing an agency

he marketing manager will need to give the agency a comprehensive brief
etting out the objectives for the campaign, as discussed above. Wilmshurst
uotes Maurice Drake's headings for a brief to a creative agency:

- Why we are advertising.
- What the advertising must achieve.
- Definition of the prospect: the consumers' age, social group, sex,
  family status but also their aspirations, hates, loves, habits –
  anything that can help the creative people not only to identify them
  but to understand them.
- Promise: 'why to buy', i.e. what the product can do for the consumer.
- Reason why: some firm reason why the consumer should believe that
  the product will keep its promise.[9]

he creative task is to turn this information into communication. Bernstein
escribes the process as using *reason* to define the proposition (the message),
nd then using *imagination* to turn it into an idea. The idea then becomes an
dvertisement through the *craft* skills of the agency.[10] It is imagination that

characterizes the best advertising. This is not the same as cleverness o
fantasy. Imagination, as the poet Wordsworth said, enables us to 'see int
the life of things'.[11] The best advertising ideas are basically simple, but mak
us think of the product in a different way, a way that makes its benefit
clearer to us.

Media selection

The choice of media on which to spend the advertising budget is increasin
almost daily. Technology and deregulation have made it easier to start a nev
newspaper, magazine, radio station or TV channel. The supply o
advertising space has increased much faster than the demand, so that eac
new publication or channel can only succeed by taking advertising revenu
away from an existing one. The proliferation of media also means that th
audience is fragmenting, and even the so-called mass media can only delive
a small percentage of the audience. It is therefore very important that th
choice of where to advertise is based on a thorough knowledge of the targe
market segment. The key factors in choosing a medium are:

- *Coverage*: will it reach the right audience?
- *Cost effectiveness*: will it do so at an affordable price?
- *Impact*: can it communicate the message in an effective way?

Coverage

There is a plentiful supply of statistical data available to aid media selectior
usually produced by bodies set up by the media owners.

For the printed media, the *circulation* (i.e. the number of copies sold
is measured by the Audit Bureau of Circulation. The ABC also audits fre
distribution newspapers and issues Verified Free Distribution figures fo
these publications.

The National Readership Survey, based on a sample of 30,000 adults
calculates the *readership* of the publications – the number of people wh
read or look at a copy – which typically is two or three times the circulatior
The NRS gives a detailed analysis of these readers by age, geographical area
and socio-economic group. (The ABC1C2DE system was invented for th
NRS.) It also analyzes their purchasing or ownership of consumer durables
A more comprehensive cross-referencing of media usage with purchasin;
habits is available from the *Target Group Index* (see Chapter 5).

Television viewing figures are based on research by the Broadcasters
Audience Research Board (BARB), which monitors electronically th
television sets of a representative sample of 2,500 homes, whose household
also keep a diary of who watched which programmes. BARB is able t

record the number of sets tuned to each channel at any given minute and so can produce viewing figures for each commercial. These are published as television rating points (TVRs), giving the percentage of the total potential TV audience tuned into that channel at the time. These are also broken down by age and socioeconomic group.

Radio audiences are measured by RAJAR and the audience reached by outdoor poster sites is sampled by OSCAR.

It is therefore possible for agencies with access to these data to calculate in detail the number in the target market who are likely to see each advertisement in the campaign.

Exposure or opportunities to see

The advertisement needs to be seen more than once to have its effect. Kotler quotes Krugman's theory that three exposures is the optimum number: the first time attracts attention, the second time is necessary for the full message to be absorbed, and the third serves as a reminder. After that, the repetition can begin to be tedious.[12] The exact figure may vary, and British advertising is often more subtle than American, needing more exposures to be fully understood and continuing to entertain through more repetitions than a more blatant sales message. For newspaper advertisements, there is also a distinction to draw between buying the paper and actually reading the advert, meaning that it might have to appear more than three times to achieve three exposures. Agencies will use the media data described in the previous paragraph to calculate the number of opportunities to see (OTS) that the campaign will provide its target audience.

With a limited budget the campaign has to choose between concentrating too much on one medium or publication, and spreading the exposures too thinly. Broadbent expresses this choice as a tension between four conflicting objectives: coverage, continuity, frequency and dominance, as illustrated in Figure 15.1.[13]

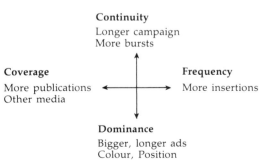

FIGURE 15.1   The four conflicting objectives of media selection.
Source: Broadbent and Jacobs (1984) *Spending Advertising Money.*

The size of the advertisement also comes into this calculation, as it influences how dominant the campaign will be. Is it better to make a big impact with a few full-page colour spreads or to aim to remind people regularly by frequent smaller advertisements? Much depends on the product and the decision-making process. Bournemouth Tourist Office places large 'brand image' advertisements to create awareness and interest at the peak booking season, and follows them up with smaller ads in the holiday sections to remind people and tell them where to send for a brochure. A visitor attraction would probably choose to advertise regularly in the local press during the season to reach the new set of holidaymakers arriving in the area each week.

Cost effectiveness

The prices of all the British media are quoted in a monthly directory known as BRAD (British Rate and Data). The cost obviously depends on the size, or length, of the advertisement. Press ads are sold by the single column centimetre (sccm: the number of columns wide times the depth in centimetres), or by full, half or quarter page. There are extra charges for special positions, e.g. on the TV page or the front cover, and for the use of colour. There is often a special price for the entertainments and holidays sections. Classified advertisements, sold by the line or number of words, are usually cheaper than display advertisements, but have less impact.

Television and radio ads are priced according to length and the time of day. Radio rates are highest in the morning 'drive time', TV rates are highest in the early evening. As mentioned earlier, TV commercial slots are sold by a kind of auction system with a scale of prices for the same slot. The agency bids for the slot and chooses a point on this scale. If another agency wants the same slot, it can put in a bid at the next point above. Broadbent says that the same slot is sold and resold an average of five times.[14]

All media offer special deals for volume, as well as local and first time advertiser discounts. Bournemouth Tourist Office say that they expect agencies to be able to negotiate discounts to give an overall cost around 40% lower than the published rate cards.

The advertiser can compare the cost effectiveness of different media by looking at the cost per thousand, that is, the cost per 1,000 readers or viewers. The true comparison must be not the cost per 1,000 readers, but per 1,000 readers in the target market segment.

A mail-order company offering classical CDs could advertise in the *Sun* or the *Independent*. The *Sun* is read by 9.2 million people, including 453,000 in social classes AB; the *Independent* by 1.1 million, of whom 560,000 are ABs. The cost of a 30 sccm advert would be £3,300 in the *Sun* and £840 in the *Independent*, giving costs per thousand ABs of £7.28p in the *Sun* compared with £1.50p in the *Independent*. Although the *Sun* reaches almost as many ABs as the more 'up-market' paper, it is not cost effective as a means of targeting that specific group in isolation.

A more useful way of comparing the two papers might be to look at the data in the NRS for readers who spend £20 or more a year on CDs, records or tapes. The *Sun* could deliver 2.7 million at a cost per thousand of £1.22, compared to 600,000 at £1.40 in the *Independent*.

However, there are other considerations to take into account in choosing between the two papers. The advertisement in the tabloid would appear in what is regarded to be a 'down-market' publication, and the AB music lovers would not regard the mail-order company with the same prestige it would carry if it were advertising in a broadsheet. It would have a different impact in each paper because of the context in which it is seen.

Impact

The impact that the advertisement will have on its audience depends on the technical capabilities of the medium, and the context in which it is seen.

The different *capabilities* of press, TV, cinema, billboards and radio are self-evident. Press can carry more detail and remains around the house for longer, but obviously lacks the movement, colour and drama of television. Radio lacks the visual elements of television, and yet can be more imaginative because the pictures are all inside the listener's head. The reader can work out the advantages and disadvantages of the other media. The choice will depend on which medium will 'give the message the best chance of being expressed clearly', to quote Wilmshurst, who goes on to say that this is very often a matter of judgement.[15]

The *context* in which the advertisement is seen, and therefore the way in which it is viewed, will depend on three things:

First, *what it appears alongside*. Probably one of the reasons why the *Sun*, the bestselling newspaper in the UK, does not carry the most advertising, is that many advertisers do not want their products to be associated with the Page Three girls, the down-to-earth style and the scandal stories on which its mass appeal is based.

Secondly, *the purpose for which the medium is used*. Television and cinema are used primarily for entertainment and viewers are not in the mood to pay close attention to the detail of the commercials, which therefore need to entertain to gain attention. Local commercial radio is used partly for information – local news, weather and traffic reports. News of local events and bargain offers fit well into this context. Radio also plays in the background while we drive to work or do the housework, so that the advertisements are absorbed almost unconsciously. Local papers are often bought specifically for advertising information – what's on at the cinema, which houses and gardens are open this weekend. The Friday night paper is likely to remain around the house for this reason. Once again, it is important to understand the customer's information search patterns (see Chapter 7).

Thirdly, *the attention the user pays to it*. The morning paper is often scanned over the breakfast table, on the train to work, or during a break. The reader does not have time to study advertisements carefully, and is not likely to be thinking about holidays or leisure. At the weekends there is more time to read the papers, and to think about the non-working side of life. For this reason holiday and leisure features and advertising tend to appear on Saturdays and Sundays. During the week, the readers are in a state of low involvement as far as leisure is concerned, whereas at the weekends they are highly involved and actively seeking information (see Chapter 7).

When to advertise

Advertisements will have maximum effect if they appear at the time when the consumer is likely to be making the decision and is therefore in a state of high involvement. This optimum time will vary according to the product and requires careful research.

In the case of holidays, there are traditionally three peak booking periods. The first is in late August when the customer returns from this year's trip with clear ideas, positive or negative, of what he or she wants to do next year. This is when tour operators tend to launch their brochures. The next peak is in January. The Christmas festivities are over, and thinking ahead to the summer holiday relieves the January gloom. The New Year papers and TV guides are oversubscribed with travel advertisements.

In recent years, a third peak has developed in the spring when the tour operators introduce their bargains to shift unsold capacity. More and more people are waiting for these bargains, particularly at times when they are uncertain about their jobs or their overtime earnings. Nevertheless research has shown that the actual decision on where to go is still made in the autumn even though the booking is not made until the spring. As mentioned earlier, Bournemouth advertises in the autumn and winter to create a desirable image for the resort, but follows it up with smaller reminders in the spring.

Handling and evaluating responses to advertising

If the advertisement is well designed and well placed, it should result in a noticeable upsurge in business. The organization needs to ensure that it is able to cope with this. There is no point in advertising if you cannot meet the resulting demand. To help companies handle the enquiries and orders, advertising agencies may offer a *fulfilment service*. Instead of the calls jamming the switchboard and diverting the company's staff from other work, a special number is provided by the fulfilment agency, whose staff take the callers' details and dispatch the brochures on the company's behalf.

As well as easing the company's workload, this service also provides a record of the number of calls in response to the particular campaign. Other methods of isolating the response to the campaign from normal enquiries include coupons with a code in the corner, or an address with a named individual, possibly fictitious, that is used only on a particular advertisement. If the campaign is not designed to produce a direct response then the organization has to rely on the monitoring methods discussed in Chapter 14, or instruct its staff to ask all callers, 'How did you hear about us?'.

Summary

This chapter has set out the process by which an organization plans and implements its media advertising. In general, the design and placement of advertisements is best handled by an agency. However, before appointing the agency, the marketing manager must clearly define the objectives of the campaign and set realistic and affordable budget limits. The response to the campaign needs to be carefully handled and monitored to ensure that the money is being spent cost effectively.

Notes

1. Kotler, P. (1994) *Marketing Management*, p. 596.
2. Rossiter, J. and Percy, L. (1987) *Advertising and Promotion Management*, p. 132.
3. *IPC Marketing Manual 1973*, MEAL quoted in Wilmshurst (1992), *The Fundamentals of Advertising*, p. 35.
4. Mitchell, L. (1993) 'Setting the advertising budget', *European Journal of Marketing* 27(6).
5. Broadbent, S. and Jacobs, B. (1984) *Spending Advertising Money*, p. 208.
6. White, R. (1993) *Advertising: What it is and how to do it*, p. 24.
7. For a fuller explanation, see Wilmshurst (1992), *op. cit.*, p. 75.
8. *The Independent on Sunday*, 26 February 1995.
9. Wilmshurst (1992), *op. cit.*, p. 133.
10. Bernstein, D. (1974) *Creative Advertising*, quoted in Wilmshurst, *op. cit.*, p. 129.
11. Wordsworth, W. (1798) 'Lines written a few miles above Tintern Abbey', *Lyrical Ballads*.
12. Krugman, H. (1975) 'What makes advertising effective?', *Harvard Business Review*, March–April, quoted in Kotler (1994), *op. cit.*, p. 640.
13. Broadbent and Jacobs (1984), *op. cit.*, p. 248.
14. *Ibid*, p. 284.
15. Wilmshurst (1992), *op. cit.*, p. 83.

16 Direct marketing

Integrated direct marketing systems
Direct response advertising
Direct communication methods
Summary

Integrated direct marketing systems

Direct marketing is one of the fastest growing areas of marketing and probably one of the least understood by outsiders. It is often confused with direct mail, and is therefore dismissed as junk mail. In fact direct mail is only part of direct marketing.

Gross defines direct marketing as 'Any form of marketing communication which allows marketers to talk directly to existing or potential customers, and/or obtain a direct response from them'.[1] There are three main elements in direct marketing:

- direct response advertising,
- direct communications methods,
- database marketing.

The three elements can be used separately or as an integrated direct marketing system.

A tour operator may use *direct response advertising* to launch its programme. A newspaper advertisement may include a telephone number or a coupon for the readers to use to get the brochure direct from the advertiser rather than through a travel agent. The advertisement may even offer a specific holiday, perhaps as a 'reader's offer' promotion with the newspaper, and include a booking form for the reader to send direct to the operator with a deposit.

After the first year of operation, the company will have compiled a list of names and addresses of those who sent for the brochures and those who then booked a holiday. It is commonsense to use this to *mail* subsequent tour offers *direct* to them. Some specialist operators, for example Vacances

Franco-Britannique (VFB) claim 70% of their bookings now come from previous customers or their friends.

As we saw in Chapter 5, the records of these customers represent an invaluable source of market information. The company could convert its mailing list into a comprehensive *database*, using the booking forms and end of holiday questionnaires to build up a profile of each customer: last purchase, preferred destinations and travel dates, special interests, dietary and health needs, the ages of each family member and their birthdays, their newspaper reading and TV viewing, the make of car, and so on.

This information can be used to *target* special offers, such as off-season reductions, special activity breaks, birthday specials and so on, to those most likely to be interested. It can also be used to build up personal relationships with customers by sending birthday and Christmas cards, and by recalling personal details next time they call.

The details of existing customers on the database can help to produce a *profile* of the market segments the company is reaching. This profile can then be used to target other potential customers. In Chapter 8 we described how *geodemographic systems* such as ACORN can be used to analyze the mailing list into areas with the highest concentrations of customers. Postcode areas of the same ACORN types can then be targeted for mailshots.

This can be done in two ways, either by *door-to-door distribution* of unaddressed material by local distributors or the Royal Mail Household

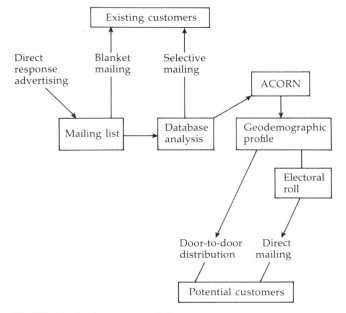

FIGURE 16.1   An integrated direct marketing system.

Delivery Service, or by personally addressed *direct-mailing* using the electoral roll to provide the names of the people living in the targeted area.

The elements in this integrated direct marketing system are shown in Figure 16.1. Such systems are used by Regional Tourist Boards and the English Tourist Board, who also offer special terms to their members for the use of geodemographic systems on their mailing lists. Database marketing is used by venues such as the Poole Arts Centre, who record all bookings on a computer database so that details of particular types of performance can be mailed to customers who attended previous shows of that type. A computer is not essential. Howard and Wright advise travel agencies to keep the names of customers on a card file by type of holiday and mail them with a selection of suitable offers. They also suggest writing to local clubs and businesses with special offers for their members, offering local restaurants and shops the chance to do joint promotions, and identifying the best types of housing in the locality for a leaflet drop.[2]

Direct response advertising

The reasons for choosing direct response advertising rather than marketing through retail channels has been discussed in Chapter 13. The general principles of advertising explained in Chapters 14 and 15 apply to direct response advertising as well. The main difference is that in order to encourage the customer to respond direct it will have to include more detailed information from which the customer can make the choice.

A number of devices are available to make it easy for the customer to respond. Coupons are expensive in terms of space but encourage the customer to fill them in immediately without the bother of composing a letter. A 'Freepost' address can also save the time and expense of buying a stamp. A telephone number which allows a free (0800) or reduced-rate (0345) call makes it even easier. If the aim is to get an immediate order, the facility to pay by credit card is essential.

Direct communications methods

Direct mail

According to the Advertising Association, expenditure on direct mail is higher than on any advertising medium other than press and TV. At £895 million in 1991, it exceeded expenditure on outdoor posters, radio and cinema put together.[3]

Direct mail has many advantages. It allows more detail about the offer to be conveyed, and it offers a wide range of creative possibilities. It is not confined to the two dimensions of a sheet of paper. The envelope can carry free gifts, samples and other gimmicks. Friends of the Earth recently mailed potential donors small pieces of chalk from Twyford Down to dramatize the effect of road building on the landscape. It can also contain a reply-paid envelope to facilitate reply.

If the mailing list is well-targeted and up-to-date it can also be less wasteful than media advertising. It is less likely to be seen by those who are not potential customers, and even if they only glance at the envelope or its contents, they are paying it more attention for a longer time than they would give to most press ads. Moreover, they are giving it their undivided attention in the home or office where the decision is likely to be made.

The big disadvantages would appear to be its poor image as junk mail, and the fact that many envelopes will go straight into the bin unopened. However, a survey by the Direct Mail Information Service in 1991 found that only 20% of people did not open direct mail items; 63% said they opened and read them; while 17% opened but did not read them. ABC1 people were more likely to open the envelope than C2DE. The Direct Mail Information Service also found that, contrary to popular belief, British people are not submerged in heaps of unwanted mail. In a four-week period the average household received 5.1 free newspapers, 5.5 leaflets/coupons, and 5.8 items of direct mail.[4] Each item of direct mail is therefore likely to be on its own on the doormat, increasing the likelihood that it will be read.

Obtaining mailing lists

Mailing lists can, as we have already said, be created by direct response advertising, and a home-grown mailing list can be used to profile and identify other potential customers. Sales promotions and competitions are also useful ways of obtaining the names of people who are interested in the product. In one promotion, secretaries were offered a free gift of a red rose in return for providing the names of those in their organization who were frequent business travellers.

Another alternative is to buy or rent a mailing list. List brokers can provide lists of customers who have dealt with similar organizations in the past or are interested in particular activities. These lists are either bought from other companies or compiled by means of consumer surveys.

NDL Ltd send questionnaires to people asking about their consumer preferences and leisure interests. In return for completing it they are promised a large number of discounts and coupons for products in which they have expressed an interest. The respondents are therefore proven to respond to direct mail and to be interested in further offers. The

names and addresses are entered in the Lifestyle Selector system, which i:
used to supply companies with lists of named individuals who hav‹
specifically declared an interest in the product. The lifestyle selection
include a wide range of interests from bingo and bowls, to wines an‹
wildlife.

Whether the mailing list is self-compiled or bought, care must b‹
taken to eliminate duplications and to weed out those who do not reply t‹
any mailings. By law people must be told if their names will be used fo‹
mailing purposes and could be offered to similar organizations. They mus
be able to register, usually by ticking a box, if they do not wish their name
to be used in this way. It is also possible to register with the Mailin›
Preference Service that you do not wish to receive *any* commercial mailin›
Companies are obliged to check their lists against the MPS register befor‹
using them. All computerized lists must be registered under the Dat‹
Protection Act, which gives people the right to know what personal detail
are being held.

The contents of the envelope

Direct mailing has tended to become rather stylized and unoriginal. Reader‹
will recognize the envelope with the incentive that screams 'Open Now t‹
Win Vast Prizes!', the four-page 'personalized' letter, double-spaced with th‹
key selling points underlined, a glossy leaflet and a reply-paid envelope
These follow the AIDA principle and are proven to be successful. Howevei
one wonders why the wit and ingenuity displayed by other forms o‹
advertising is not tried more often in direct mail.

Door-to-door distribution

Door-to-door distribution is very easy for local businesses to do, but it lack‹
the personal touch of an addressed envelope. As mentioned earlier, th‹
Royal Mail offer a complete service, identifying the most suitable areas fo‹
the product through the *Target Group Index* and ACORN, sorting an‹
delivering the leaflets with the normal post.

Telemarketing

Cold calling on the public by telephone in their own homes meets witl
considerable resistance in Britain, in contrast with the United States, and i‹
not widely practised. It is more frequently used in business-to-busines‹
selling to canvass appointments for sales representatives. Telemarketing ca›
be effective in selling to carefully screened lists of prospective customers
especially as a follow-up to an enquiry, or can be used to clean lists prior to
mailing, for market research or for setting appointments.

Fliers

Handing out leaflets in the street is a basic form of direct marketing used by some leisure organizations, such as nightclubs, restaurants and attractions. It can be very wasteful and present a poor image of the company, particularly if the leaflets are seen littering the street afterwards. Fliers can however be useful if they are distributed at times and in places where the target customers are concentrated, e.g. in colleges, or as people emerge from a venue or an event similar to the one targeted. Care must be taken not to risk prosecution for obstruction, nuisance or trespass.

Loose leaflets can also be included in newspapers and magazines. As they fall out they attract attention, but again risk annoying the customer and being left as litter. They can offer more scope creatively than an advertisement in the publication itself, e.g. pop-ups, samples, scratch 'n' sniff, etc. Because a reply-paid card can be included, they can be effective in generating enquiries, and despite the extra cost can prove more cost effective than space in the newspaper itself.

Fliers can also be included in carrier bags at shops, or in mailings from other organizations, e.g. with telephone or credit card bills, or AA/RAC subscription renewal notices.

Summary

Direct marketing is a large and growing form of promotion. It is heavily used by certain sectors of the leisure industries – holidays and travel, music and book clubs – which have computerized integrated direct marketing systems of the kind developed by the mail-order catalogue giants. It can also be used effectively on a local scale by small organizations, particularly those with a membership scheme or mailing list. It is simply a matter of keeping accurate records of past customers and using them selectively to generate future business.

With the proliferation of media and the fragmentation of audiences noted in Chapter 15, direct marketing will appear increasingly attractive. Direct marketing allows the organization to learn more about its customers and to respond to them in a more personal way. It is therefore an effective way of achieving long-term customer relationships.

Notes

1. Gross, M. (1992) *The Direct Marketer's Idea Book*.
2. Howard, M. and Wright, R. (1994) 'Going for the direct approach', *Travel Agency*, April.
3. Advertising Association (1992) *The Media Pocket Book*.
4. *Ibid*, pp. 122–24.

17 Sales promotion

What is sales promotion?
Pricing down or packaging up?
The economics of sales promotion
The effect of sales promotion on brand image
Objectives of sales promotion
Trade promotions
Joint promotions
What makes an effective sales promotion?
Case Study 17.1: Pickfords Christmas Day promotion
Summary

What is sales promotion?

Sales promotion is a term which confusingly can have several meanings.
Literally, it could mean anything that promotes sales, including advertising.
It is usually confined to the so-called below-the-line activities which do not
include provision for commission to be paid to advertising agents. This
definition could include promotional literature, exhibitions, familiarization
visits and point of sale material. However, its most common usage is to refer
to the promotion of additional sales through incentives and discounts. It is in
this sense that it will be used here.

   The Institute of Sales Promotion defines it as 'a range of *tactical*
marketing techniques designed within a strategic marketing framework to
add value to a product or service in order to achieve *specific* sales or marketing
objectives'. The key words are in italics.

Added value

Sales promotion comes after the product features have been designed, the
unique selling points identified and the brand image established by an
advertising campaign. It is the additional incentive or discount offered to

persuade the customer to buy now, from this company, rather than later, from someone else. In terms of AIDA and other hierarchical models (see Chapter 14), sales promotion is often designed to turn desire into action, although, as we shall see, it can play a role at any stage of the communications process.

Limited tactical objectives

Sales promotion works because it offers the customer a bargain and creates a sense of urgency. The offer only stands for a limited period and the customer therefore has to act quickly to take advantage of it. If the promotion were not limited it would become part of the normal product/price offer. It would lose its urgency and would simply add to the cost or reduce the price without stimulating sales. Sales promotions therefore have to be used sparingly; otherwise, consumers will come to expect discounts and will not buy at the full price. As we noted earlier, this has happened with the late-sale bargains offered by tour operators.

Another risk with promotions is that they will simply give added value, or reduced prices, to those who were going to buy anyway. To prevent this, they are often limited in validity as well as duration.

Pricing down or packaging up?

Sales promotions come in two basic types. They can offer a reduction in price, or they can include something extra in the 'package' at the normal price. Examples of the latter include offers such as 'two-for-the-price-of-one' or '15% extra free', free gifts, vouchers and competitions.

Price-based promotions are easy to understand and have an immediate appeal, so will probably have a greater impact on sales. On the other hand, a price reduction is easy for a competitor to copy, and so risks provoking a price war. Price cuts can devalue the image of the product, low price being popularly equated with low quality, as in the phrase 'cheap and nasty'. There is also the risk already mentioned of customers coming to expect the lower price, making it difficult to increase it again.

Added-value packages avoid these dangers and if used imaginatively can help to attract attention to the product and reinforce the brand image. The difficulty is finding an additional incentive that is desirable enough to stimulate purchase in the way that a cash saving does. The prize or gift has to be valuable enough to attract the customer, but the costs to the company must not outweigh the value of the extra business generated, as happened with the disastrous Hoover promotion offering free flights to the USA for any purchase worth over £200. This was such an attractive offer that it drew more people than Hoover could cope with administratively or financially. They attempted to control demand by introducing restrictions on the time and date of the flights, something that had not been mentioned in the offer. This made matters worse by attracting widespread media criticism and law suits. There has to be a balance between making the gaining of the prize or gift too easy, so that it becomes uneconomic for the company, and making it too difficult, so that the customers do not think it worth trying for.

The economics of sales promotion

The ISP definition emphasizes that a sales promotion campaign has specific objectives. Unlike brand image advertising, the effects are easy to measure and evaluate (see Case Study 17.1: Pickfords). If the value of the extra business gained during the period of the promotion exceeds the costs of the promotion – e.g. the gifts or discounts plus the advertising and administrative costs – then the campaign has succeeded. This makes it an attractive form of marketing particularly at times of recession when sales are down and budgets are tight. A sales promotion campaign can boost flagging sales and pay for itself in a short time.

It is also useful in selling off surplus capacity, and as such is, as Middleton says, a vital weapon of the travel industry in manipulating demand in response to unforeseen fluctuations.[1]

An extreme case of this was the 1986 'Go for it, America!' promotion mounted by British Airways to counter the slump in US travel to Europe as a result of a series of terrorist attacks. BA announced that all seats to the UK on 10 June 1986 would be free, allocated to the winners of a nationwide sweepstake. In addition, all passengers that summer took part in competitions to win prizes that epitomized British quality – a round trip on Concorde, a £100,000 shopping spree in Harrods, a Rolls-Royce car, the lease on a Chelsea town house, and an investment portfolio of UK stocks and shares. Some of the winners were also invited to tea with Margaret Thatcher at 10 Downing Street. The positive publicity gained by the advertising campaign and the news media coverage it attracted were probably more important than the incentives themselves in reversing the decline in bookings.[2]

The effect of sales promotion on brand image

The promotion must be designed, as the definition says, within a strategic marketing framework. The additional offer must enhance rather than contradict the brand image. The gift or prize must be appropriate to the image of the product and the lifestyle aspirations of the target market, as illustrated by the BA example above.

Pickfords, in a joint promotion with Cosmos Holidays, offered a Sony Walkman for those who booked early, before 30 November 1987. This targeted the younger end of the holiday market: 'to get you in the mood for all that sun, sea and sand, we'll give you a summertime hits cassette to play on it'. It also provided the opportunity for an eye-catching and memorable slogan: 'Walk into Pickfords, Walk out with a Walkman'.

Similarly, with the headline 'Some holidaymakers will have more to smile at than others', Thomson offered a free 35 mm Opus camera to those booking a Villas and Apartments holiday in April. They also offered a prize of a free holiday for the best photo taken with the camera.

The prize is often used to convey a message about the product, to create a conditioned response to the prize which will transfer itself to the product (see Chapter 14). Leisure and tourism prizes, particularly holidays, are often used in this way by other types of product. Cadbury's 'Mum in a Million' prize draw in March 1989 invited people to nominate their mothers for a prize of a week's holiday for four in a European city of their choice. This was part of a continuing strategy to associate Cadbury's with Mother's Day gifts. The entry form included a push-out 'Mum in a Million' sticker, and bouquets of flowers by Interflora were the runners-up prizes.

Objectives of sales promotion

It will be apparent from the examples that sales promotion can be used to achieve a number of different marketing objectives, as well as that of creating an immediate purchase.

To create awareness and promote trial of a new product: Just as consumer goods manufacturers use free samples and coupons, leisure attractions can use free or discounted tickets to get people to try a new product, as in the example of the Sheffield Steelers ice hockey team described in Chapter 8.

To differentiate the product from competitors' offerings: Where the products are all similar, as with beach holiday packages, the free gift or discount can be the deciding factor.

To retain and reward regular customers: A club may include an incentive offer with its subscription renewal notices to persuade waverers to remain members; a promotion that requires a number of visits to obtain will encourage more frequent use and discourage brand switching. Newspaper reader offers that require coupons from several editions of the paper, and schemes such as Air Miles that involve collecting stamps or coupons towards an expensive item, are examples of loyalty-building programmes. Recently

242 PART 4 THE PROMOTIONAL MIX IN LEISURE

stamps have been replaced by smart cards. Customers of Shell or Tesco are given plastic cards which are swiped through a machine each time they make a purchase.

To change or reinforce the brand image: Mateus Rosé achieved great success as 'a wine for those who don't know much about wine' in the UK in the 1960s. Eventually, as wine drinking became more widespread, people were expected to know about wines, and drinking Mateus Rosé became a joke. To change its image, Mateus ran competitions to win gourmet holidays in Portugal, positioning the wine as a distinctive part of Portuguese gastronomy.

To sell excess capacity or channel demand to less popular periods (see the discussion of price discrimination in Chapter 12).

To obtain names and addresses for database marketing (see Chapter 16). Vauxhall ran a competition with *The Observer* newspaper to win a new Omega car and a trip to the Rugby World Cup finals in South Africa. As well as naming their all-time world rugby XV, entrants were asked to state what type of car they currently owned and when they planned to replace it. Rugby supporters and *Observer* readers matched the profile of the target market for the new executive car.

To encourage personal recommendation: The Queens Park Health Club in Bournemouth offered members a luxury branded bath towel as a gift if they gave the name of a friend who subsequently joined the club.

To reach new markets: Joint promotions can reach segments that cannot be isolated by other means. Anyone buying a house from Ealing estate agents Sinton Andrews will be entitled to a year's free membership of the local Questors Theatre. This introduces newcomers to the area to the concept of a members-only theatre club.

To generate publicity and goodwill: The British Airways 'Go for it, America!' campaign is a good example of this. Promotions linked to a charity are also likely to gain favourable press coverage and enhance the image of the company (see Chapter 18).

Trade promotions

So far we have been talking about promotions aimed at the consumer. Sales promotions can also be targeted at the intermediaries in the distribution channel. These can take various forms of incentive:

Encouraging retailers to participate in consumer promotions: These are known as two-tier promotions. Fuji films offered Air Miles vouchers to anyone taking their film to be developed and printed at a Fuji dealer between July and August 1989 (Air Miles are vouchers each giving one mile free travel on British Airways and other flights). As well as receiving a small number of Air Miles automatically, customers were also entered into a draw with 25 prizes of 1,000 Air Miles. To encourage the dealers, mystery shoppers (i.e. Fuji personnel posing as customers) awarded 450 Air Miles (enough for a trip to Paris) to those dealers judged to be handling the promotion well.[3] Without the cooperation of the dealers, the promotion would fail.

Encouraging retailers to sell the product more actively: Promotions can act as incentives for retailers to reach a sales target. Balkan Holidays, for example, offered free skiing holidays for travel agency staff who sold a certain number of holidays. (Such promotions need to be sensitive to the relationships within the retailer, so as not to be seen as bribing the counter staff to divert from company policy.) Some tourist attractions reward the managers of hotels and pubs who display their leaflets with free tickets and invitations to end-of-season parties.

Rewarding sales and other staff for performance: Travel and foreign conferences are often used by companies as incentives for their staff to reach high performance targets. A whole sector of the travel industry is dedicated to supplying the demand for incentive travel packages.

Joint promotions

Many of the above examples are joint promotions in which two organizations with similar target markets combined their resources to their mutual advantage. This collaboration can reduce the cost of the incentives offered.

During summer 1995, Wimpy International joined forces with Buena Vista International (UK), the film distribution arm of Disney, in a deal that gave Wimpy exclusive rights to use Disney's latest films to promote children's meals. 'We see ourselves perfectly matched with the Disney market because we are both associated with traditional values, family entertainment and educational advancement', said a Wimpy marketing manager.[4]

A common form of joint promotion is that used to promote a brand of drink in a pub or wine bar. The pub attracts extra custom because of the cheap drinks offer, and the drinks company gets people to sample the product.

What makes an effective sales promotion?

From the examples of sales promotions given in this chapter, certain general lessons can be drawn as to the criteria for a successful campaign:

1　The offer must be desirable to the target market.
2　The promotion must not be too arduous for the customers to participate in, and they must feel they have a credible chance of gaining the 'prize'. Small consolation prizes for all participants help.
3　The promotion must enhance the brand image.
4　The campaign should offer opportunities for creative advertising and for PR coverage.
5　Staff and retailers should be given an incentive to promote the offer vigorously.
6　The offer should be limited in duration and validity in order to limit the extra costs to the company, and to avoid devaluing the product in the eyes of the consumers.
7　The promotion campaign should be carefully costed to ensure that the extra business gained will outweigh the extra costs.

QUESTION

1　Find examples of current promotions in the consumer or trade press. What would their objectives appear to be? Evaluate them against the criteria for effective sales promotion given above.

CASE STUDY 17.1　*Pickfords Christmas Day promotion*

In December 1987, readers of the Sunday papers were startled to read an advertisement announcing 'This Year Christmas Day Will Be On 28th December'. It turned out to be a Pickfords Travel promotion offering £50 off summer holidays and a £5 deposit, for one day only.

Traditionally, the peak season for booking holidays started after the New Year, and the days between the Christmas and New Year holidays were slack times for travel agents. By enticing people to book earlier than usual, Pickfords were not only hoping to fill their own offices but also to attract custom away from their rivals.

The offer was heavily criticized, especially by independent travel agents, as buying business at low or non-existent profit margins. Pickfords' marketing director Kevin Welch, recently recruited from Weetabix, declared that the branches had been as busy on that one day as they would normally have been for the whole week, and that the promotion had paid for itself. Pickfords therefore followed it up with a similar offer, '£20 off leap year holidays – up to and including February 29th 1988', linked to Horizon holidays.

At first sight, the accusation of buying business appears justified. An average-priced summer holiday for two at £500 would earn a travel agency 10% commission, i.e. £50. The small print at the bottom of the ad showed that the Christmas reduction was £50 per booking form for two or more people, not per person, but that would still would leave Pickfords with nothing. However, multiples like Pickfords use their buying power to negotiate 'over-rides', i.e. extra commission from preferred operators (see Chapter 12) at around 12.5%. On £500 this would be £62.50. In addition, the offer was tied to the purchase of Pickfords travel insurance at the time of booking, which would cost around £20 per person. The commission rates on insurance are considerably higher than on the holidays themselves, up to 50% in some cases; taking an average rate of 20%, Pickfords would earn £8 on insurance for two.

The relative costs of the promotion for a £500 booking are shown in Table 17.1. From these figures it would be necessary for Pickfords to take four times as many bookings as normal to show a profit on the promotion.

Table 17.1   The Pickfords Travel Christmas offer

	Normal price (£)	Christmas offer (£)
Commission on holiday	62.50	62.50
Commission on insurance	8.00	8.00
Less Christmas offer		50.00
Pickfords' earnings	70.50	20.50

The trade press coverage of the offer revealed that it formed part of Pickfords' strategy of winning market share from the independent sector and rival multiple travel agency chains such as Thomas Cook and Lunn Poly. It marked the beginning of a phase in the UK travel industry when the focus of price competition shifted from the tour operators to the travel agents. The other chains followed suit until charts showing a scale of discounts according to the value of the holiday became permanent features of the agency windows. The resulting growth of multiple branch travel agencies at the expense of independents was described in Chapter 9 (Table 9.2).

By 1992 Pickfords were in financial difficulties, and were acquired by AirTours. The brand name was changed to Going Places. Kevin Welch was retained as marketing manager.

Summary

The ability of sales promotion to make an immediate, measurable effect on sales makes it a heavily used marketing tool. However, it must be used carefully as a tactical weapon, adding value for a limited period or in carefully defined circumstances to achieve specific objectives. Otherwise, it can lead customers to expect the offer or reduction as a permanent part of the product package.

The message that the sales promotion conveys must reinforce rather than contradict the brand image conveyed by advertising. It should conform to and play a part in achieving the strategic objectives of the brand. For this reason the sales promotion should be designed and planned as part of an integrated marketing communications strategy, rather than be used as simply a short-term expedient.

Notes

1. Middleton, V. (1994) *Marketing in Travel and Tourism*, p. 178.
2. Teopaco, J. and Greyser, S. (1988) 'British Airways' "Go for it America" promotion' in Greyser, S., *Case Studies in Marketing*.
3. Sambrook, C. (1990) 'Hard sell holidays', *Marketing*, February, p. 31.
4. *Leisure Week*, 13 January 1995.

18 Public relations

Who are the public?
The functions of PR
How to obtain marketing publicity
Using a PR agency
Advantages and disadvantages of PR as a promotional tool
Case Study 18.1: Changing the image of Majorca
Summary

Public relations (PR) includes all the activities designed to 'establish and maintain mutual understanding between an organization and the public', to use the Institute of Public Relations definition. PR is not an optional part of the marketer's armoury. All organizations have public relations, even if they do not consciously engage in PR activities (one is tempted to say *especially* if they do not engage in PR activities).

The organization's actions and communications are unconsciously judged by everyone with whom it comes into contact, whether as direct customers or casual passers-by who notice the logo on the premises or vehicles. PR is concerned with controlling the impression thus created, to ensure that the image of the company is positive rather than negative.

Who are the public?

The organization is seen by a number of different publics who may have an influence over its fortunes. Figure 18.1 shows Wilmshurst's diagram of the 'PR universe'.

Let us apply this diagram to a private company that has taken over the management of a local authority leisure centre under compulsory competitive tendering (CCT) The company will obviously need to impress the customers that the new management is an improvement on the old one. The local council will be watching carefully for reassurance that they have made the right decision in choosing the company, and some members of

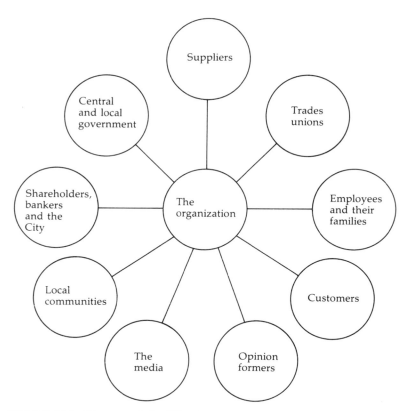

FIGURE 18.1   Diagram of the PR universe.
Source: Wilmshurst (1992) *The Fundamentals of Advertising*, p. 106.

the council may well be critical of the CCT policy. Employees will be anxious about the change, and will tell their families and friends if anything upsets them. If the staff belong to a union, the officials will be suspicious of the new management's intentions and will react to any proposals that seem to threaten their members' interests. The local press will be keen to pick up any criticism or controversy from any of these sources and give it a wider public. If there is any implication that the company needs to reduce costs in order to remain viable, this may affect their credit rating with suppliers and alarm their bankers and others with a financial stake in the company. All of these parties are therefore the receivers of the company's PR message.

The problem is that many of these people do not wear uniform. The man who brings his daughters swimming on a Saturday may also be a local councillor, the chairman of a social club, and on the committee of a local charity the company has just refused to help! An aggrieved employee may go to the pub and sound off about the organization to someone he meets, who just happens to be considering hiring the venue for a function.

To counteract these potential difficulties, PR aims to present a positive image of the company, as, in the words of David Bernstein, 'a good guy, making worthwhile products in a responsible manner. He must also be seen as a good neighbour'.[1] The last aim is important if the venue causes parking problems, litter or late-night noise that upsets those who live nearby.

The functions of PR

PR, then, is concerned with the image of the whole company and as such is sometimes regarded as separate from the marketing function, located under such headings as corporate affairs. The work of the PR department can include:

- Corporate identity
- Lobbying
- Crisis management
- Internal communications
- Customer relations
- Marketing publicity

All of these elements play a role in maintaining the credibility of the company in the eyes of the public. As we saw in Chapter 14, the credibility of the source of the message has an important influence on whether the message is accepted. PR in its widest sense lays the foundations on which other forms of marketing communication build.

Corporate identity

The objectives of establishing a corporate identity are similar to those of branding (see Chapter 10): to create an image of consistency, reliability and professionalism which is easily recognized by the public. Everything that the company owns or produces has to project the same image. The central symbol of the image is the logotype (usually referred to as the logo), which should appear on all the publicity, correspondence, buildings, vehicles, uniforms, merchandise, etc. There may be a Corporate Identity Manual specifying how the logo is to be used in different situations, the colour schemes to be used on vehicles or in premises, and the house style to be used in written communications. The corporate image can be reinforced by advertising, by obtaining favourable news coverage and analysis in the media, and by sponsorship of charity and community ventures.

A change of corporate identity can be used as part of relaunching or repositioning a company. The Owners' Abroad group recently changed their name to First Choice Holidays, bringing all their brands together under one corporate name. Such changes need considerable advertising expenditure to succeed. British Rail changed the name of their package holiday organization from Golden Rail to Gold Star Holidays to indicate a wider product range including non-rail holidays. When the organization was privatized and acquired by Superbreak, the new owners found that the public still remembered the old name but did not recognize the new one. Accordingly, they changed the name back to Goldenrail.

Lobbying

The organization's business may be affected by changes in the law or in government policy. It needs to make sure that the politicians are aware of the impact their decisions will have. Lobbying can be done by individual companies, professional bodies or by specially formed groups such as the Flexi-link consortium set up by the ferry companies to argue against building a Channel tunnel. Local organizations need to build good relations with their local councils, particularly in relation to planning decisions.

Crisis management

When a serious incident occurs, it is the job of the PR department to take the pressure off operational managers by handling media enquiries and ensuring that the organization's version of events is presented. This will be easier to do if the the PR staff already has good relations with the local and trade press.

The organization needs to be seen to be acting swiftly, efficiently and responsibly to deal with the problem. P&O diffused much of the unfavourable impact of the Zeebrugge disaster on the company reputation by immediately accepting responsibility and promising adequate compensation. In contrast, Union Carbide is still contesting legal claims arising from the Bhopal chemical works explosion.

Internal communications

Since the staff play an important role in creating the image of the company and the quality of the customers' experience, it is important that they are kept fully informed and made to feel part of the team. The PR function often includes producing staff newsletters and briefing presentations.

Customer relations

Answering customer complaints and claims promptly and fairly can limit the bad word-of-mouth publicity dissatisfied customers can cause. This may be the responsibility of operations managers, a separate customer relations department, or the PR department.

Marketing publicity

Marketing PR is part of the wider remit of the PR function and is part of the promotional mix. Its objective is to secure editorial space to achieve marketing goals. Editorial space in a newspaper, or indeed in a TV broadcast, is written or presented by a journalist as a news or feature story. As such, the story is likely to be perceived as unbiased, factual and more credible than an advertisement.

How to obtain marketing publicity

There is an inherent conflict between the aims of the organization to achieve maximum favourable publicity for its products, and the journalist's need to retain his or her reputation for impartiality. The PR executive needs to respect this, and so needs to present the journalist with material that can be used in an objective news story. There is a great difference in style between advertising copy and a news report.

Journalists, particularly those covering leisure, tourism and the arts, or writing for trade journals, receive large numbers of press releases from PR people. They will reject any press releases that:

- are not relevant to the readers of the publication,
- do not contain any real news,
- cannot be included in the publication without considerable rewriting, or
- come from a source that is unknown, or is known to be unreliable.

PR must follow the basic principles of marketing and be designed with the need of the customer in mind. In this case, the customer is the journalist, whose need is for news stories that will interest the readers and so help to sell papers.

Finding news

Leisure and tourism organizations have a great advantage over those in other industries. People enjoy reading about travel, holidays, sport, the arts and entertainment. The media devote pages or programmes to each of these areas, and their specialist correspondents are always looking for stories. (The names of these correspondents can be found in the latest edition of PIMS UK Media Directory.) New products, programmes and services are real news which should easily gain media coverage.

To keep the organization in the public eye at other times, the press should be informed of any changes in the management team, long-service awards and other staff achievements, and any unusual or amusing incidents that occur. The Sea Life Centres regularly receive unusual sea creatures (for example, a crab with three claws) from local fishermen, which can provide them with stories and pictures to give to the local media.

Creating news

Leisure and tourism organizations are also adept at creating news stories. Anniversaries, presentations to the thousandth or the millionth visitor, appearances by guest celebrities, all attract media coverage. Regional TV stations like to have something with a strong visual content to end their news broadcasts – vintage vehicles, children's performances, senior citizens' outings and the like.

Events such as parades, opening ceremonies and brochure launches can be staged to give a reason for inviting journalists to visit the company. As well as enjoying the show and the hospitality, they can be given a press release conveying the marketing message behind the event. Such events need careful planning and stage-managing to avoid embarrassing mistakes that could be seized on gleefully by the media. Charity events and sponsorship deals also provide opportunities for media publicity.

The press release

The press release is the principal weapon of PR. To be effective it must be as carefully targeted as an advertising media schedule. It should be sent to the right publications, and be written in a style that those publications would use. Press releases usually take the following form.

Headline.   The headline should give a clear idea of the subject. It is not necessary to try to think of witty puns or other gimmicks. The paper will have its own style for these.

First paragraph.   The first paragraph may be all that gets printed, so it should contain the essential facts of the story – who, what, when, where, why – and the name of the organization or brand.

Style.   The style should be that of a news report, factual, written in the third person, and free of hyperbole. Commands such as 'Thrill to the excitement of the Ride of Death!' and over-enthusiastic adjectives (brilliant, stupendous, unprecedented, etc.) belong in advertising copy, not in journalism.

Story angle. The story should be genuinely interesting to the paper's readers. Ideally, it should tell them something new that is happening, and contain a strong human angle, preferably concerning someone they have heard of (a celebrity) or someone with whom they can identify (a local person, someone of the same age or background). Children and animals always generate interest and sympathy.

Quotations. The way to get a subjective, enthusiastic comment into the story is to put it in quotations, attributed to a company spokesman, preferably named; or better still, a satisfied customer.

Length. A press release should normally take one side of A4 paper, double spaced to allow the journalist to amend it and mark it up for printing.

Contact. A contact name and telephone number for further information should be given.

Photos. A good picture is worth, as the saying goes, a thousand words. The press release should either enclose a clearly focused photo with a caption, or a precise time for a photo-call. The PR person should take care that the press photographer is given an accurate list of names and other essential details.

Follow-up. After the press release has been sent out, a follow-up phone call can be made, ostensibly to offer further information or to finalize details for a photo-call. This will be more effective if the journalist is a regular contact.

Reviews

Reviews of books, plays, films, concerts and other events are a powerful, if double-edged, form of publicity. Sending out free review copies or tickets to the appropriate media is an important part of the work of the marketing department of these types of organization. A good review can be recycled by using quotations from it on posters, book jackets, etc. There is, however, also the risk of a bad review.

Using a PR agency

PR agencies offer a range of services which the organization would find time consuming to handle itself. For the opening of a new nightclub in Leicester, a PR agency offered the following campaign:

- Full use of local media within the catchment area of the club, using a variety of promotions and events, each targeted at the various age groups the club was aiming to attract.

- Competitions in the local press (pinpoint the new nightclub on a specially drawn map of the city centre; spot the champagne glass in a drawing of the nightclub) and with local radio stations (phone-in with the name of a record/artist or to answer quiz questions). Prizes to include a free bottle of champagne, to be served before 10 p.m. to highlight the club as an early evening pub-style venue as well as a late nightspot. Top prizes would be a weekend in Amsterdam, or a trip to a West End show.
- A pre-opening press visit to view the final stages of the decoration and fitting out of the club. The Mayor would be invited and a press conference organized.
- A pre-opening press evening when the media would be invited to attend with guests. This would demonstrate the club in action, with special dancers among the crowd to create 'a real glitzy evening'.
- An opening night to be publicized as 'the biggest thing to hit the city', with a celebrity to open it and well-known guests invited. A theme, such as a black and white party, would be adopted and a competition prize offered 'to encourage a massive attendance'.

For such a campaign the agency would handle all the arrangements, design the publicity, send out the press releases and invitations, and contact the media, for a set fee.

Advantages and disadvantages of PR as a promotional tool

PR publicity is often regarded as free publicity. In fact, it can be quite expensive in terms of staff time and hospitality, particularly in the case of specially staged press receptions, trips or other events. However, it can be more cost effective than advertising if measured in terms of the column centimetres of media space obtained. Editorial coverage also carries greater credibility than advertising.

There is, on the other hand, no guarantee that the story will be printed. Even if it is, the newspaper may leave out vital information or add unfavourable comments to demonstrate its independence. Press releases generally convey good news, which is much less dramatic and interesting than bad news, and will get less prominent coverage.

Most leisure organizations will find it relatively easy to get coverage from the local media and trade journals. The national media have space only for major news stories and controversies. The holiday pages and programmes offer the best chance, but they can choose from a very wide range of competing products. Opportunist PR coverage may be gained by inviting a TV programme to use the premises; for example, the Channel Tunnel terminal at Cheriton recently hosted the National Lottery Live. While establishing good relations with the media can help to win such opportunities, they cannot be relied upon. Media advertising offers a much more certain way of reaching a national audience.[2]

CASE STUDY 18.1 *Changing the image of Majorca*

The Spanish Balearic Island of Majorca is one of the UK holidaymakers' most popular destinations, and as such has felt the full effects of the fluctuations in demand for inclusive holidays which were described in the case studies in Chapters 7 and 9.

During the boom years 1985–88, visitor numbers to Majorca threatened to outstrip the supply of beds, as more and more people took advantage of low-priced holidays in the sun offered by the competing tour operators. In response, new hotels were built in and around the popular resorts, adding 70,000 extra beds to the island's tourist accommodation.

This success brought with it a share of the negative coverage that the package holiday generally was receiving in the UK press. Stories included tourists arriving to find hotels overbooked or unfinished; the beaches full of litter and overshadowed by towering hotels; poor fire, safety and hygiene standards in the hotels; and the bars and streets full of drunken louts. 'The island represents some of the worst excesses of the tourism industry', wrote one journalist, 'and is often cited as the classic example of how not to go about tourism.' A TV holiday programme asked a young man on holiday there, 'What's the best thing about Majorca?', and received the reply, 'Me, getting drunk'.

As early as 1985, the Balearic Islands' regional government was aware that something had to be done to check the spread of tourist developments around the islands and to improve the quality of the tourism product. Planning laws restricting new developments to three storeys high and requiring a plot of land equivalent to 30 m^2 per guest were introduced in that year.

As visitor numbers began to fall in 1989 and 1990 the problem became more urgent. Something had to be done to improve the image of the islands. Development controls were further tightened, effectively limiting new developments to four-star quality or higher. Development was banned completely in conservation areas which covered 30% of Majorca's surface. Legislation was introduced to encourage older hotels to be upgraded, shut down, or to be converted to other uses. Enforcement of stringent safety and comfort standards aimed to eliminate some of the excess capacity now estimated to be around 50,000 beds.

A £115 million programme of refurbishment was begun to improve the resorts' environment and infrastructure. This was funded by the regional government and the local district councils. Starting with one of the most popular, and notorious, resorts, Magaluf, the improvements included new promenades and landscaped pedestrian areas with palm trees, seats, lamp-posts and litter bins installed at frequent intervals. Extra policing and new noise abatement rules were designed to curb the nuisance caused to other visitors by rowdy drinkers in all-night disco-bars.

These improvements formed the basis of the promotional campaign mounted by the Fomento del Turismo de Mallorca (the Majorcan Tourist Board, a state-funded but privately owned consortium) and the Balearic Islands Tourism Council (Ibatur). With a promotional budget of only £2.15 million to cover the whole of Europe plus a conferences and groups campaign in the USA, they could not afford media advertising on the scale needed to make an impact. PR was therefore the main weapon. The objectives of the PR campaign were as follows:

1   To draw attention to the determination of the island authorities to make improvements to the environment and the quality of the tourism product.

2   To counter the 'lager lout resort image' by creating awareness of the island's other attractions:

   •   the spectacular mountains with unspoilt villages on the west coast;
   •   the historic city of Palma;
   •   artistic associations with Chopin, Miro and Robert Graves;
   •   wildlife in the mountains and coastal nature reserves; and
   •   the more architecturally and environmentally sensitive resorts on the east coast.

3   To attract back the family and older markets repelled by the current image.

A new corporate identity was sought. The island referred to itself as Mallorca, using the spelling of the local language (Mallorquin, a variant of Catalan) to emphasize its cultural identity. Some of the resorts also rebranded themselves. Magaluf and Palma Nova were labelled Costas de Calvia (the name of the district council), and the other notorious resort of Arenal became Playas de Palma (Beaches of Palma)

Print played an important role in the campaign. A brochure entitled 'Magaluf's Dressing Up' showed plans and artists' impressions of the new-look resort. This was aimed at journalists, and the travel trade, as was a special edition of the *Destination Spain* magazine published for the World Travel Market in London. A series of leaflets showing the conservation areas and Blue Flag clean beaches, birds and flowers of the island, and walking trails were made available to the trade and the public.

Exhibitions were the main means of reaching the travel trade. As well as attending all the travel trade fairs in Europe as part of the Spanish

National Tourist Office stand, Majorca sponsored the central area of the London Earls Court Boat Show in 1991, turning it into a Mallorcan harbour.

Special events were used to highlight the diversity of the tourism opportunities. These included the Pollensa Music Festival, which was attended by the King of Spain, and major golf and yachting competitions. The island also attracted the ABTA conference in 1993.

Press releases were issued with news of the improvements under titles such as 'BITC sets standards for high quality tourism'. These were used, together with the printed material, in press packs for press conferences by tourism minister Jaime Cladera at travel fairs, and were given to journalists on press trips to the island.

Mallorca's efforts were supported by Thomson Holidays, whose Sun Hotels scheme (see Chapter 9) was addressing the same problem in creating a quality image. Thomson MD Charles Newbold was photographed with Sr Cladera in the trade press and quoted as saying that Mallorca was showing the way for other Mediterranean resorts.

The press trips, targeting travel journalists from the broadsheet newspapers in the UK, concentrated on parts of the island less well known to the tourists, in the mountains for example, in conjunction with special interest tour operators or exclusive hotels.

The outcome was extensive coverage, usually contrasting the present image of Majorca with its unspoilt areas and with the plans to improve the main resorts. Headlines included 'Different Coasts for Different Folks', 'Balearic Island on Trial', 'Sun, Sea and Sewage', and 'Civilization will resume as soon as possible'! TV holiday programmes also featured Majorca's programme of improvements.

Since 1992, British visitor numbers to the island have recovered, although the Mallorcan Tourist Board insist that numbers are now less important than attracting higher-spending visitors. With the growth in visitors from other parts of Europe, and a recovery of the other main market, the Germans, the stories from Majorca in the summer of 1994 were once again of full hotels and fears of overbooking.

It is difficult to attribute the revival entirely to the PR campaign, as Spain and the Balearics have undoubtedly been helped by political events elsewhere. With the wars in former Yugoslavia, terrorism in Turkey and Egypt, and tourist kidnappings and murders in African countries, the Spanish islands appear to be a safe place to holiday. For holidaymakers, the feeling of safety is probably now linked with a feeling that they will also get a reliable, value-for-money, good quality product.

Sources: Morgan, M. (1991) 'Majorca: Dressing Up to Survive', Tourism Management, 12(1), March, and subsequent research. Thanks to Anna Skidmore of Fomento del Turismo de Mallorca for information supplied over a number of years.

258 PART 4 THE PROMOTIONAL MIX IN LEISURE

QUESTIONS

1 What lessons does the case of Majorca hold for other resorts seeking to change or improve their image?

2 Discuss the relationship between PR and other parts of the marketing and promotional mixes as illustrated in this case study.

3 Identify the roles of the different organizations, public and private sector, involved in this campaign.

4 What risks were there in relying on PR to get the message across? How could these risks be minimized?

Summary

Public relations activities are designed to establish good communications and goodwill between the organization and its various publics. These include not only customers, but suppliers, buyers, politicians, financial institutions, employees and local residents. Marketing PR is just one aspect of the role of PR, which also includes corporate identity, lobbying and crisis management. Marketing PR aims to create editorial coverage of the organization's products in order to achieve promotional objectives. Editorial coverage can be very cost-effective because it is seen as unbiased and factual. However, it is not possible to guarantee that it will be favourable and accurate. A well-written press release and good relations with media correspondents can minimize these problems.

As with the other promotional tools, PR is more effective if it is used in an integrated marketing communications strategy to deliver a single persuasive message to the customer.

Notes

1. Bernstein, D. (1984) *Company Image and Reality*, p. 53.
2. Further reading: French, Y. (1994) *Public Relations for Leisure and Tourism*.

19 Promotional literature

The role of print in leisure and tourism
Designing the packaging
The future of print
Summary

The role of print in leisure and tourism

Brochures and leaflets play a more important role in leisure and tourism than in most other industries. As previously noted, the aim of much travel advertising is to persuade the customer to get the brochure; it is the brochure that actually sells the product. For many small tourist attractions, the leaflet in the tourist information centre, pub or hotel is a more effective means of communication than media advertising. The production and distribution of brochures is often the largest item in the marketing budget.

General books on marketing do not give much space to printed publicity materials (often referred to as 'print') as a marketing tool. Print is seen as a minor element of below-the-line promotion, useful in direct mail, exhibitions and point-of-sale displays. In leisure and tourism, however, its role is central, and more analogous to that of packaging in manufactured goods. As Oliver says, 'modern packaging is viewed as a vital part of the communications mix. It has strategic significance in so far as it reflects and reinforces brand and corporate identities, and it has operational significance in that it provides point of purchase stimulation'.[1] The same is true of the holiday brochure.

Designing the packaging

People choose to buy package holidays for the same reasons as they choose to buy branded breakfast cereals in packets. The package offers them reliability and consistency, it is more convenient to buy, it is more prominently displayed and, because it is mass-produced, it is probably cheaper.

The word package is used in two senses. The package, as in package deal, is the totality of the features and elements included in the price. The package in the physical sense is the wrapping which encloses these elements and enables them to be transported and displayed. A holiday brochure both describes the package in the first sense and acts as the package in the second sense, enabling the holiday offer to be made available for the customer to inspect.

According to Kotler, packaging decisions are part of product management, linked with decisions on branding and positioning.[2] In fact, the design of the packaging, or in our case, the brochure, involves almost every aspect of the marketing mix, as shown in Figure 19.1.

Product influences

The packaging has to inform the potential customer of what is inside. European law obliges manufacturers to include a full and accurate list of the ingredients. In the same way, a brochure or leaflet is subject to the Trades Descriptions Act 1968, Section 14 of which expressly forbids the making of false statements concerning the provision of services. A leaflet or brochure which invites the customer to make a booking in advance is also subject to the law of contract. A contract is an agreement between two parties which is marked by the exchange of money in return for a promise to perform certain services. The seller is legally obliged to make the buyer aware of the terms and conditions of the contract; hence the pages of small print conditions in the holiday brochure. The ABTA Code of Conduct requires tour operators to

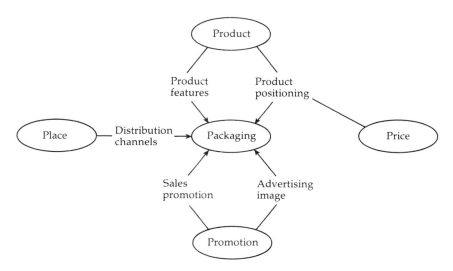

FIGURE 19.1   Marketing mix influences on packaging design.

give a full description of what a tour includes, and to show pictures of the hotels.

Print, therefore, has to be informative and accurate, which can make for dull reading. There is a tension between the need for accurate detail and the desire to make the product attractive, which a skilled designer has to resolve.

It is important to succeed in this, since the customer has only the brochure from which to make the choice to buy. The product, the experience he is buying, does not yet exist, and will continue to be a future promise even after he has paid for it. In this situation the brochure acts as a product substitute, as Middleton put it.[3] The brochure therefore needs to reassure the customer, before and after purchase, that it is a reliable and trustworthy product. Just as the cornflakes packet carries guarantees and royal coats of arms, the brochure will carry information on the company's track record, testimonials from satisfied customers, and seals of approval from trade and licensing bodies such as ABTA, the Civil Aviation Authority, or the tourist board.

The brochure also has to convey the positioning of the product. It has to establish expectations of quality and value for money, to distinguish the brand from its competitors and to appeal to the right target market. This is done partly by what is offered – the contents of the package, and partly by the style in which it is presented – the brand name, logo, colour scheme, and the choice of words and pictures.

Place influences

The brochure is, in Middleton's words, an access/purchase mechanism. Its task is first to make the product available to the customers and then to make it easy for them to purchase it. To do this, it must be easy to obtain, easy to understand, and easy to use.

Packaging of manufactured goods is designed to make distribution easy. The packets can be stacked together on pallets, loaded by forklift trucks into standard containers and shipped anywhere in the world. They can then be unloaded, and displayed on the shelves of the shop, without at any time damaging the contents.

The design of promotional literature also has to take into account the way it will be distributed and displayed. Travel brochures have to be A4 size if they are to fit into the the travel agent's racks. Only those designed for direct mailing can experiment with different sizes or formats, as Tjaereborg did when first entering the UK market with a landscape rather than portrait format (i.e. long-side at the top).[4] Holloway describes how they eventually changed to the conventional format. The reason was that they had reduced the thickness of the paper to minimize postal charges and the thinner pages flopped badly in the wide format.

Leaflets can be displayed in tourist information centres in either a single A5 sheet format or A4 three-folded. The A5 sheet allows a larger, more striking image to attract attention on the shelf. The A4 folded leaflet involves the customer in discovering more by unfolding it to reveal a centre spread. It can also unfold to form a poster for display or souvenir purposes. To encourage displays at pubs, hotels and other places, an attraction may design a cardboard holder for the leaflets.

Having reached the potential customer, the brochure or leaflet plays an important part in facilitating the purchase. Even the simplest leaflet must always tell the customer how to get to the attraction, usually by means of a map. The brochure must contain a booking form and easy-to-follow details of the booking and payment process.

Promotion influences

As we saw in Chapter 14, advertising's role is often to make the potential customer remember a message about the product, which is then recalled at the point of sale. The packaging should therefore remind the customer of the advertising. It should carry the same logo and brand image, and if possible some echo of the slogan or imagery of the advertising.

In travel this is not easy to do. The tour programme and the brochure have a long planning cycle, whereas the advertising is quicker to produce. It is often the advertising that echoes the design of the brochure rather than vice versa.

Cornflakes packets also frequently carry a sales promotion offer – a free gift in the packet, a competition, or a coupon for example. Brochures and leaflets also carry sales promotions, often announced dramatically on a flash across the cover. Early editions will offer a limited number of free places for children, or larger group discounts for early booking. The travel agency may add a sticker with its own incentive discounts. Visitor attractions often offer a reduction for customers producing the leaflet. This acts as an incentive and also provides a means of monitoring the effectiveness of the leaflet and the distribution method.

Barbara Conroy points out that travel brochures often resemble the magazines that their target market reads.[5] Mass-market brochures use brighter colours, have a higher picture to text ratio, and use simpler language than those aimed at more exclusive markets. This is because they have to 'get on the same wavelength' as those with whom they are trying to communicate.

Price influences

Price is part of the positioning of a product. An expensive product has to be packaged in a way that communicates quality, exclusivity, luxury. Up-market tour brochures are printed on expensive glossy paper and use a few pictures surrounded by white space, just as an expensive clothes shop displays only a few dresses in the window.

The price of the product also determines the revenue potential, and thus the budget available for promotional literature. The cost of producing the print must be kept within a figure partly set by the value of the sales that will result. The costs of print vary according to a number of factors:

- the weight/thickness of the paper,
- whether a gloss or matt finish is required,
- the number of colours,
- the number of photographs and artwork,
- the number of pages, and
- the number of copies to be printed.

For simple leaflets, the organization may produce its own camera-ready artwork and order copies from a printer. Since brochures and leaflets play such a central part in leisure and tourism promotion, it is usual to engage the services of a design agency who will work to a brief in a similar way to the advertising agencies discussed in Chapter 15.

The future of print

Ever since the computer became part of business life, there have been forecasts that the printed word will become redundant. It is possible to imagine a time when all the functions carried out by the brochure will be performed by the computer. Instead of going to the travel agent to pick up brochures, customers will request details of holidays over the Internet and watch video pictures of the accommodation before booking with the swipe of a credit card. It seems more likely that even if the system was in place, users would still print out the details in order to study them at leisure in places the VDU cannot reach!

Summary

Promotional literature plays a more important role in leisure and tourism than in other industries as it acts as a tangible and immediate substitute for an intangible experience which is being promised for the future. It provides the detailed information on which the purchase decision is based, information that is often too complex to be conveyed by media advertising.

The design of the printed material, like the design of packaging in other sectors, is influenced by all the elements of the marketing mix. It must clearly describe the product, convey the positioning and reinforce the advertising message, while being of the right size and shape for the distribution outlets.

The design of the brochure must reconcile the legal requirements for accurate and complete descriptions with the need to present the product to the target market in an attractive, easy-to-read way. As such, it is best left to a skilled designer working to a well-prepared brief.

Notes

1. Oliver, G. (1990) *Marketing Today*, p. 250.
2. Kotler, P. (1994) *Marketing Management*, p. 457.
3. Middleton, V. (1994) *Marketing in Travel and Tourism*, p. 192.
4. See Holloway, C. and Plant, R. (1992) *Marketing for Tourism*, p. 151.
5. Conroy, B. (1987) 'Design of Brochure Covers'.

20 Meeting the customer face to face

Personal selling
Sales techniques
The sales encounter
The changing role of personal selling
Point-of-sale promotion
Front-of-house management
Exhibitions
Case Study 20.1: Sunseeker at the Boat Show
Summary

Personal selling

Types of selling in leisure and tourism

Personal selling is often associated in marketing texts with the work of the sales representative, but many other staff are involved in selling as part of their job. There are a number of different types of sales encounters in the leisure industry:

- *Retail selling*: across the counter in a gift shop, ticket office or travel agency.
- *Telephone selling*: initiated either by the customers, in order to book tickets or order from a catalogue, or by the organization perhaps following up a mailshot or canvassing prospective trade customers.
- *Trade selling*: by a sales representative to an organization, for example a tour operator to a travel agent, or a visitor attraction to a coach company or a group travel organizer.
- *Supplementary selling*: where a member of staff who is in contact with the customers for some other reason uses the opportunity to sell an additional product or service. Examples would be the tour operator's

resort representative or the coach driver selling optional excursions; an instructor in a leisure centre selling sports clothing, equipment or additional classes; or a band selling recordings of their music at a gig.

In addition to these direct sales encounters, it can be argued that every member of staff who comes into contact with the customers can act as a sales person even if they do not actually take the money themselves. They can help to sell partly by creating a positive image of the company by their actions, but also by informing or reminding customers of the products and benefits on offer. For example, a 'cast member' at Disneyland Paris, overhearing guests talking about the need to buy gifts before the park closed, reminded them that the shops at Festival Disney outside the theme park gates remained open until midnight.

Each situation requires different sales techniques which take account of the customer's needs and state of mind at the time. Not all selling is hard selling. Kotler quotes McMurray's classification of sales positions, which can be adapted to the leisure industry:[1]

Deliverer. The job is predominantly to deliver the product. This could apply to coach drivers or instructors engaged in supplementary selling.

Order taker. The main job of counter staff in retail outlets is to take the customer's order rather than to create demand for other products. Some sales visits have the same main purpose.

Missionary. The purpose of the encounter is to build goodwill or to educate potential users rather than to make an immediate sale. Talks to schools, social clubs or other meetings by representatives of travel, sporting or arts organizations have mainly a missionary function.

Technician. The main emphasis of the job is placed on technical knowledge. The tour operator's sales staff spend much time advising agencies on booking and accountancy procedures, or answering specific questions or problems relating to a customer's holiday. The initial fitness assessment on a new customer at a health club is also a technical selling situation. In these situations the customer seeks the expertise of the sales person to solve a problem.

Demand creator. Unlike the technical selling situation, the customer has not asked for help, and may not be aware of the need for the product. This is the classic position of the door-to-door or cold-calling representative who has to persuade an uncommitted customer that she needs the product.

In practice, all these types of selling may be involved in the same job. A technician or order taker can be alert for opportunities to create demand for another of the organization's products or services.

Advantages and risks of personal selling

Personal, face-to-face selling can be the most effective form of marketing communication, because the seller gets instant feedback and so can adapt the message to meet the specific needs of the buyer (see Schramm's model in Chapter 14). The buyer gets the benefit of personal attention, answers to specific problems, and the reassurance of dealing with a person rather than a distant organization. It appears to have advantages on both sides.

The face-to-face sales encounter also carries risks to both sides because of its personal nature. The buyer fears that she will be pressured to buy because it is harder to say no to someone's face. The salesman is invading her personal space, whether in the workplace or on the doorstep at home. It may also be a waste of her valuable time, which puts her on the defensive to a greater extent than when watching an advertisement or reading a mailshot.

To the seller, the sales encounter carries the threat of rejection. Having offered both the product and his personality, it may be psychologically hurtful to be turned down.

The sales encounter therefore needs to be managed in a way that minimizes the risks to both parties. There needs to be what Holloway calls a rapport, a relationship of mutual respect and trust, before the sales sequence can begin.[2]

Sales techniques

Good sales technique minimizes both the risk to seller and the threat to the buyer. The key is preparation.

Preparing by promotion

A good relationship depends on mutual understanding. McGraw-Hill business magazines ran a much-quoted advertisement in which a surly, balding buyer says to a young salesman:

> I don't know who you are.
> I don't know your company.
> I don't know your company's product.
> I don't know what your company stands for.
> I don't know your company's customers.
> I don't know your company's record.
> I don't know your company's reputation.
>
> Now – what was it you wanted to sell me?[3]

As we said in Chapter 2, the purpose of marketing is to avoid putting salesmen in that kind of embarrassing position. Selling is the final element in the promotional mix, after the other elements have established the company's image and selling points. Asking 'Have you seen our advert?' or 'Did you receive our brochure?' is a useful opening. (If the buyer is already a customer, then she will know of the company's record. It is usually easier to sell new or additional products to existing customers than to find new customers – another reason for the importance of secondary selling, and of good customer care.)

Preparing by research

The other side of the relationship is that the seller must understand the needs of the buyer. The seller should approach the encounter knowing as much about the buyer's business and personal interests as possible. As well as using information based on formal primary and secondary research provided by the company, the seller should keep up-to-date by reading the trade and local press and by listening to trade gossip. (In secondary selling situations, a great deal of useful information can come from casual conversations with guests.)

Identifying the DMU

Part of the research for trade selling should be to identify the right person to sell to. In Chapter 7, we looked at the different roles that each member of the family has in the decision-making process. Organizations also operate as decision-making units (DMUs), both formally and informally. The sales person needs to identify the MAN, the person with the means, the authority, and the need to buy. As we saw in the example of Pickfords Travel in Chapter 13, this may lie at different levels of the organization. The main negotiation would be with the top management at head office, but the branches would still need contact with the tour operators for technical advice, problem solving and delivery of brochures.

The sales encounter

Whether it is a negotiation between trade buyer and seller or an informal conversation aimed at a secondary selling, the sales encounter will progress through similar stages. These follow what could be called the ABC model, which draws on the work of Macdonald and Leppard.[4] Selling is basically a simple matter of gaining Attention, presenting the Benefits, and then Closing the sale. In the process, it will also be necessary to overcome the buyer's objections.

Gaining attention

To be physically in the same room as the customer is not the same as to be on the same wavelength. Before beginning the sales talk, a good salesperson will make sure that he has the customer's full attention. This is done by raising a topic which will interest the customer, and the topic she is likely to find most interesting of all is herself.

The aim of the various types of opening recommended by Macdonald and Leppard, and countless other sales books, is to get the customer not only to listen but also to talk about her needs. Devices to do this include questions (about the business or her personal interests), references (to advertising, competitors, trade gossip), sales aids (photos, models, etc.), or new information that the customer will find relevant.

A good salesperson is a good listener, because it is by active listening that he can understand exactly what the customer is looking for. It is then an easier task to choose the right product and present it in terms of the right solutions to the particular customer's needs. As the old sales dictum put it, 'Find out what they need, and then sell it back to 'em!'

Presenting the benefits

The style of presentation will vary with the situation. The important thing to remember is the basic marketing principle that people buy benefits not products. If the 'sales pitch' is in danger of getting too technical, the little phrase 'which means that ...' will focus it back on the relevance to the customer. Macdonald and Leppard recommend subjecting the sales presentation to the 'So what?' test. This involves getting someone to interrupt at any time with the question 'So what?', forcing the presenter to translate his description of the product into benefits to the user.

Overcoming objections

It is inevitable that the customer will come up with objections, if only as a defence against being swept into a decision before she has had time to think about it. The salesperson will anticipate what the most likely objections are, and will be able to answer them and turn them to advantage. Among the most common objections are

Objection	Answer
It's too expensive	Not compared to the savings
	Not compared to the alternatives
I can't afford it	We can offer easy payment terms
It isn't exactly what I want	We have an alternative
It's too complicated	We can offer training and a helpline
I need to consult X	I can arrange a demonstration
The other brand is better	Not according to these press reviews

Answering objections can provide an opportunity to point out further advantages of the product. From the nature of the objections, it can become clear what the customer is thinking and how close she is to committing herself to buying the product.

Closing the sale

The whole purpose of the sales process is to reach an agreement, or as the sales manuals put it, to close the sale. Yet it is a common fault of sales people to delay asking directly for the order for fear of rejection. To overcome this risk, they should watch for signals that the buyer is near to commitment. These signals can be in the form of body language and tone of voice, or in the nature of the objections, questions and statements made.

A trial close can avoid the danger of a direct refusal by asking the customer questions of detail which assume that she has decided to buy. For example, these can be questions of which dates she would prefer, what colours, how she will pay, and the like. These can follow naturally from the answers to objections, for example 'We offer easy terms. Would you be paying over two years or three?' It is not easy to answer 'no' to this kind of question.

A summary of the customer's needs and the benefits of the product is another way of concluding the interview by demonstrating the logic of agreeing to buy. If the customer is still unconvinced, a concession on price or an additional element thrown into the package may be needed. The salesman needs to know the extent to which he can vary the offer – there is no point in offering a concession the company will not honour.

Some approaches to selling urge employees never to take no as the answer and to keep on until the customer gives in. Sean Philips of Fitness First tells of an American health club staff member who, when the customer said that he couldn't buy membership now because he didn't have his cheque book, insisted on driving him round to his apartment to collect it! Philips acknowledges that such an approach would not work in Britain. The customer may need time to think in order to reassure herself that she is not being pressured into a decision. There may genuinely be others whom she needs to consult. In these situations it may be counterproductive to keep pressing for an answer, but neither should the matter be dropped. Another appointment should be made and the offer should be put in writing.

The sales sequence is summarized in Figure 20.1.

Transaction versus relationship-oriented selling

What has been described above is a process aimed at making a single sales transaction. In many leisure cases this can be a short-sighted approach. A person who feels she has been pressured into joining a health club will come to use it in a hypercritical frame of mind, and is less likely to renew membership. While the same techniques will still be useful, the emphasis

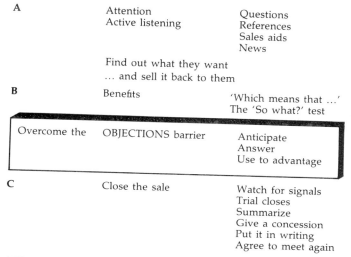

A   Attention   Questions
            Active listening   References
                             Sales aids
                             News

            Find out what they want
            ... and sell it back to them

B   Benefits
                             'Which means that ...'
                             The 'So what?' test

Overcome the   OBJECTIONS barrier   Anticipate
                                      Answer
                                      Use to advantage

C   Close the sale
                             Watch for signals
                             Trial closes
                             Summarize
                             Give a concession
                             Put it in writing
                             Agree to meet again

FIGURE 20.1   The sales sequence.

should be more on creating a personal relationship of trust rather than on making a quick deal.

Relationship marketing is increasingly important in trade selling where, as previously stated, the buying power is becoming concentrated in the head offices of a few large retail chains. In these situations, the 'LGD approach' may be important.[5]

Controlling the costs

One-to-one sales encounters are expensive. Sales staff have to be paid, trained, equipped (with cars and expense accounts, perhaps). These costs are justified only if the revenue they produce is considerably higher than the expense. This is likely to be where a large order can be won by negotiation with an individual buyer, where a complex message has to be explained, or where a high volume of business can be generated. Sales representatives have to be managed carefully, ensuring that they are well trained, motivated, allocated efficiently (by area, product or customer) and monitored against realistic targets.

The changing role of personal selling

The cost of sales staff and the concentration of buying authority have reduced the role of the salesperson in many industries including travel. Twenty years ago, each tour operator and transport company had a sales force organized on a regional basis to call on every travel agent. As multiple agencies began to adopt centrally-devised racking policies, the sales visit to the branch became of less value both to the tour company and to the busy agent with little time to chat to the rep. 'Isolated one-off calls from reps are of no value at all', said Lunn Poly director John McNeill in 1985. 'Companies that have a guy calling just once are wasting their money. It is increasingly important that a rep should know what he is talking about, because the product is so varied. In general, sales reps are not that good at disseminating information'.[6]

The travelling sales rep has increasingly been replaced by other means of servicing travel retailers, such as:

- *Merchandisers*, employed solely to deliver brochures and erect point of sale displays, 'deliverers', to use McMurray's classification.
- *Field marketing agencies*, employed on short-term contracts to deliver a new brochure, explain it to retail staff, and provide display material.
- *Computer reservations systems*, which among other things issue tickets, handle the accounts, record the agents' sales performance and deal with orders for brochures. This should result in fewer problems requiring a rep as trouble shooter, and provide more detailed market information than the reps did.
- *Agency sales teams*, operating from an office to deal with agents' problems, monitor their performance and organize promotional events, educational visits and incentives.

Retail selling is also changing. Counter staff in supermarkets, for example, have been replaced by checkout operators, who themselves may be replaced by the latest technology where the customers electronically record the barcodes as they buy. Vending machines in leisure centres dispense not only drinks and snacks, but also clothing and equipment. Formule 1 hotels have even replaced the hotel receptionist for much of the day with an automatic check-in using the customer's credit card.

Employing a person to serve the customer face to face can now only be justified by the added value the human element brings to the transaction. This may be either by raising the level of service offered to command a higher price (see Chapter 11) or by using personal selling to persuade the customer to buy more.

Point-of-sale promotion

As the human element in retailing becomes less apparent, the use of point-of-sale promotion is growing in importance. In some product areas, such as food and groceries, 80% of purchase decisions are made at the point of sale, and there is a wide range of publicity material to help sway the choice. These include posters, window pelmet stickers, window displays, dump bins (temporary cardboard dispensers), illuminated shop signs, open/closed notices, note pads, pens, ashtrays, pen holders, etc., all branded with logos and slogans and offered free by the producer to the retailer.

The point-of-sale material often aims to remind customers of the current advertising campaign. In 1985, Sealink Channel Islands services produced a window display with a cuddly soft toy version of a ferry. It was illustrating a campaign slogan that 'There are no hardships with Sealink'!

The use of these items is changing, with the balance of negotiating power shifting from the manufacturer to the retail chain. Shop interiors are designed to create a particular image to differentiate the retail brand and to create an ambience in which customers will enjoy spending money. The multiple travel agencies have followed Next and River Island in exerting total design control over the appearance of their branches. Point-of-sale displays now have to harmonize with this design environment, and with the company-wide policy on product racking. The displays are now as likely to be promoting the agency brand as the operator's.

Front-of-house management

Front-of-house management is a term used in the theatre to cover everything on the audience side of the stage. The concept of treating the box office, foyer, bar and entrance area as a single unit can be usefully applied to other leisure venues. All work together to create the customer's first impressions before reaching the core experience. As discussed in Chapter 11, the tangible and the human elements both play a part in forming the customer's perceptions.

Front-of-house design and management have a number of objectives:

- *To sell tickets, to give information, and to provide a collection point for pre-booked tickets.* The three functions may need to be split at busy times.

- *To attract passers-by in so they can find out what the venue has to offer.* The location, the exterior displays and the access can help this, but so too can the provision of refreshment areas, displays and events that are open to all, not just to those with tickets for the main performance area. This is the policy of the Pompidou Centre in Paris, the theatres and concert halls on London's South Bank, and numerous regional arts centres. If people find the centre a pleasant place to have lunch they are more likely to return for the evening performances.

- *To direct the flow of people to avoid congestion and conflicting movements, and to reduce queuing, particularly outside the building.* In UCI cinemas the traditional wet cinema queue has been abolished. The new layout of the foyers allows people to buy tickets as they arrive and then wait for their chosen film inside. Where queues are inevitable, displays, entertainment and regular information can help to reduce irritation. In Disney's Star Tours simulator ride, for example, the waiting area is designed as the space port terminal with announcements, videos and animated figures creating the atmosphere well before people reach the ride itself.

- *To create opportunities for secondary spending*. As well as the traditional ice cream, popcorn and hot-dog vendors, entrance areas can include shops selling souvenirs, memorabilia and recordings of the artists. The Royal Festival Hall has fully stocked book and record shops, while Old Trafford has two supermarkets selling Manchester United branded gifts to the fans.

These functions may seem to be as much the responsibility of the operations as the marketing department. However, the front-of-house area can provide opportunities for point-of-sale promotions, for personal selling and for creating an image of a quality service.

Exhibitions

Exhibitions also provide an opportunity for personal selling and promotional displays. They are particularly useful in enabling marketing and operations staff to come into direct contact with customers they would not normally meet in person. The unique advantage of an exhibition as a promotional medium is that it has a self-selecting audience. Everyone at a holiday exhibition is actively interested in some sort of holiday. It is then just a question of interesting them in yours.

The publicity for the Recman exhibition in 1993 promised stand holders:

> The opportunity for your company to meet thousands of genuine sales prospects in person. A self-selecting audience whose buying power is guaranteed. In just three days an exhibition can enable you to reach your market in a way that no advertisement or direct mail can.

The organizers' research will stress the business that is done as a direct result of the exhibition. However, it is unlikely that the majority of visitors come with the intention of placing orders. Research for the Southern Tourist Board Days Out Fairs for group organizers, teachers and coach operators found the following reasons for attending:

To seek information and literature	98%
To find out what is new, to compare	95%
To discuss business	15%
To make or renew business contacts	7%
To place orders	3%

The reasons for attending will differ according to the type of exhibition, and the design of the stands will vary accordingly. The public exhibition will have stands like three-dimensional adverts and plenty of brochure displays. Stands at trade shows like the World Travel Market have more space to entertain clients and discuss business.

The leisure and tourism industries support a wide range of exhibitions: trade exhibitions, public exhibitions, and exhibitions devoted to particular activities and destinations. Exhibitions are organized by specialist exhibition companies, by national and regional tourist boards and by individual leisure and tourism companies. In tourism there are national and international circuits of exhibitions which can keep a resort or major attraction's marketing team busy all winter, handing out brochures, loading and unloading vans, and running up bills for food and accommodation.

Exhibitions are a form of promotional medium, and the same principles of media selection discussed in Chapter 15 apply. The organization should examine the costs, the coverage obtained, and the context in which their stand will be seen. The results of attending the exhibition should be carefully monitored both in terms of the initial contacts made and the business that resulted (see the Case Study 20.1: Sunseeker and the Boat Show).

The advantages and disadvantages of exhibiting are listed in Table 20.1.

The exhibition should be part of an integrated promotional campaign. It is no use just turning up. The company's presence should be

Table 20.1   Advantages and disadvantages of exhibitions.

Advantages	Disadvantages
A self-selecting audience	Can attract brochure-grabbers and free-gift collectors
An opportunity to make sales leads and build up mailing lists	The competitors may also be there
An opportunity for detailed sales presentation and negotiation	Takes up marketing staff time – lost opportunity costs
Creative possibilities of a three-dimensional display, use of videos, figures in costume, etc.	Expensive: space rental, services, display design, brochures, gifts and hospitality, staff time, expenses and accommodation, transport associated promotions, etc.
'Synergy': the size of the event, the media coverage, the main-stage entertainment create a greater combined impact than the individual stand could on its own	Dependent on the exhibition organizers to attract the right visitors
Opportunity for PR events, brochure launches, tie-in media advertising	Decision may be political ('We have to be seen to be there') rather than commercial.

advertised in the local or trade press; trade contacts should be sent invitations to call in on the stand, possibly for a drinks reception; and competitions should be used to encourage people to spend longer looking at the stand and to leave their names and addresses.

After the exhibition, leads should be followed up and requests for information supplied quickly. Competition winners should be notified promptly and the opportunity taken for media coverage.

As usual in marketing, the staff are the key to exhibition success. They need to have the right product knowledge and negotiating authority to deal with the type of customers expected. They also need to enhance the visual appeal of the stand! Waterhouse talks of the three S's of exhibiting: smiles, shoes and sleep. The first is obvious. The second are important as the exhibitors should be on their feet ready to greet visitors rather than sitting reading the paper. Sleep is important as they need to be bright and cheerful the next morning, not hungover from a night of partying. Waterhouse also warns against groups of stand personnel huddled together in conversation, thus discouraging visitors from interrupting them or ranged across the front of the stand as if ready to repel boarders.[7]

CASE STUDY 20.1   *Sunseeker at the Boat Show*

Sunseeker International of Poole are a leading manufacturer of luxury motor yachts. The International Boat Show at Earls Court is an obvious opportunity for them to meet prospective customers from all over the world. But it is an expensive form of promotion. Sunseeker's costs for the 1994 Boat Show are shown in Table 20.2.

Table 20.2   Sunseeker's costs for exhibiting at the 1994 Boat Show.

	Cost (£)
Space for exhibiting five boats and two stands	14,064.00
Electricity supply	265.52
Flooring	578.00
Printed signs, brochures, leaflets, displays	2,800.00
Staff expenses (travel, accommodation, meals)	5,400.00
Insurance	2,434.00
Transportation costs	5,000.00
Photography, new design launch	287.00
Complimentary tickets	110.00
Competition prizes	430.00
Total	**31,421.52**

In ten days of exhibiting, Sunseeker received 3,840 enquiries. Of these 1,280 were serious enough to require a written quotation after the exhibition, from which 52 (4%) eventually placed orders. 23 orders were placed at the Boat Show itself. Three staff therefore achieved 75 orders in ten days. The cost per order for the exhibition was only £418.95. The orders were worth a total of £7 million.

QUESTIONS

1 What alternative media coverage could Sunseeker have bought for £31,000? What would the likely response rate have been?

2 Yacht buyers evidently go to the Boat Show to place orders. Is the same true of visitors to other exhibitions, e.g. the World Travel Market, Recman, or a regional holiday exhibition open to the public? How should exhibitors at these exhibitions evaluate the success of their stands?

Summary

Personal selling in leisure is not only the job of designated sales representatives. Any staff who come into contact with the public can perform a sales role. Talking face to face with a potential customer has many advantages, but also carries potential risks for both parties. The purpose of the planned approach to the sales encounter described in this chapter is to minimize these risks.

The sales encounter should not be approached as a one-off transaction, where the seller has to win at the buyer's expense. Rather, it should be seen as part of an on-going process of relationship management.

Changes in the relationship between retailers and suppliers have reduced the role of the travelling sales representative in travel and leisure. The major deals are agreed between executives at the company headquarters level, and branches communicate with the suppliers via computer links and are serviced by contract field sales teams.

Many customer decisions are made at the point of sale. The retail environment – the design and styling of the premises – plays an important part in conveying the company's message to its customers. The front-of-house aspects of leisure venues need to be planned and managed in the same way.

Personal selling should be seen as the culmination of the organization's marketing effort. All the research, planning, product design, pricing and promotion should result in an offer that meets the needs of the customer. All the salesperson then has to do is communicate clearly with the customer.

Note: To avoid accusations of being exclusively male-oriented and to distinguish the seller from the buyer clearly, I have referred to the former as 'he' and the latter as 'she'. This is not intended to imply that all sellers are thrusting males seeking to take advantage of passive female buyers. The gender roles are often reversed in modern business.

Notes

1. McMurray, R. (1961) 'The mystique of super-salesmanship', *Harvard Business Review*, March/April, adapted by Kotler, P. (1994) *Marketing Management*, p. 685.
2. Holloway, C. and Plant, R. (1992) *Marketing for Tourism*, p. 108.
3. Kotler (1994), *op. cit.*, p. 684.
4. Macdonald, M. and Leppard, J. (1988) *How to Sell a Service*.
5. Lunch, golf and dinner!
6. Papworth, R. (1985) 'Death of the salesman?', *Travel Agency*, September, p. 12.
7. Waterhouse, D. (1987) *Making the Most of Exhibitions*, p. 165.

PART 5

Implementing the Marketing Concept in Leisure

21 Cooperative marketing

Joint marketing ventures
Sponsorship
Case Study 21.1: Arts sponsorship: Eldridge Pope and the
Dorchester community play
Summary

Joint marketing ventures

Advertising can be very expensive and it is difficult to make a great impact with the average budget of £40,000. Inventive marketing managers are therefore always looking for ways to make their money go further by collaborative or cooperative joint marketing ventures.

Joint marketing ventures involve cooperation between independent organizations to communicate with a common target audience to their mutual benefit. There are several forms this cooperation can take. Cooperative partnerships can be based on:

1   *Geographic location.* Brian Cooper of the Weymouth Diving Museum formed the Weymouth Old Harbour Association to promote all the attractions round the harbour through signposting, posters, leaflets, joint-ticketing, special events, and even a sponsored ferry (rower-powered) linking the two sides of the harbour. The aim was to establish the harbour as a day-trip destination.

2   *Similar products.* Hotel consortia like Best Western are formed by independent hotels of a similar character and quality to provide a central marketing and reservations service.

3   *Supplier–retailer collaboration*, e.g. drinks promotions in pubs, point-of-sale displays, joint advertising by tour operators and travel agents.

4   *A shared market.* As illustrated in Chapter 17, many promotions involve two companies with very different products but a common target market. This is the relationship in sponsorship, to which we shall return later.

The cooperation can take several forms, with increasing degrees of commitment:

- a one-off joint promotion,
- a trade association campaign,
- a trade association with an 'umbrella' brand name, or
- a consortium with its own corporate identity and standards.

Using the public sector tourist office

It is often the role of the public sector tourist office for the area to provide the umbrella brand and to coordinate the marketing, The Southern Tourist Board, for example, publish, promote and distribute a wide range of brochures and leaflets aimed at different market segments. These publications include Main Holidays, Short Breaks, Conference Venues, Educational Visits, Travel Trade Manuals, Best of Hampshire Attractions, Historic Churches and Cathedrals, and various themed motoring trails. They promote these at exhibitions aimed at travel trade buyers, group organizers and teachers, tourist information centre staff and at overseas exhibitions with the BTA. They are distributed via tourist information centres, travel agents and by direct mail using an extensive database. For the individual business, buying space in these publications gives:

- a wider circulation than they could reach on their own for the same cost,
- increased public awareness of the generic product and their own brand, and
- the enhanced credibility and quality image that comes from being associated with the Tourist Board.[1]

Unfortunately, in England particularly, there is a confusing choice of joint promotion opportunities offered by the various levels of the public sector. An attraction like the Weymouth Diving Museum could advertise in publications produced by Weymouth and Portland Borough Council, Dorset County Council, and either the Southern or the West Country Tourist Board, Weymouth being on the boundary of the two regions! It could also seek to be featured in the brochures of coach operators offering holidays in the area, ferry companies using the port, and holiday centres in the area.

The choice requires research into their customers' decision-making processes (see Chapter 7), their perceptions of the various brochures and brands, as well as the comparative costs and coverage.

Sponsorship

Sponsorship is a particularly high-profile form of collaborative marketing between organizations with only a market in common. It is defined as:

> Financial or material support of an activity unconnected with the sponsor's main business, but from which he hopes to gain significant benefits.

This distinguishes it from patronage, philanthropy and charity. Companies may support the arts and sports for purely altruistic motives, but that is not sponsorship. A sponsorship deal is an exchange between two parties who both intend to benefit from it.

Sport and the arts are the principal beneficiaries of sponsorship. 55% of sponsorship money goes to sport,[2] amounting to £250 million in the UK in 1991.[3] The sponsorship can be of

- *the event*: e.g. the Embassy World Darts Championship,
- *the player*: e.g. Nike and Ian Wright,
- *the team*: e.g. Holsten Pils and Tottenham Hotspur,
- *the competition*: e.g. the FA Carling Premiership (Bass),
- *the stadium*: e.g. Fosters and the Oval Cricket Ground,
- *coaching schemes*: e.g. Dairy Crest in athletics.[4]

(For the sake of brevity we shall use 'the event' to stand for any of these.)

Sponsorship has become part of a symbiotic relationship on which the survival of professional sport depends. Spectators will only come to watch star players so the event needs sponsorship to pay the appearance fees. Sponsors want TV coverage, which will only be attracted to events with large audiences and star players. This is shown diagrammatically in Figure 21.1. The Palais Omnisport, Bercy, Paris, France's main international indoor arena, has a marketing team dedicated to finding sponsors for the sports governing bodies and other promoters of events. Without the sponsorship, the events would be uneconomic even with 14,000 ticket sales.

Arts sponsorship in Britain was worth £58 million in 1992, or 29% of all sponsorship. Private sector sponsorship represents almost 11% of the total non-box-office funding of arts venues. The visual arts received the highest percentage (30%) followed by music (26%), festivals (19%) and theatre (10%).[5]

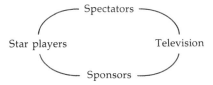

FIGURE 21.1   The relationship between sport, TV and sponsorship.

The benefits of sponsorship

Sponsoring the arts or sport can offer a number of benefits to the company.

1. *Publicity.* The brand name will be seen and read by the public before, during and after the event. They will become conditioned (see Chapter 14) to associate it with the emotions and image of the event. This will enable the sponsors to achieve a number of communications objectives:

(a)   Increased awareness.
(b)   Changed attitudes. An unexciting product like insurance or banking can enliven its image by becoming associated with Test cricket (Cornhill) or motor rallying (Lombard RAC). A brand like Yardley cosmetics targeting a new male audience can gain a new masculine image by sponsoring motor racing. Oil companies like BP can counteract fears over the environmental effects of oil drilling by sponsoring local community events and environmental projects.
(c)   Targeting specific audiences. Lager brands can reach an audience of heavy users by sponsoring football. Opera and ballet sponsorship reaches heavy concentrations of ABC1 over-55s in the market for financial services. Coca Cola and Pepsi sponsor pop artists like Michael Jackson to reach their main target market.
(d)   Reaching audiences not accessible through other media. Sports sponsorship really became significant after the voluntary ban on tobacco advertising on television. It is now estimated that tobacco sponsorship of sport is worth £6–£9 million a year. Durex sponsored motor racing when other forms of advertising were barred to their product.

2. *Community public relations.* Sponsorship of local events can help to build the image of the organization as a good neighbour (see Chapter 18), as well as keeping the brand name in the public mind. It can also be good for staff morale to see their firm involved in the community.

3. *Promotional entertaining.* Sponsorship of an event usually brings with it the right to free tickets and hospitality facilities. These can be used to entertain important clients, or as prizes for staff incentive schemes. This would mainly be of benefit to established firms seeking to enhance good customer and staff relations.

4. *Sales and merchandising opportunities.* If a brewery sponsors a football team it will expect to have exclusive rights to sell its products in the club's bars. Any sponsor may have a stand to sell its goods or distribute publicity at the event.

5.   *Linked advertising.* To exploit the full benefits of the association with the sponsored event, the organization will need to carry out advertising and other promotions. Mintel report that 1.8% of the total expenditure on arts sponsorship was spent on supporting media advertising.[6] Bass sponsored the FA Carling Premiership for £12 million over four years, but spend £4 million per year on support promotions including special Premiership cans, a 'Fan of the Week' competition with the *Daily Mirror*, and sponsoring the sports programmes on Virgin and Capital Radios.

Attracting sponsors

A sponsorship agreement needs to be marketed like any other form of exchange. The organization seeking sponsors needs to set out clearly not only why it needs sponsorship but also how sponsorship can benefit the sponsor. It should prepare a concise document including:

- details of the event or organization to be sponsored,
- evidence of its reputability, e.g. patrons, previous sponsors, well-known names involved,
- its track record, if any
- actual or projected audiences, preferably with demographic profile,
- expected media coverage, and
- facilities offered to sponsors.

This document should be sent to any companies who are likely to benefit from contact with the audience, association with the image of the event, or who have connections with the local community. As in selling to an organization, it is important to identify the right decision maker with the means, the authority and the need to make sponsorship agreements. While we have stressed that this decision will be made on commercial grounds, the personal interests of a chairman, or other senior manager, may influence him to give a sympathetic hearing to particular forms of sport or the arts.

The Association for Business Sponsorship of the Arts (ABSA) is a body set up by the government to encourage business sponsorship. As well as providing a register of members, the ABSA administers the Business Sponsorship Initiative matching pound for pound the money donated by a first time sponsor of an arts event or organization, and £1 for every £4 of additional sponsorship from a previous sponsor. Following the success of ABSA, the Central Council for Physical Recreation (CCPR) administer the Sports Match scheme which will match pound for pound any sponsorship of sports schemes to benefit young people or inner city areas.

Some ideas for firms that may support sponsorship can be found in *A Guide to Company Giving* from the Directory of Social Change.

Sponsorship terms

It is important to define precisely what the sponsor will get for the money. Sponsorship agreements may include:

- Use of the sponsor's name in the title of the event, on all publicity and advertising for the event, at the event, on hoardings, vehicles and team shirts.
- Entertainment and publicity facilities at the event.
- Sales outlets at the event.
- Whether the sponsorship is exclusive or will be shared with other sponsors (it is normal to exclude any others from the same or similar industries who could be direct or indirect competitors).
- Whether the performers will be available to take part in photo-calls and other publicity for the sponsor (this is a delicate area as the performers may have agreements with their own sponsors).
- Clauses limiting the sponsor's right to intervene in matters that might prejudice the artistic or sporting integrity of the event (artistic freedom is jealously guarded by performers and directors).
- The duration of the agreement and the renewal terms.

Trends in sponsorship

Sponsorship of the arts and sport on the scale it is used today is relatively new. More and more organizations from the national to the local level are seeking sponsorship, often as a substitute for reducing state subsidies. Sponsorship is also being sought to underwrite commercial entertainment ventures, such as TV programmes. The Beamish sponsorship of the TV series *Inspector Morse* is a well-known recent example.

The increasing use of sponsorship means that its impact is being diluted as it becomes part of the normal trappings of a sporting or artistic event. Every inch of a Formula One racing car and much of the driver's clothing appears covered in company logos. As mentioned earlier, a televised football match may involve separate sponsors for the programme, the competition, the team, and the individual players, not to mention the match ball.

Another implication is that sponsors may turn from traditional sporting competitions and arts performances to specially created events designed for maximum popular appeal and televisual quality. Kellogg's recently withdrew their sponsorship of the Tour of Britain cycle race to concentrate on the TV spectacular contest series *Gladiators* and tours by teenage pop idols Take That.

In the future both sides of a sponsorship deal will need to treat it as a serious form of marketing communications, little different from media advertising.

CASE STUDY 21.1 *Arts sponsorship: Eldridge Pope and the Dorchester community play*

Community plays involve a small core of professional theatre people harnessing the enthusiasm and hidden talents of the people of the community to produce a work that celebrates the area but also has intrinsic artistic value. The form was developed, almost by accident at first, by playwright and director Ann Jellicoe in Lyme Regis, Dorset, from her involvement in a school play. She went on to found the Colway Trust, which produced a series of community plays in towns and villages in West Dorset and East Devon.

She was invited to Dorchester on the initiative of councillor and former mayor Trevor Jones. A proposal was drawn up for a play to be written by David Edgar, well known for his work with the National Theatre including a highly successful adaptation of Dickens' *Nicholas Nickleby*. The play would be performed, in autumn 1985 in a local church, directed by Jellicoe with a professional composer/musical director and designer, working with a cast and backstage team that eventually included nearly 400 local people. As Table 21.1 shows, even with the benefit of their free labour, a production of this scale costs a considerable amount of money.

Grants were received from South West Arts and the district council, and a number of imaginative fundraising events were held. These were more successful in raising awareness than money, but served to demonstrate the degree of involvement of local people in the project. Without sponsorship, however, the play could not have taken place.

The main sponsor was the local brewery, Eldridge Pope, who provided £5,000. Their involvement was encouraged by the interest of their chairman, Christopher Pope, who revealed considerable acting talent in a cameo part as Mayor of Dorchester. At the time the sponsorship was agreed, the team of local researchers came up with the idea of a storyline involving the troubled life of the founder of the brewery, Sarah Eldridge. David Edgar, a left-wing writer, had some qualms about the danger of making the play into a commercial for the brewery, but was attracted by the contrast between Mrs Eldridge the brewer and the other leading character, a puritanical (and teetotal) clergyman called the Reverend Henry Moule. The central event of the play was a cholera epidemic in 1854, which led the townspeople to see the vicar in a new light.

The play project received regular coverage in the local press during the 18-month period of research, fundraising and recruiting of volunteers.

Table 21.1   The costs and revenues of a community play in £ (based on 11 weeks' rehearsals, 3 weeks' performance, half a week clearing up; figures for 1989).

Costs:

Professionals

Writer's fees and royalties	6,500	
Director	6,500	
Composer/musical director	3,150	
Designer	3,000	
Stage manager/lighting staff (3)	6,150	
Total professionals		25,300

Administrative staff

(employed on Job Creation for 34 weeks)	5,500	

Production costs

Costumes	3,300	
Scenery/staging	4,700	
Lighting	3,200	
Administration and publicity	9,000	
Fundraising expenses	6,000	
Miscellaneous	5,500	
Total production costs		31,700
Total cost		**62,500**

Note: 400 actors, costume makers, stage hands, props and scenery makers, fundraisers, ticket sellers, baby-sitters, etc. (68,000 person hours) *free*.

Where does the money come from?

15 performances × 300 audience = 4,500 tickets; to cover costs, the ticket price would need to be £14.

Sponsorship and grant aid is therefore essential to keep the prices affordable by the community.

Sponsorship

Major sponsors, e.g.

Eldridge Pope	8,000	
Barclays Bank	8,000	
Marks and Spencer	1,000	
Minor sponsors (local businesses)	4,400	

Grants

Regional Arts Association	2,500	
District council	7,500	
Business Sponsorship Incentive Scheme	3,500	
TVS Trust	3,000	
Donations	500	
Local fundraising (gross)	8,600	
Total donated		**47,000**
Tickets and programme sales		16,000
Total		**63,000**

Source: Dorchester Community Plays Association, budget for a second play in 1989.

The Eldridge Pope logo appeared on all the adverts and handbills for workshops, auditions and fundraising events, as well as for the play itself. There were ingenious efforts, aided by the brewery PRO, to create good stories including a rumour of a ghost of one of the characters haunting a building which was being used as a workshop for the play; and an audition for sheep, one of which was to be used in a crowd scene. According to the report, Caroline the sheep got on well with the cast, 'especially after she knocked back a pint of Dorchester bitter brewed by Eldridge Pope who are sponsoring the play'.

The reputation of David Edgar was expected to gain national arts page coverage for the play, but the news value of the event was raised when South West Arts cut their grant to the Colway Trust. Ann Jellicoe announced her resignation in protest, and the arts press, radio and TV programmes were full of stories using the Dorchester play as evidence of the value of this type of community arts work.

Entertaining Strangers, as the play was called, played to full houses and was seen by 4,000 people over its ten-day run. It was extensively reviewed by the national press, with critics like Michael Billington of the *Guardian* praising Dorchester's beer as well as its play.

David Edgar subsequently adapted the play for a smaller cast at the National Theatre with Dame Judi Dench playing Sarah Eldridge. Eldridge Pope won an ABSA award for the best new sponsorship of the arts, and Councillor Trevor Jones quickly persuaded them to agree to sponsor a second Dorchester community play four years later.

Sources: Jellicoe, A. (1987) *Community Plays*, and numerous articles and documents collected by the author.

QUESTIONS

1   What benefits did the brewery get from its sponsorship?

2   To what extent were these benefits predictable, and how far was the success of the play the result of unforeseen external factors?

3   In what other ways could Eldridge Pope have spent £5,000 of their promotional budget to achieve similar objectives?

4   How far is it acceptable for a play or other work of art to include references to the sponsor's name and products?

Summary

Sponsorship is the best-known example of collaborative marketing, which we define as cooperation between independent organizations to communicate with a common target audience to their mutual benefit. Other forms include joint promotions, trade associations, marketing consortia. Public sector tourist boards exist partly to coordinate collaborative marketing ventures with the commercial tourist businesses in their region.

The search for sponsors or other partners should be approached as a marketing task. The potential sponsor is a customer seeking to satisfy his needs and obtain benefits from the deal. The sponsorship offer should therefore be presented in terms of the benefits to the sponsor rather than as an appeal for charity.

A public sector tourist board, or a commercial marketing agency, which produces brochures and guides, has two relationships that require marketing. One is obviously with the end-users, the members of the public who use the guide to choose holidays or day-trip destinations. The other is with the businesses that buy space in the guide. These businesses will have to be persuaded of the benefits they will gain by being included.

The main benefit of any collaborative venture is that by pooling their promotional budgets, organizations can reach a wider target audience than they could otherwise afford to. However, each organization needs to be sure that they have chosen the right partners, the best means of reaching the right audience in the most cost-effective way and with the maximum impact for their particular product.

Notes

1. See Wood, M. (Ed.) (1980) *Tourism Marketing for the Small Business*, ch. 13–22.
2. KeyNote (1992).
3. Institute of Sports Sponsorship.
4. Shaw, R. (Ed.) (1993) *The Spread of Sponsorship*.
5. Mintel (1993) Arts Sponsorship report, *Leisure Intelligence*, **1**.
6. *Ibid*.

22 Marketing in leisure organizations

Marketing and the management process
Case Study 22.1: Marketing Portsmouth
Marketing and the organizational structure
Control and monitoring of the marketing effort
Marketing and organizational culture
Coda: Marketing – a long-term investment

This book has been an account of the marketing process as it is applied in the leisure and tourism industries. It has described what needs to be done to identify, anticipate, and satisfy customer needs. These activities have to be performed by someone we have referred to as the marketer or the marketing manager. This chapter looks at who this person might be, and how he or she fits into the organization.

The management of an organization can be described in terms of:

- *the process*: what tasks are performed,
- *the structure*: who is responsible for each task,
- *the culture*: the beliefs and attitudes that determine how the organization behaves.

This chapter will examine the place of marketing in each of these views of the organization. In doing so, it will be necessary to look at the barriers to implementing the marketing process, and how the marketing process has to be adapted to different types of organization, particularly small businesses and public sector organizations.

Marketing and the management process

In Chapter 3, illustrated by Figure 3.1, the management process of a product-oriented organization was compared to that of a marketing-oriented organization. The work of the marketing manager or department will be very different in the former, where the job will be seen in terms of selling what has already been provided, than in the latter, where marketing will have an important role in determining what should be provided.

There have been many attempts to define what exactly characterizes a marketing orientation. Kotler defines the pillars of the marketing concept as target markets, customer needs, coordinated marketing and profit through customer satisfaction.[1] Narver and Slater identify customer orientation, competitor awareness, and interfunctional coordination as the key components.[2] Middleton's four key elements are similar but stress the need to be outward-looking and innovative towards customers and the business environment, and to look to the future, the long-term interests of customers and the social and environmental constraints.[3]

The practical implications of this orientation, therefore, are that the organization should engage in the following activities:

1   Systematic analysis of the customers, the competition and the business environment (regular primary and secondary research as part of a marketing information system).

2   Planning to meet the opportunities and threats identified (a marketing or business plan).

3   Reviewing and updating the products and services offered in the light of changing customer demands (product planning and development).

4   Communicating what the organization offers in terms that are relevant and appealing to the target markets (a promotional strategy based on a brand image).

5   Ensuring that what is delivered to the customers meets their expectations (customer care as part of a quality assurance system).

6   Monitoring the effectiveness of these activities.

As leisure and tourism organizations are competing for the customers' spare time and money among an almost endless choice of alternatives, this flexible, forward-looking, customer-oriented approach would seem to be essential to survival. Yet there are many leisure organizations that do not carry out all of these key activities.

Barriers to implementation of the marketing concept

Jobber identifies five barriers that prevent the implementation of the marketing concept:[4]

1   High-cost solutions: giving greater satisfaction to the customers may cost more money.

2   Unquantifiable benefits: the exact return on this additional cost may be difficult to quantify, particularly in the short term.

3   Personal ambitions: individuals in the organization may put their own priorities above that of satisfying the customer. These may be a narrow obsession with technical aspects of the work, preserving or expanding personal empires, or simply a desire for an easy life.

4   Reward systems that discourage the marketing-oriented approach: these may encourage maximizing sales or cutting costs without concern for the quality offered.

5   Saying rather than doing: top managers may pay lip service to customer satisfaction and then cut back the funds needed to achieve it.

These traits may be particularly prevalent in small businesses.

Marketing in small businesses

Many leisure companies are small businesses. Writers on small businesses point out that they are necessarily constrained by a shortage of resources, time, money and expertise, leading to a suspicion of high-cost, unquantifiable solutions. They are likely to concentrate on a niche market where they have a distinctive advantage over their larger competitors.[5] The nature of the firm is bound up with the personal ambitions of the owner or manager, who may be in the business through personal interest in the sport or activity as much or more than through the profit motive.[6] For these reasons they tend to stick to tried and tested products and rely on established customers. Research for Bournemouth University by Sheathe[7] into small tourist attractions, and by Abbott[8] into equestrian centres, confirm that very few small businesses carry out market research, or have a formal marketing plan. 'Marketing' means a leaflet in the local tourist information centre, and an ad in the local paper.

In the small business, there may not be a separate marketing manager but the owner/manager still needs to carry out marketing activities. Customers do not make allowances for small businesses. They expect the same quality, the same professionalism at the same prices as they would from a larger company. In fact, they expect a higher standard of personal service. Otherwise they might as well opt for the security of dealing with a large well-known organization.

Marketing in the public sector

Saker and Smith's work mentioned in Chapter 3 shows that a marketing orientation is difficult to detect in local authority leisure services departments. Although most carried out occasional market research, very little of that research was directed at obtaining information about specific user segments or non-users. Only 14% of local authorities had a written marketing strategy or marketing plan. The main reasons for this were not a lack of awareness of the importance of marketing, but a lack of support from the elected council, leading to a lack of resources for specific marketing posts, research, training or promotion. High-cost solutions and unquantifiable benefits do not appeal to councillors struggling with a shortage of funds, and the threat of government capping on their spending. As Saker and Smith say, the marketing function within a local authority 'is often trapped in a cycle where it is poorly resourced, seen as a cost, unable to develop a convincing strategy for its own development, and thus poorly positioned to argue its benefits and the case for more resources'.[9]

The other problem is that public sector organizations often do not have direct control over the product they are marketing. The leisure and tourism product labelled Bournemouth, for example, consists of a large number of hotels, guest houses, shops, restaurants, leisure and entertainment venues owned by the private sector, as well as the beaches, parks, conference centre and infrastructure for which the council is directly responsible. Summing up the appeal of the resort in a single advertising message is very difficult, and controlling the quality of the visitor experience even more so. The personal ambitions and reward systems of the individual proprietors may work against them supporting a marketing initiative for the whole town. Nevertheless, Bournemouth is in the process of developing a comprehensive leisure strategy based on extensive research and analysis of customer needs. This includes the formation of a marketing plan and the appointment of specific leisure marketing posts.

The marketing objectives of a local authority are necessarily more complex than those of a commercial organization. Figure 22.1 shows the customers and exchanges involved. The mission of any council must be to make the area a pleasant and prosperous place to live and work. The leisure and tourism department can help to achieve this mission by meeting the following objectives:

1   to provide leisure facilities to meet the needs of the residents;
2   to bring economic benefits to the area by attracting visitors; and
3   to create new jobs by attracting new companies to locate their businesses in the area.

As Figure 22.2 shows, these objectives are all interlinked. The leisure attractions satisfy the residents, attract visitors, and by making the area seem

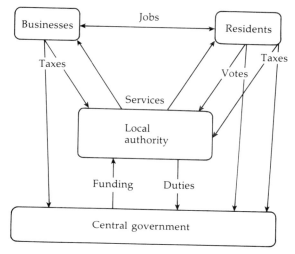

FIGURE 22.1   The customers and the exchanges in local authority marketing.

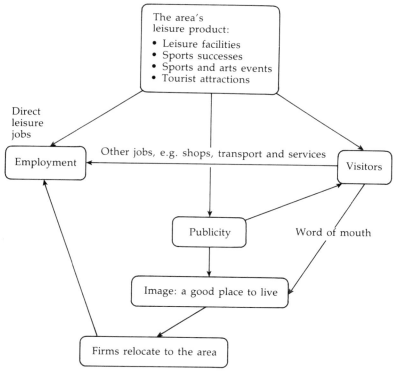

FIGURE 22.2   The role of leisure in an area's economy.

a pleasant place to live, help to attract new industries. The local authority can influence this process in a number of ways:

1. *By direct investment*. In the past, the authority would invest directly in leisure and tourism facilities, such as the Portsmouth D-Day Museum or the Bournemouth International Centre. Cities spend millions of pounds in bidding for major sporting events, as did Manchester for the Olympic and Commonwealth Games, and Sheffield for the World Student Games. Such expenditure may be restricted by central government controls over council spending.

The authority can also invest in the infrastructure of the area to make it a more pleasant place for visitors. This can include roads and public transport, pedestrian precincts for shopping, parks and esplanades, street furniture, or the refurbishment of historic public buildings.

Public sector investment is usually designed to act as a stimulus for private sector investment in the area. The improvements to the resort infrastructure in Majorca, for example, were designed to stimulate reinvestment of hotels and creation of more up-market packages to the area. The Bournemouth International Centre was designed to attract more conferences and so benefit the local economy by creating business for local hotels and other services.

2. *By creating themes and brand images for the area*. This is the traditional role of the council's tourist marketing department, to find a slogan and produce guides, posters, exhibition stands, etc., to promote the image of the place. This, it is hoped, will generate enquiries for promotional literature, which will then result in bookings for the private sector advertisers. In this respect, the tourist office can be seen as a promotional agency providing a service for the local tourist industry.

3. *By encouraging high quality standards*. The advantage the public sector tourist offices have over commercial marketing agencies is that their publications are seen as official and carry a quality assurance for the customer. In many countries all tourist accommodation has to be approved and graded by the state. In the UK, only a voluntary inspection and classification scheme operates.

The local authority can also encourage improved quality standards by grants, for conversion of hotels to provide en-suite facilities or to provide access for the disabled, for example, if the political climate allows. It can also discourage inappropriate or substandard developments through the planning regulations, and in extreme cases close down unsatisfactory establishments. The planning laws have been used extensively to improve the quality of the tourist accommodation and to protect the environment in the Balearic Islands in recent years.[10]

4. *By acting as a facilitator of exchanges between commercial sector tourism organizations.* Middleton points out that public sector tourist offices usually have too limited a promotional budget to make a major impact through media advertising. Instead, they use a strategy of marketing facilitation.[11] This aims to provide a bridge between, for example, local hoteliers and incoming tour operators, so that the two parties can create and promote a package to the area. This may involve producing a trade manual, providing a travel trade liaison service, and organizing press and trade familiarization visits, exhibitions and workshops. It will involve bringing the local trade into cooperative marketing campaigns. If the private sector is not offering the right products for the area it may even include providing a reservations service or putting together their own package holidays. This is frequently the case with domestic holidays, which are not as readily available through travel agents.

It will be seen from this list that the work of marketing managers in the public sector will be different from, but no less challenging than those of their private sector counterparts.

Portsmouth is a city which has adopted the marketing approach with success, as can be seen in Case Study 22.1. Another unlikely success story is Bradford, which has innovatively used its links with the Brontë sisters, its industrial heritage, the surrounding moorland scenery, and the sheer novelty value of selling short breaks to a Yorkshire mill town to great effect. (Despite this success Bradford Council's Business Development Unit was closed down in 1994 as a means of meeting reduced spending targets. In a political environment that requires short-term results, the long-term investment required for marketing can seem a luxury.)

CASE STUDY 22.1   *Marketing Portsmouth*

For centuries, Portsmouth's business was naval warfare. At the end of the second world war 23,000 men were employed in the naval dockyard, a figure which had declined to 7,700 by 1982. The declining role of surface warships in modern warfare and a continuing review of Britain's defence needs led to the announcement in that year that the naval base would cease to carry out major refits and the workforce would be cut to 3,300.

The city council, looking to diversify its economic base, identified tourism as a potential growth industry, and appointed Sunny Crouch as chief marketing and tourism officer at the head of a Tourism Section of 7 posts. The city's traditional tourism product was 'Sunny Southsea', a stretch of mainly shingle beach with the usual facilities of a British seaside resort. Its unique selling point, however, was its trio of historic flagships of the Royal Navy: Nelson's HMS *Victory* (1765), Britain's first ironclad warship

HMS *Warrior* (1860), and Henry VIII's *Mary Rose* (1545) which amid great public interest had been raised from the seabed on prime-time live television in October 1982.

Taking up an English Tourist Board marketing theme 'The Year of Maritime England', in 1982 Portsmouth decided to market itself as 'The Flagship of Maritime England' which appeared on all its brochures and posters. A further product was added to this range in 1984 when the City Council built a £1.4 million D-Day Museum to capitalize on the interest in the 40th anniversary of the Normandy landings. In addition, the large number of minor maritime historic sites in the area were marketed under the brand of 'The Defence of the Realm' in a joint initiative by Portsmouth, Hampshire County Council and the Southern Tourist Board. The areas around the historic ships were improved by use of 'authentic' paving, Victorian-style lamp-posts and signing. A new Tourist Information Centre was opened.

To make it easy for visitors to buy the product, Portsmouth created its own inclusive short-breaks product, Portsmouth PopAways, and was a founder member of 'The Great English City Breaks' promotion with 12 other cities and Goldenrail, the short-break operator. This produced a product of sufficiently wide appeal to gain rack space in retail travel agents. (The brochure is still produced as 'Great British Cities', including Scottish and Welsh cities.)

A travel trade executive was appointed to promote Portsmouth as a destination to tour operators, coach, ferry and rail transport operators, and incoming tour ground-handling agents.

The results were an increase in visitor numbers and expenditure, and rising hotel occupancy rates in the off-season months. The *Mary Rose* now attracts 3.5 million visitors a year and the D-Day Museum over 750,000. This had a stimulant effect on private sector tourism investment:

- upgrading of 5 existing major hotels (£5.5 million in 1986/87),
- opening of the Portsmouth Hilton in 1981 at a cost of £5 million,
- a £1 million Sea Life Centre for Southsea seafront (opened 1986),
- two marina projects providing 1,000 berths (1988),
- a new water-based leisure and conference facility, the Pyramids (1988),
- a £1 million new caravan and camping centre, and
- a major £140 million new leisure and shopping development in the city centre.

Research by Portsmouth Polytechnic showed that in 1986 tourism-related activity accounted for 10% of local income and jobs, and that the new developments would result in a 33% increase in expenditure over a three-year period, generating over 3,000 permanent jobs at a cost of less than £2,000 of public money per job created.

Source: Presentation by Sunny Crouch to the British Institute of Management, May 1988.

The author would like to thank Sunny Crouch (now Director of Marketing, London Docklands Development Corporation) for permission to use this material.

Marketing and the organizational structure

Once the organization gets too big for one person to run, it begins to need a structure. Organizational structures have two dimensions: horizontal and vertical.

Horizontal structures divide the organization into sections responsible for different functions, e.g. finance, personnel, operations, marketing and sales. Each function is also divided horizontally into a number of sections according to the work to be done. A basic marketing department might be divided into research, product planning, promotion and sales.

Vertical structures create levels of command and responsibility, from the teaboy to the managing director. A marketing department may have a marketing manager, assistant managers for each function, and possibly a layer of office supervisors in charge of the clerical workers.

Structures have a number of purposes:

- to allocate responsibility,
- to define lines of communication,
- to ensure supervision and control, and
- to retain staff by giving them the opportunity of promotion.

Bureaucracy is now a dirty word, but the concept was originally a good one, a rational way of organizing work after the irrational and corrupt courts of kings and princes. People tend to work better when they know what is expected of them.

A good organization should be cost-effective, accountable and coherent. It should also be responsive to customer needs and market trends. The trouble with structures is that they become too rigid; they develop demarcation disputes and empire building; and they obstruct new ideas that threaten the reasons for their existence. In all organizational structures there is a tension between a number of conflicting needs:

specialization versus integration
control versus delegation
efficiency versus responsiveness.

Marketing tends to favour the right-hand qualities, accountants and operations people tend to be on the left.

Even within marketing there can be forces pulling in both directions. There is an argument for strong central control to ensure a coherent strategy, brand image and quality standards. Centralization, however, can mean that the organization becomes too remote from the customers and too slow to adapt to market changes. A structure which gives managers delegated authority to respond to the needs of their particular market can avoid this.

Marketing responsibilities can be divided horizontally in a number of ways:

1   By marketing specialism – market research, product planning and development, advertising, PR, etc.

2   By geographic area.

3   By type of customer or market.

4   By product.

Sealink Ferries used a combination of these divisions of responsibility. It had central planning, reservations, advertising and public relations sections, but delegated responsibility for budgeting, pricing, timetable specification, and promotion to route (product) managers (Short Sea, Anglo-Dutch, Irish Sea and Channel Islands). The sales force was divided by customer type (coach and tour operators, freight, and travel agencies). The travel agency sales staff were allocated to geographical areas. There was also an 'inclusive holidays' product that was managed as a separate profit centre.

It is clear from this example that, however the organization is divided, the different departments need to work together and establish

Product managers

		Short Sea	Irish Sea	Anglo-Dutch	Channel Islands
	Travel agencies				
Marketing managers	Coach and tour operators				
	Freight hauliers				
	Sealink Holidays				

FIGURE 22.3   A matrix organization for a ferry company.

networks that cross the formal divisions. This is sometimes described as a matrix organization, as illustrated in Figure 22.3.

The advantage of such an organization is that there are clear lines of communication from the marketing department both to the customers through the market managers and to the operations departments through the product managers. Within the department, however, there are many potential conflicts of interest. The product managers will complain that the market managers are not selling their particular routes hard enough to the customers, and the market managers will insist that their particular customers should take priority over other types of traffic on the routes.

An alternative structure for an organization with a range of products is to treat each product as a separate profit centre. The product manager is then responsible for running the route as a separate business, 'buying' marketing services from the central in-house departments. In some organizations the product managers are encouraged to buy from outside if it is cheaper, and to compete with other products in the range for customers. The abrasive style of management this creates is used to drive down costs and reduce overheads. However, it can also lead to unnecessary duplication. There is also a danger that quality of service will be sacrificed and that the customers will be confused by the different messages coming from different product managers within the same organization. Nevertheless it is an approach, sometimes known as an internal market, increasingly favoured by the government to be adopted by public service organizations.

Control and monitoring of the marketing effort

One of the key objectives of organizational structure is control. The managers and staff are given responsibilities and are expected to achieve certain performance targets. Those above them in the organizational structure are expected to monitor their performance and to take action where necessary to praise, reward, correct or discipline their subordinates. As was said in our discussion of Quality Management in Chapter 11, this ought to be a shared process, with the individuals involved in agreeing the specifications and performance indicators for their work.

This raises the question of how to set performance indicators to control the marketing effort. The success of each of the various marketing functions can be measured against their objectives which have been discussed in preceding chapters on pricing, distribution, advertising, sales promotion and service quality. A number of general indicators can also be used to evaluate the overall success of the marketing effort:

- *company success indicators*: profitability, sales trends, market share, brand awareness;

- *customer satisfaction indicators*: repeat purchase percentage, brand ranking against competitors, customer satisfaction questionnaire results, number of complaints;
- *marketing efficiency indicators*: marketing costs as a percentage of sales, broken down into component costs such as sales force, advertising, sales promotion, market research, and marketing administration. The costs per advertising response, positive sales lead, and ultimately per sale (visitor, booking, etc.) should also be monitored.

These indicators will only be meaningful if they are compared over a period of time or against industry norms, if these are known.

Where there is a social or political element to the objectives, monitoring may be more difficult, but most of the above indices will still be relevant. The private contractors managing local authority leisure centres may be set additional targets in terms of utilization by specific types of people. As well as making a profit at the contract price, they also have to meet performance targets in terms of the quality of the service provided. BS 60001 sets out a detailed inspection process to be carried out by the client authorities.

Marketing and organizational culture

Organizational cultures, like any cultures (see Chapter 7), grow from the particular circumstances in which people interact with each other. The history and development of the organization, the tasks to be performed, and the degree of competition will all affect the priorities of the people in it. These priorities will be expressed in the structure of the organization and the management style.

The author noticed a significant difference in culture between British Rail and its former subsidiary Sealink Ferries. Trains run on a complex network of fixed tracks. Each movement has to be carefully integrated into all the others, and thousands of staff over a wide geographic area need to be informed. As a result, the culture of the organization stressed safety, operational efficiency, and strict lines of demarcation, communication and control. The marketing departments operated within a bureaucratic, operations-oriented organizational structure, and much of their time was spent in specifying customer requirements for detailed planning and costing by the operations departments of several regions. Even with the change from regional to product management (Inter-City, Network South East, Regional Railways, etc.), response to changing customer demand remains a slow process.

In contrast, within Sealink Ferries, each ferry route, indeed each ship, is a self-contained profit centre, and changes in the times and frequency of one operation can be quickly costed, evaluated and implemented without an impact on the rest of the fleet. As a result, the structure was one of delegated authority to the route managers who encouraged a culture of marketing-led innovation, introducing new inclusive tour and excursion products, sales promotions and publicity events each year. The effectiveness of these efforts quickly became apparent in the numbers boarding the ship, so that evaluation and control were rapid.

The culture of an organization is clearly linked to its general orientation. Marketing-oriented companies should have a culture of pride in the quality of the customer service they provide, and should therefore work together to achieve it. However, as Jobber has pointed out, there is a difference between saying and doing, and personal ambitions may work against the best interests of the customer. Marketing orientation cannot be created by issuing a mission statement and making promises in brochures. The whole organization needs to be involved in the process through the type of quality training and management schemes described in Chapter 11.

The first and most important task of the marketing manager is to sell to his colleagues the benefits of putting the customer first.

Coda: Marketing – a long-term investment

One thing that should be noticed from this review of the place of marketing in the organization is that it needs to be seen as a continuing investment. Marketing may increase costs in the short term, and may not result in any short-term improvement in the balance sheet. Marketing may require investing in a long-term brand-building campaign, rather than a price-led promotion. It may involve changing traditional ways of doing things. It may require collaboration rather than competition. In the public sector, for example a local authority, marketing expenditure may not result in any direct revenue to the authority and can therefore only be evaluated in terms of long-term benefits to local residents or businesses.

This emphasis on the long-term benefits of marketing places it in conflict with the chronic short-term orientation which is prevalent in UK industry because of the demand by financial institutions for short-term returns on investment, and which is prevalent in politics because of the politicians' need to win the next election. This short-term mentality prefers price-led sales promotion to brand image advertising, and cost-cutting to reinvestment in quality.

However, to ignore the changing and rising expectations of consumers, and to fail to invest, to adapt and improve the services offered, can only lead to a spiral of declining standards, declining sales and profitability.

Notes

1. Kotler, P. (1994) *Marketing Management*, p. 19.
2. Narver, J. and Slater, S. (1990) 'The effect of marketing orientation on business profitability', *Journal of Marketing*, October, pp. 20–35.
3. Middleton, V. (1994) *Marketing for Travel and Tourism*, p. 15.
4. Jobber, D. (1995) *The Principles and Practice of Marketing*, p. 599 ff.
5. Davis, Hills, La Forge (1985). 'The marketing/small enterprise paradox', *International Small Business Journal*, 3(3).
6. Collins, M. and Randolph, L. (1991) 'Business or hobby? Small firms in sport and recreation', *Leisure Tourism: Social and Environmental Change*.
7. Sheathe, R. (1991) *What Role does Market Research Play in the Marketing of Attractions in the Southern Region?*
8. Abbott, V. (1995) *Equestrian Centres: The Value of Small Business Marketing*.
9. Saker, J. and Smith, G. (1993) 'Selling leisure', *Leisure Opportunities*, September–December.
10. See Morgan, M. (1991) 'Dressing up to survive: Marketing Majorca anew', *Tourism Management*, March; see also Case Study 18.1.
11. Middleton, V. (1994), *op. cit.*, p. 233.

Bibliography

Abell, D. (1980) *Defining the Business: The Starting Point of Strategic Planning.* Englewood Cliffs, NJ, Prentice Hall.

Abbott, V. (1995) *Equestrian Centres: The Value of Small Business Marketing,* Dissertation, BA Leisure Marketing, Bournemouth University.

Advertising Association (1992) *The Lifestyle Pocket Book 1992.* Henley, NTC Publications.

Advertising Association (1992) *The Media Pocket Book 1992.* Henley, NTC Publications.

Allied Dunbar (1992) *National Fitness Survey 1992* (Summary). London, The Sports Council and the Health Education Authority.

Ansoff, I. (1957) 'Strategies for diversification', *Harvard Business Review*, Sept./Oct., pp. 113–24.

Astles, R. (1989) 'Overseas package holidays: Where next?', *Leisure Intelligence*, 2: 4.3.

Audit Commission (1991) *The Road to Wigan Pier: Managing Local Authority Museums and Art Galleries.* London, HMSO.

Audit Commission (1991) *Review: Local Authorities, Entertainment and the Arts.* London, HMSO.

Audit Commission (1993) *Realising the Benefits of Competition: The Client Role for Contracted Services.* London, HMSO.

Baker, M. (1985) *Marketing: An Introductory Text.* Basingstoke, Macmillan.

Barksdale, H.C. and Harris, C.E. (1982) 'Portfolio analysis and the product life cycle', *Journal of Long Range Planning*, **15**(6).

Barrett, C. and Winnifrith, T. (1989) *The Philosophy of Leisure.* London, Macmillan.

Bernard, M. (1993) 'Leisure defined: A review of the literature', *Leisure, Recreation and Tourism Abstracts*, **8**(1). Oxford, Commonwealth Agricultural Bureaux.

Bernstein, D. (1974) *Creative Advertising.* London, Longman.

Bernstein, D. (1984) *Company Image and Reality.* London, Cassells.

Boon, G. (1993) *Survey of Football Club Accounts.* Manchester, Touche Ross.

Bottomley, R.M. (1992) *The Travel Agent.* Sunderland, Business Education Publishers.

Bournemouth Borough Council Leisure and Tourism Directorate (1993) *Business Plan 1993.*

BQA Leisure Services Quality Committee (1992) *Quality Assurance for Leisure Services.* London, Sports Council.

Bradshaw, J. (1972) 'The concept of social need', *New Society*, **30**(3): 640–43.

British Film Institute (1995) *Film and TV Handbook 1995.* London, HMSO.

British Market Research Bureau (annual) *Target Group Index.* London, BMRB.

British Tourist Authority (1991) *Digest of Tourism Statistics,* London, BTA.

British Tourist Authority (1993) *Digest of Tourism Statistics.* London, BTA.

Broadbent, S. (1984) *Twenty Advertising Case Histories*. London, Holt, Reinhart and Winston.

Broadbent, S. and Jacobs, B. (1984) *Spending Advertising Money*. London, Business Books.

Burak, P. and Bennetts, A. (1985) 'Designing products for the leisure travel market', in Mill, R.C. and Morrison, A.M. (Eds) *The Tourism System*. Englewood Cliffs, NJ, Prentice Hall.

Burton, T.L. (1971) *Experiments in Recreation Research*. London, Allen and Unwin.

Butler, R.W. (1980) 'The concept of a tourist area cycle of evolution: Implications for the management of resources', *Canadian Geographer*, 24: 5–12.

Caie, G. (1991) 'Poised to strike', *Leisure Management*, **11**(3): 63.

Central Statistical Office (1993) *Social Trends 23*. London, HMSO.

Chisnall, P.M. (1985) *Marketing: A Behavioural Analysis*. London, McGraw-Hill.

Coalter, F. (1990) 'The mixed economy in leisure', in Henry, I. (Ed.) *Management and Planning in the Leisure Industries*. London, Macmillan.

Collins, M. and Randolph, L. (1991) 'Business or hobby: Small firms in sport and recreation', *Leisure Tourism: Social and Environmental Change*. World Leisure and Recreation Association Congress, Sydney, Australia.

Congreave, I. and Jackson, R. (1972) *The Geography of Recreation and Leisure*. London, Hutchinson.

Conroy, B. (1987) 'Design of brochure covers', presentation at the Tourism Society Conference, University of Surrey.

Cooke, A. (1994) *The Economics of Leisure and Sport*. London, Routledge.

Cooper, P. (1992) 'The life cycle concept and tourism', in Johnson, P. and Thomas, B. (Eds) *Choice and Demand in Tourism*. London, Mansell, p. 154.

Corry, D. and Williamson, P. (1994) *A Game without Vision: The Crisis of English Football*. London, Institute of Public Policy Research.

Cowell, D. (1978) 'Marketing's application to public authority sport, recreation and leisure centres', paper presented at the Marketing Education Group Conference, quoted in Torkildsen (1983) *Leisure and Recreation Management*. London, Spon.

Cox, B. and Ennis, K. (1988) *Marketing Classics*. Needham, MA, Alleyn and Bacon.

Crimp, M. (1981) *The Marketing Research Process*. Hemel Hempstead, Prentice Hall.

Crouch, S. (1986) *Marketing Research for Managers*. London, Heinemann.

Dahringer, L.D. and Muelbacher, H. (1991) *International Marketing*. Wokingham, Addison-Wesley.

Davidson, L. (1979) *Offensive Marketing*. London, Pelican.

Davis, Hills, La Forge (1985) 'The marketing/small enterprise paradox', *International Small Business Journal*, **3**(3).

de Bono, E. (1977) *Lateral Thinking*, Harmondsworth, Penguin.

Dibb, S. and Simkin, L. (1993) 'Strategy and tactics: Marketing leisure facilities', *Service Industries Journal*, **13**(3): 110–24.

Drucker, P. (1954) *The Practice of Management*. New York, Harper & Row.

Drucker, P. (1973) *Management: Tasks, Responsibilities and Practices*. London, Heinemannn.

Dumazedier, J. (1960) 'Current problems in the sociology of leisure', *International Social Science Journal*, **12**: 522–31.

Dumazedier, J. (1967) *Towards a Sociology of Leisure*. New York, Free Press.
Engel, J.F., Blackwell, R.D. and Miniard, P.W. (1990) *Consumer Behavior*, 6th edn. Orlando, FL, Dryden.
Family Expenditure Survey 1992. London, HMSO.
Festinger, L. (1957) *A Theory of Cognitive Dissonance*. Stanford, CA, Stanford University Press.
First Leisure plc (1990) *Annual Report 1990*.
Fishbein, M. (1963) 'An investigation of the relationships between beliefs about an object and attitudes towards that object', *Human Relations*, **16**: 233–40.
Ford, H. (1923) *My Life and Work*. New York, Doubleday, Page.
French, Y. (1994) *Public Relations for Leisure and Tourism*. Harlow, Longman.
General Household Survey 1990. London, HMSO.
Giblin, D. (1986) 'Customer care in British Rail', in Moores, B. (Ed.) *Are They Being Served ?: Quality Consciousness in Service Industries*. Oxford, Philip Allan.
Gratton, C. (1993) *Transnational Corporations in the Leisure Industries*, paper presented at the Leisure Studies Association Conference (unpublished).
Gratton, C. and Taylor, P. (1985) *Sport and Recreation: An Economic Analysis*. London, Spon.
Gratton, C. and Taylor, P. (1987) *Leisure in Britain*. Hitchin, Leisure Publications.
Gratton, C. and Taylor, P. (1988) *Economics of Leisure Services Management*. Harlow, Longman/ILAM.
Greyser, S. (1992) *Case Studies in Advertising and Communications Management*, Englewood Cliffs, NJ, Prentice Hall.
Grönroos, C. (1984) *Strategic Management and Marketing in the Service Sector*. Bromley, Chartwell-Bratt.
Grönroos, C. (1989) 'Defining marketing: A market-orientated approach', *European Journal of Marketing*, **23**(1): 52–59.
Gross, M. (1992) *The Direct Marketer's Idea Book*. New York, AMACOM.
Hanna, M. *Leisure*, IPC Sociological Monograph No. 12.
Haywood, L.J., Kew, F.C. and Bramham, P. (1989) *Understanding Leisure*. London, Hutchinson.
Headland (1993) *Women Keeping Fit*, New Leisure Markets Report. Cleveland, Headland.
Henley Centre for Forecasting (1994) *Leisure Futures*, **1**: 16.
Henry, I. and Spink, J. (1990) 'Planning for leisure', in Henry, I. (Ed.) *Management and Planning in the Leisure Industries*. London, Macmillan.
Herzberg, F. (1966) *Work and the Nature of Man*. Cleveland, Collins.
Hofstede, G. (1980) *Culture's Consequences: International Differences in Work-related Values*. Beverley Hills, CA, Sage.
Holloway, J.C. (1990) *The Business of Tourism*. London, Pitman.
Holloway, J.C. and Plant, R. (1992) *Marketing for Tourism*. London, Pitman.
Hooley, G. and Saunders, J. (1993) *Competitive Positioning: The Key to Market Success*. Hemel Hempstead, Prentice Hall.
Howard, J.A. (1989) *Consumer Behavior in Marketing Strategy*. Englewood Cliffs, NJ, Prentice Hall.
Howard, M. and Wright, R. (1994) 'Going for the direct approach', *Travel Agency*, April.
Hughes, A. (1994) 'A family business', *Leisure Management*, July.

Hughes, E. (1994) *Travel Agents and Overseas Tour Operators*. Hampton, Keynote Publications.

Hyman, H. (1942) 'The psychology of status', *Archives of Psychology*, **38**.

Inglis, S. (1994) 'A whole new ball game', *Leisure Management*, July.

Jellicoe, A. (1987) *Community Plays*. London, Methuen.

JICNARS (annual) *National Readership Surveys*.

JICNARS (1982) *Social Grading in the National Readership Survey*. London, JICNARS.

Jobber, D. (1995) *The Principles and Practice of Marketing*. London, McGraw-Hill.

Johnson, S. (1991) 'Attractive experiences', *Leisure Management*, **5**: 42–45.

Keynote (1991) *Market Review: UK Leisure and Recreation*. Hampton, Keynote Publications.

King, S. (1973) *Developing New Brands*. London, Pitman.

Kotler, P. (1994) *Marketing Management: Analysis, Planning, Implementation and Control*, Englewood Cliffs, NJ, Prentice Hall.

Krugman, M. (1965) 'The impact of television advertising: Learning without involvement', *Public Opinion Quarterly*, **29**(Fall): 349–56.

Krugman, M. (1975) 'What makes advertising effective?', *Harvard Business Review*, March/April.

Lancaster, G. and Massingham, L. (1993) *Essentials of Marketing*. London, McGraw-Hill.

Lannon, J. and Cooper, P. (1983) 'Humanistic advertising', *International Journal of Advertising*, July.

Lavidge, R. and Steiner, G. (1961) 'A model for productive measurement of advertising effectiveness', *International Journal of Advertising*, July.

Leisure Consultants (1994) *Leisure Forecasts 1994–98*. Sudbury, Leisure Consultants.

Levitt, T. (1960) 'Marketing myopia', *Harvard Business Review*, reprinted in Cox, B. and Ennis, K. (Eds) (1988) *Marketing Classics*. Needham, MA, Alleyn & Bacon, p. 10.

Local Government Act 1988: Competition in Sport and Leisure Facilities Order, 1989.

McCarthy, E.J. (1981) *Basic Marketing: A Managerial Approach*. Homewood, IL, Richard D. Irwin.

Macdonald, M. (1989) *Marketing Plans: How to Prepare Them, How to Use Them*. Oxford, Butterworth Heinemann.

Macdonald, M. and Leppard, J. (1988) *How to Sell a Service*. Oxford, Heinemann.

McGuire, W.J. (1990) 'Some internal psychological factors influencing consumer choice', *Journal of Consumer Research*, **2** (March), quoted in Engel *et al.* (1990), p. 63.

McMurray, R. (1961) 'The mystique of super-salesmanship', *Harvard Business Review*, March/April.

Marcuse, H. (1964) *One-Dimensional Man*. London, Sphere Books.

Market Research Society (1977) *Handbook for Researchers*. London, MRS.

Martin, W. and Mason, S. (1992) *The Thatcher Years*. Sudbury, Leisure Consultants.

Martin, W. and Mason, S. (1994) 'Current trends in leisure: Taking account of time', *Leisure Studies*, **13**: 133–39.

Masarini, D.M. (1994) 'The new age', *Leisure Management*, **14**(9), September.

Maslow, A. (1954) *Motivation and Personality*. New York, Harper & Row.

Mayo, E. (1949) *The Social Problems of Industrial Civilizations*. London, RYP.

Meyersohn, R. (1961) 'Leisure', in Campbell, A. and Converse, P.E. (Eds) *The Meaning of Social Change*. New York, Russell Sage Foundation.

Middleton, V. (1994) *Marketing for Travel and Tourism*. Oxford, Butterworth Heinemann.

Middleton, V. and Astles, R. (1994) 'Marketing IT products: Thomson Sun Hotels', *Marketing in Travel and Tourism*. Oxford, Butterworth Heinemann.

Mills, P. (Ed.) (1992) *Quality in the Leisure Industry*. Harlow, Longman.

Mintel (1991) 'Leisure time 2: Age and leisure', *Leisure Intelligence*, 2.

Mintel (1993) 'Arts sponsorship report', *Leisure Intelligence*, **1**.

Mitchell, A. (1985) *The Nine American Lifestyles*. New York, Collier Macmillan.

Mitchell, A. (1990) 'Marketing out of the downturn', *Marketing*, 26 April, pp. 25–26.

Mitchell, L. (1993) 'Setting the advertising budget', *European Journal of Marketing*, 27(6).

Moores, B. (Ed.) (1986) *Are They Being Served?: Quality Consciousness in Service Industries*. Oxford, Philip Allan.

Morgan, M. (1991) 'Dressing up to survive: Marketing Majorca anew', *Tourism Management*, March.

Morgan, M. (1990) 'Moving ferries upmarket: The Starliner experiment', *International Journal of Physical Distribution Management*, 20(5).

Morgan, M. (1994) 'Homogeneous products: The future of established resorts', in Theobald, W. (Ed.) *Tourism: The Next Decade*. Oxford, Butterworth Heinemann.

Morgan, M. and Vaughan, R. (1993) 'Market trends in leisure', *ILAM Guide to Good Practice in Leisure Management*, Release 3. Harlow, Longman.

Mullin, B., Hardy, S. and Sutton, W. (1993) *Sports Marketing*. Champaign, IL, Human Kinetics Publishers.

Narver, J. and Slater, S. (1990) 'The effect of marketing orientation on business profitability', *Journal of Marketing*, October, pp. 20–35.

New Earnings Survey 1993. London, HMSO.

O'Shaughnessy, J. (1992) *Competitive Marketing: A Strategic Approach*. London, Routledge.

Ogilvy, D. (1963) *Confessions of an Advertising Man*. New York, Atheneum.

Oliver, G. (1990) *Marketing Today*. Hemel Hempstead, Prentice Hall.

Palmer, A. (1994) *Principles of Service Marketing*. London, McGraw-Hill.

Papworth, R. (1985) 'Death of the salesman?', *Travel Agency*, September.

Peisley, T. (1992) 'Ferries, short sea cruises and the Channel tunnel', *Travel and Tourism Analyst*, No. 4, pp. 5–23.

Plog, S.C. (1973) 'Why destination areas rise and fall', *Cornell Hotel and Restaurant Administration Quarterly*, Nov. 1973, pp. 13–16.

Plummer, J.T. (1974) 'The concept and application of lifestyle segmentation', *Journal of Marketing*, January, p. 34.

Porter, M. (1980) *Competitive Strategy: Techniques for Analyzing Industry and Competitors*. New York, Free Press.

Prochnik, W.-O. (1975) 'Urban planning for leisure', *Ekistics*, **40**(236): 60–62.

Quinlan, F. (1981) 'The use of social grade in marketing', *Quarterly Review of Marketing*, Autumn.

Rapaport, R. and Rapaport, R.N. (1975) *Leisure and the Family Life Cycle*. London, Routledge & Kegan Paul.

Reeves, R. (1961) *Reality in Advertising*. New York, MacGibbon and Kee.

Renshaw, M.B. (1992) *The Travel Agent*. Sunderland, Business Education Publishers.

Ries, A. and Trout, J. (1982) *Positioning: The Battle for Your Mind*. New York, Warner.

Roberts, J. (1979) *The Commercial Sector in Leisure*. London, Sports Council/SSRC.

Rodger, L.W. (1971) *Marketing in a Competitive Economy*. London, Cassell.

Rogers, E.M. (1962) *The Diffusion of Innovations*. New York, Free Press.

Rossiter, J. and Percy, L. (1987) *Advertising and Promotion Management*. New York, McGraw-Hill.

Rottenberg, S. (1956) 'The baseball players' labor market', *Journal of Political Economy*, **63**: 243.

Russell, B. (1960) *In Praise of Idleness, and Other Essays*. London, George Allen & Unwin.

Saker, J. and Smith, G. (1993) 'Selling leisure', *Leisure Opportunities*, **115–118**. September–December.

Saker, J. and Smith, G. (1993b) 'Marketing activity', *Leisure Opportunities*, **116**: 34–35.

Sambrook, C. (1990) 'Hard sell holidays', *Marketing*, February, p. 31.

Schramm, W. (1961) *The Process and Effect of Mass Communication*. Urbana, IL, University of Illinois Press.

Seabrook, J. (1988) *The Leisure Society*. Oxford, Blackwell.

Seward, K. (1994) 'Interview: Ken Heathcok', *Leisure Opportunities*, 25 July.

Shaw, R. (Ed.) (1993) *The Spread of Sponsorship*. Newcastle upon Tyne, Bloodaxe.

Sheathe, R. (1991) *What Role does Market Research Play in the Marketing of Attractions in the Southern Region?* Dissertation, BA in Tourism Studies, Bournemouth University (unpublished).

Sloane, P. (1980) *Sport in the Market*, Hobart Paper. London, Institute of Economic Affairs.

Strong, E.K. (1925) *The Psychology of Selling*. New York, McGraw-Hill.

Taylor, F.D. (1964) *Scientific Management*. London, Harper & Row.

Terpstra, V. and Sarathy, R. (1994) *International Marketing*, 6th edn. New York, Dryden.

Torkildsen, G. (1983) *Leisure and Recreation Management*. London, Spon.

Veal, A. (1989) 'Leisure, lifestyle and status', *Leisure Studies*, **8**: 141–53.

Veal, A. (1992) *Research Methods for Leisure and Tourism: A Practical Guide*. Harlow, Longman/ILAM.

Waterhouse, D. (1987) *Making the Most of Exhibitions*. London, Gower.

Welburn, H. (1987) 'Travel selling and distribution', *Travel and Tourism Analyst*, July, pp. 3–15. The Economist Publications Ltd.

White, R. (1993) *Advertising: What It Is and How To Do It*. London, McGraw-Hill.

Wilmshurst, H.J. (1992) *The Fundamentals of Advertising*. Oxford, Butterworth Heinemann.

Wood, M. (Ed.) (1980) *Tourism Marketing for the Small Business*. London, English Tourist Board.

Wordsworth, W. (1798) 'Lines written a few miles above Tintern Abbey', *Lyrical Ballads*.

Zeithaml, V., Berry, L. and Parasuraman, A. (1990) *Delivering Quality Service*. New York, Free Press.

INDEX

Notes: Separate indexes of Authors, and of Companies and Organizations follow this main subject index, for the benefit of readers wishing to look up the theories of a particular author (e.g. Porter, Ansoff) or find particular case studies (e.g. British Airways).

A few research bodies and publications in wide use by leisure marketers are included in the main subject index as are generic leisure activities (e.g. ten-pin bowling, theatres).

Where an entry is a paragraph, section or chapter heading in the text, it is shown with initial capitals. Bold page numbers indicate a complete chapter on the topic.

Index of Authors

Index of companies and organisations